CIVIL SERVICE HANDBOOK

EVERYTHING YOU NEED TO GET A CIVIL SERVICE JOB

Edited by
Gabriel Heilig

THOMSON

ARCO

Australia • Canada • Mexico • Singapore • Spain • United Kingdom • United States

An ARCO Book

ARCO is a registered trademark of Thomson Learning, Inc., and is used herein under license by Peterson's.

About The Thomson Corporation and Peterson's

With revenues of US$7.2 billion, The Thomson Corporation (www.thomson.com) is a leading global provider of integrated information solutions for business, education, and professional customers. Its Learning businesses and brands (www.thomsonlearning.com) serve the needs of individuals, learning institutions, and corporations with products and services for both traditional and distributed learning.

Peterson's, part of The Thomson Corporation, is one of the nation's most respected providers of lifelong learning online resources, software, reference guides, and books. The Education Supersite[SM] at www.petersons.com—the Internet's most heavily traveled education resource—has searchable databases and interactive tools for contacting U.S.-accredited institutions and programs. In addition, Peterson's serves more than 105 million education consumers annually.

For more information, contact Peterson's, 2000 Lenox Drive, Lawrenceville, NJ 08648; 800-338-3282; or find us on the World Wide Web at www.petersons.com/about.

Fourteenth Edition

Library of Congress Number 97-80438

ISBN 0-02-863541-8

Printed in the United States of America

10 9 8 7 6 5 4 3   04 03 02

CONTENTS

PART TWO
Getting a Job with the U.S. Postal Service

Working for the U.S. Postal Service 75

The Facts About Postal Service Examinations 91

PART THREE
Getting State and Municipal Civil Service Jobs

Finding Jobs with Your State or Municipal Government 99

Sample Civil Service Job Announcements at the State and Local Level 107

PART FOUR
Examination Preparation

How to Prepare Yourself for Civil Service Examinations   133

Preparing for Multiple-Choice Tests   137

Sample U.S. Postal Service Examination—Exams 470 and 460   171

Biographical/Achievement Inventory   203

Important Civil Service Employment Contacts   207

Webliography of Federal Employment Web Sites   213

Federal Occupations That Require Examinations   215

Glossary of Civil Service Hiring Terminology   223

INTRODUCTION: How This Book Helps You Launch a Career in Civil Service

Any time you search for a new career, you should consider civil service employment. This is true whether you're a new graduate hunting down your first full-time position or you're a veteran worker trying to change jobs or even careers. Why? There are several important reasons:

First, there is the sheer size of the civil service network. The U.S. Federal government is the country's largest single employer. Similarly, the state government is often one of, if not *the* biggest employer within each state; likewise, the county government one of, if not *the* biggest employer within each county; and so on. For you, size means opportunity—a constant stream of job vacancies as civil service employees retire or leave for private-sector jobs. Size also means variety. No matter what academic degree, work experience, or personal skills you have, there is likely a place within the government you can fill.

Second, there is security associated with civil service careers. Civil service employment is not subject to the same trends as private-sector employment—the buying and selling of companies, the tyrannies of personal likes and dislikes that can result in firings or layoffs. With civil service, you can have—if you choose—the "lifetime employment" that was once taken for granted in the private sector, but is now a thing of the past.

Third, there are the benefits connected to civil service work. Government employment provides solid salaries, health and life insurance, time off, and retirement plans. In many instances, these benefits are superior to any you will find in private-sector employment.

For all these reasons, you should seriously consider civil service work, if not aggressively search for such a position.

What Your New ARCO Book Will Do for You

The *Civil Service Handbook* takes you step-by-step through the process of finding and applying for government jobs. The handbook begins with an overview of civil service employment and helps you decide whether consideration of such jobs should become a serious pursuit. How does civil service employment stack up against private-sector employment? This should be applied not only in the areas of salary and benefits, but also in the equally important area of temperament. (In other words, do you have the type of personality that will work well within a civil service environment?)

The handbook goes on to explain—from *your* end—how to find the type of Federal job that matches your background and experience. It also explains—from the *government's* end—the process of finding and hiring the right person. You'll get tips on making your way through the maze of paperwork when filling out applications—and actual samples of filled-in applications and forms. You will also get proven advice on avoiding common mistakes that can bump you out of consideration.

Included is a separate section on finding employment in the United States Postal Service. This is handled separately because, while postal workers enjoy the same benefits as Federal workers, the Postal Service itself is an independent agency. Your handbook describes the jobs available through the Postal Service and the typical working conditions of those jobs. It helps you find out about openings, how to apply for them, and finally, what to expect from the U.S. Postal Service Exam.

Your handbook then covers available jobs at the city, county, and state levels—again helping you find out the types of positions available, where the openings are, and how to apply for them.

The final section of the handbook brings you expert help on passing the written tests associated with each level of civil service employment. You are given samples of tests actually used by the Federal, state and local civil service, as well as the United States Postal Service. You are also provided with the answers and explanations to each sample, as well as a scoring key to let you know whether you're ready for the real thing or need more preparation.

In short, your new *Civil Service Handbook* is the best all-round guide you could possibly have for making this essential decision—and following through on it to career success.

Good luck!

ONE

The Best Job for You in Government

CONTENTS

DECIDING IF A GOVERNMENT CAREER IS RIGHT FOR YOU

Getting hired by the government is like trying to ride an elephant. It can be a safe and rather comfortable ride, and once you're on, it's not easy to fall off. But, getting *on* the elephant? Now, that's another story.

To a job-seeker, the government can seem as huge as an elephant—and as slow and ponderous in the way it responds. This will soon become apparent to you in the amount of information you'll be asked to provide when you apply for a government job—and the time it takes for the government to respond to your application. It's not like sending in your resume to an ad in the Sunday paper. In fact, many people find the process of applying for a government job so complicated, so frustrating, and so time-consuming that they often throw up their hands in disgust and decide: "This is nuts. Forget about it." This is a shame because, like riding an elephant, there are real advantages to a government career, as you'll see in the following sections. In fact, you may even decide that the best possible job for you is on the local, state, or Federal level.

When considering any job, you're likely to go through the advantages and disadvantages of the position. You compare not only the number of "pros" and "cons" on each side, but also each one's relative importance. Not every pro equals every con. For example, a particular job might have five points listed in the "pro" column and only one "con." But, if that single con can't be overcome—say, the job requires moving and you absolutely can't move—then the one disadvantage outweighs all the advantages.

Other disadvantages may not be stumbling blocks so much as they are tradeoffs for a better good. This is especially true when the job you're considering is a government job.

In considering government employment, go through the same process you would with any job, listing the advantages and disadvantages. Besides the obvious points on each side, keep in mind the intangibles. A government career brings with it a certain frame of mind, almost a lifestyle. For people who see the lifestyle as having peace of mind, this will be a definite plus; for those who see it as repetition or boredom, it will be a minus. Be honest when assessing the pros and cons and your own reactions to them.

The Advantages of Government Work

The "pros" are the easiest points to make about any job. They are what you get excited about in the first place. Listed below are the most significant pros of government work:

THE GOVERNMENT IS AMERICA'S LARGEST EMPLOYER

Nearly three million Americans work for the Federal government. That's a lot of people—and a lot of jobs. Add in jobs at the state, county, and city levels and you can understand why the government is one employment opportunity that cannot be overlooked. With this size comes diversity. Almost every imaginable occupation has its place in government work. There's room for everyone from soldiers, spies, and politicians to auto mechanics, pipefitters, and carpenters. There's room for satellite watchers and map readers, secretaries and file clerks, accountants and auditors, purchasing agents and contract administrators, scientists and medical doctors, teachers and law enforcement officers—well, you get the picture. Almost anyone can find a suitable job at some level of government.

THE GOVERNMENT IS ALWAYS HIRING

Roughly 10 percent of all currently filled Federal jobs will become vacant and open for rehiring in any given year. This is due to turnover—attrition due to retirement and to subsequent promotions "up-the-ladder," as lower-graded employees apply for the jobs that higher-graded employees have just left. This makes for a continual process of hiring, rehiring, and promotion throughout the entire Federal government. As a result, jobs are always being filled.

But what of government budget cuts?

Politicians can stand in front of the cameras and announce that they're "going to cut the bloated Federal payroll," but the fact can't be changed: People are always getting hired by the government, even during so-called "hiring freezes." Government agencies have had more than two hundred years to learn how to protect themselves from Washington politics and are very creative about protecting their payrolls. Plus, these agencies provide real services that, when cut, cause taxpayers to complain and to change their votes. This means that "when push comes to shove," politicians back off.

While hiring freezes may be felt more on the lower levels, the state and municipal levels of government are also engaged in a continual process of hiring new people—and have also learned how to survive the political axe.

A GOVERNMENT JOB IS A SECURE JOB

Although it's difficult to get a government job, once you're "on the elephant," it's likely that no one will be able to get you off until you're good and ready to get off. In other words, you can stay or leave, according to your own schedule. Reductions In Force (RIFs) happen infrequently, and when they do, most agencies achieve their goals through early retirements—often accompanied by $25,000 incentives—and by attrition (not filling the jobs left vacant by people who have taken on other careers or retired).

A GOVERNMENT JOB PROVIDES ROOM FOR MOVEMENT AND GROWTH

While you may start out in one particular position, once you're working for the government, you'll find that you have opportunities to move upward or sideways in your field—or to change fields. Advancement may not be rapid, but if you do your work well, it is almost guaranteed, as good work is generally rewarded. In addition, the security of a government position allows you to make long-term career plans. In most cases, you'll know just how to earn a promotion—as well as a raise to the next pay-grade. These procedures will be clearly defined.

GOVERNMENT JOBS PROVIDE STRONG SALARIES

All civil service jobs vary in expectations, requirements, and salary, but we can look at some specific levels of government salaries to get a good sense of the general pay scales.

As an example, below you'll find the pay schedule for most white-collar Federal employees. They're covered by the General Schedule, which is established by the Federal Wage System. Wages for the General Schedule originate from recommendations by the Federal Prevailing Rate Advisory Committee, which is made up of management and labor unions. The Committee surveys non-Federal pay for similar jobs in the same locality and then advises the Director of the Office of Personnel Management on pay policy.

GENERAL SCHEDULE BASIC PAY FOR 1999

GS-1	$13,362	GS-5	$20,588	GS-9	$31,195	GS-13	$53,793
GS-2	$15,023	GS-6	$22,948	GS-10	$34,353	GS-14	$63,567
GS-3	$16,362	GS-7	$25,501	GS-11	$37,744	GS-15	$74,773
GS-4	$18,401	GS-8	$28,242	GS-12	$45,236		

Here's how the General Schedule works:

There are 15 grades, with 5 steps in each pay grade, which increase at 4 percent intervals. At Step 2 of each grade, compensation is based on the average going rate for private-sector employees performing the same job. So while the first step may fall below the average pay-rate, it would certainly fall within the range of what an actual private-sector job might pay. At Step 5 within each grade, however, Federal employees are paid 12 percent above this average private-sector rate, which demonstrates the advantage in moving through the ranks of Federal employment.

Federal employees not only receive wages comparable to the same job in the private sector, they also receive wages comparable to the same job in each particular location. This is important, as certain areas of the country have a higher cost of living, and often pay employees higher salaries. This "locality pay" can be 5.6 to 12 percent higher than the regular General Schedule amount for jobs within the continental U.S.—and 10 to 25 percent higher for jobs outside the continental U.S.

In addition to "locality pay," certain hard-to-fill jobs in specialized scientific, technical, and medical fields begin at higher starting rates. And, as in the private sector, employees who work the night shift are paid a night differential.

GOVERNMENT EMPLOYEES GET MANY SOLID BENEFITS

Would you like paid vacations? Comprehensive health-care insurance? A secure retirement pension? Of course, you would.

With health-care costs rising—and health insurance premiums skyrocketing just as quickly—a strong benefits package is one of the most important advantages of working for the Federal government. In addition, a secure retirement is another major concern many people have. As the stock market rises and falls (and private-sector pension plans crumble under administration costs and poor investments), Federal employees have the comfort of knowing their retirement benefits are secure.

An added plus is that this solid package of benefits is available to *all* government workers, not just a selected few. This fact, combined with a sense of job security, is often enough to sway people to find a government career.

What kind of benefits do government workers receive? Below is a chart of the benefits offered to Federal employees. Packages for state, county, and city employees may differ according to location.

FEDERAL BENEFITS

Type of Benefits	Who Is Covered	Available Options
Health: *Federal Employees Health Benefits (FEHB)*	Federal Employees and Retirees and their survivors. Coverage may include: • Self only; or • Family coverage for yourself, your spouse, and unmarried dependant children under age 22	• Managed Fee for Service Plans; • Point of Service (POP) options; or • Health Maintenance Organizations (HMOs)

(continues)

FEDERAL BENEFITS (CONTINUED)

Type of Benefits	Who Is Covered	Available Options
Retirement: *Federal Employees Retirement System (FERS)*	Almost all new employees hired after 1983 are automatically covered. Employees who leave may still qualify for benefits. Builds on the Social Security benefits employees may earn in the future, or may already have earned, from non-Federal work.	FERS is a three-tiered retirement plan, consisting of these components: • Social Security benefits (available for those age 62 and retired) • Basic Benefits Plan (financed by a small contribution from the employee and the government) *A Special Retirement Supplement, for employees who meet the criteria, is paid as a monthly benefit until the employee reaches age 62.* • Thrift Savings Plan (tax-deferred retirement savings and investment plan; similar to 401(k) plans)
Life: *The Federal Employees' Group Life Insurance Program (FEGLI)*	Federal employees and retirees, as well as many of their family members are eligible for this group life insurance program.	Basic Insurance (automatic unless employee opts out; insured pays two-thirds of cost and the government pays one-third); plus Optional Insurance (not automatic; insured pays 100 percent of cost)

A GOVERNMENT CAREER IS A CAREER IN PUBLIC SERVICE

Working for the government can provide a level of satisfaction that few other careers offer. You are a public servant, in the best sense. As just a few examples, consider these important Federal agencies: the Federal Emergency Management Administration (FEMA), the Federal Aviation Administration (FAA), the Federal Bureau of Investigations (FBI), the Small Business Administration (SBA), the Center for Disease Control (CDC), or the National Institutes of Health (NIH). Each one of these agencies—and every one of its employees—is contributing to the health and welfare of the American people. In many instances, mid-career professionals who have already succeeded in the private sector want to "give something back," and will choose to work for the government, precisely for this reason.

A GOVERNMENT JOB OFFERS OPPORTUNITIES FOR ADVANCED PROFESSIONAL TRAINING

Not everyone who is hired by a government agency is fully trained to begin working their first day on the job. Additionally, many employees who are advancing within the government need substantial training to effectively handle an increase in job responsibility. In response to this need, both Federal and state agencies see to the full training of their people. As a result, multiple training and educational opportunities are available. These opportunities may include full or partial tuition reimbursement, as well as time off—sometimes with pay—to complete the programs. This is a *major* benefit, as such training helps you do your current job better and helps prepare you for future promotions.

THE GOVERNMENT HIRES PEOPLE AT ALL STAGES OF CAREER DEVELOPMENT

This is an important fact. You can be a high school graduate with virtually no work experience at all, or a recent college graduate, or a student still in college, or a veteran who is separating or retiring from the U.S. Military, and the government will have positions for which you can successfully apply. You can be a Ph.D. or a high school dropout who went back to finish the GED degree, and the government will have opportunities for you. There is almost no situation imaginable for which the Federal government does not have opportunities!

The Disadvantages of Government Work

In the previous section, you were presented with several reasons to consider working for the government on the municipal, state, or Federal levels. But what about the other side of the coin: the "con" side? There are some very important factors you need to consider before you can make an informed decision about a career in government service.

YOU WILL HAVE TO WORK IN A LARGE BUREAUCRACY

The government is a bureaucracy, an organization with a strict hierarchy. This means several things to you, the Federal employee, with regards to your ability to make a decision. First, every move you make must be approved by a rigid chain of command. Second, every action you take must have a precedent. Third, every aspect of your employment will be regulated by pre-existing guidelines and procedures that are established in your personnel manual. These regulations protect you from being fired and your job from being eliminated. However, these regulations also require you to do your work according to rules and requirements that may no longer make sense.

A bureaucracy the size of the United States government changes slowly because many of its regulations were written long ago. The situations they were to address may have changed, but the regulations and requirements remain. That's why the government is often referred to as a "dinosaur."

THE GOVERNMENT FAVORS BUREAUCRATS OVER RISK-TAKERS

A bureaucracy favors bureaucrats. It makes wonderful sense. However, if *you're* not a bureaucrat, this can become a professional challenge to your patience and persistence. If you're the kind of person who sees what needs to be done, wants to do it, and is accustomed to doing it on your own, you may find this aspect of government work intolerable. What *you* see as taking initiative, the bureaucracy may see as taking risks; after all, you're acting without precedent and without approval. Actions *you* think show you off as a "self-starter" may make you, in the bureaucracy's eyes, a "loose cannon."

CHANGE IN MOST GOVERNMENT AGENCIES IS A SLOW PROCESS

It is a general rule that as an organization grows, it becomes more cumbersome. As a result, it becomes resistant to change. With an organization as large as the government, change comes about very slowly—even on the municipal level.

On the Federal level, we're talking about a vast empire of agencies and departments, all of which are subject to regulation by the Legislative and Executive Branches of our national government. These agencies may have huge budgets, but they are not fully their own bosses. They do "the will of the people," as expressed by Congress and the Executive Branch.

On the lower levels of states and counties, agencies and departments also report to a higher authority. Even the "single person" at the top, such as the governor, listens to the ruling political party and the current mood of the people. And, in most cases, "the people" tend toward conservative changes—*slow* changes.

It all boils down to this: If you're a government worker and somewhere along the way you become dissatisfied with the status quo, you're in for a very long ride if you try to change things.

INCOMPETENCE IS EASILY HIDDEN IN LARGE ORGANIZATIONS

The larger the organization, the more "dead weight" it will carry. By "dead weight," we are referring to those employees who simply go through the *motions* of working, but who actually accomplish very little. These individuals rely heavily on the work ethic of those dedicated to their careers to cover for them.

You should be aware of this, because although most government employees will be just as diligent as you are, you may be "carrying the weight" for other, less motivated, employees. And because of all the job security that led you to the government in the first place, you may be stuck with these employees for the duration.

IT MAY BE DIFFICULT TO LEAVE A DEPARTMENT ONCE YOU'RE IN

It may come to pass during your employment that you would like to transfer into another position, or even another agency. Be forewarned, however, that receiving a transfer within the Federal government can be just as cumbersome as it was getting hired. Every personnel-related action involves large amounts of paperwork and will probably take months to process. Few bosses are likely to volunteer eagerly to get involved in instigating these paper-shuffling procedures. You may get lucky and have your transfer approved right away. Or, you may have to wait until so-and-so in the department you want finally decides to retire and frees up a vacancy.

GOVERNMENT AGENCIES ARE SUBJECT TO INTENSE POLITICAL PRESSURES

Because government agencies have so many constituencies and audiences to please, decisions can be difficult to make. The pressures governing a given situation, combined with political and/or media pressure, often cloud facts and logic—and even the purpose for which an agency exists. The "bottom line" is always changing and, in many cases, doesn't make sense.

A GOVERNMENT POSITION ON THE FEDERAL LEVEL MAY REQUIRE YOU TO TRAVEL AS PART OF YOUR WORK

Federal agencies and departments administer programs throughout the U.S. and, in many cases, overseas. Agencies need many people to ensure that these programs are operating properly and that field offices are doing what they have been asked to do.

One of the questions on the Federal application form (Form SF-171) is "Are you willing to travel?" The next question is "How frequently are you willing to travel: 1–5 nights a month, 5–12 nights a month, or more than that?" If your response is that you are unwilling to travel, you may be ruled out of consideration for the position you prefer.

The bottom line is: *Someone* needs to travel in many of these jobs. Are you willing to let that "someone" be you?

YOU MAY HAVE TO WORK HARDER FOR LESS THAN YOU EXPECT

Many people have the mistaken idea that government work is easy. Their perception may be that there is very little to do, ample opportunity for paid vacation and holidays, and unbelievable benefits. This perception is a myth—and the truth can come as quite a shock.

Government employees, for the most part, work *very* hard. And while their salaries and benefits are very good, they are not fantastic. If you're motivated by money alone and want to reach incredible professional heights very quickly, government work is not for you.

Comparing Public- and Private-Sector Employment

The "pros" and "cons" considered in the previous section address government work in and of itself. However, a career in the public sector is an alternative to a career in the private sector. So, it's useful to also look at how government work—with its advantages and disadvantages—compares to private-sector work.

GOVERNMENT JOBS ARE MORE SECURE

Government work has always been secure. In the last decade, however, security has become a rare commodity in the private sector. As a result, job security must be considered when comparing public- and private-sector employment.

Do you wake up every morning worrying whether you still have a job? Do you anxiously listen to news reports and rumors about corporate takeovers? Most of the traditionally accepted ideas of job security have been destroyed. Even the terminology has changed: "Layoff" has become "downsizing" has become "rightsizing"—as if changing the language could disguise the nightmare of losing your job. In the private sector, job security no longer exists. Period. Even a Fortune 500 company can be acquired by another company. It can always suffer huge profit downturns. And cutting payroll is one of the easiest methods for companies to show a temporary economic gain.

On the other hand, the government doesn't have to show a profit to stockholders every three months. And no one is trying to buy out the Department of Agriculture.

Because of this fact, security is one of the largest advantages of government work. With government work, you no longer have to worry about basic economic survival. You can finally have peace of mind.

GOVERNMENT PAY AND BENEFITS ARE COMPARABLE TO MOST PRIVATE-SECTOR PAY AND BENEFITS

Government salaries, at least on the Federal level, are legally required to be comparable to those in the private sector. Government pay is determined by surveying the salaries in the private sector. In addition, the government has a "locality pay differential" for areas of the country that have a higher cost of living, as well as a night differential for night shifts.

In addition, government health-care benefits are strong and consistent across all agencies and departments. This may not be the case with many private-sector jobs. Benefits in the private sector are subject to more frequent change than in civil service—or they may not exist at all.

Additionally, civil service retirement plans are very good—and they're guaranteed. Private-sector plans, on the other hand, often become uncertain when it's time to actually pay out. The private sector favors executives in both salaries and benefits, while the government offers the same benefits package to all. Of course, there are differences between the benefits on the Federal level and on the individual state, county, or city level; between the public and the private sectors; and within the private sector itself.

As a quick example of these differences, take a look at something relatively simple: the number of paid holidays a company might offer. Let's begin with paid holidays offered to Federal employees:

FEDERAL HOLIDAYS

New Year's Day	Labor Day
Martin Luther King, Jr.'s Birthday	Columbus Day
Washington's Birthday	Veterans Day
Memorial Day	Thanksgiving Day
Independence Day	Christmas Day

In a suburb of New York City, civil service employees receive the above 10 holidays, plus Lincoln's Birthday, Good Friday, Election Day (even in non-presidential election years), and the day after Thanksgiving, for a total of 14. Not every state, county, or city, however, may be this generous.

How does the private sector compare? There are wide differences. As an example, one Fortune 500 company gives employees twelve paid holidays. Six are called "national holidays" (New Year's Day, Memorial Day, Independence Day, Labor Day, Thanksgiving, and Christmas Day). In addition to these, three more paid holidays are decided upon by the employee's local branch, depending on what other companies in the area give. And still another three days are given as personal holidays, chosen by the employee, for a total of twelve. By contrast, a large national retail store has only six paid holidays—the same six listed above. And, being a retailer, this organization is open for two of those six days—Memorial Day and Labor Day. So even though an employee will be paid for the holiday, he or she may also have to work on it.

THE GOVERNMENT HAS LESS DISCRIMINATION THAN THE PRIVATE SECTOR

No one likes to talk openly about discrimination, such as sexism or racism, in the workplace. It exists in both the private and public sectors. However, because the process of hiring and promotion of government employees is ruled by precedent and regulations and is less vulnerable to individual likes and dislikes, there is less discrimination.

This is particularly true with regards to age. In the private sector, youth is prized because of its energy and enthusiasm, its up-to-date knowledge straight from college or grad school, and its lower pay ranges. Someone in his or her fifties may find it difficult to find a new position in the private sector.

In government, however, positions are graded in terms of their salaries—not in terms of age (unless a job has physical requirements). Thus, a Federal agency may have a GS-13 position to fill for an accountant. Anyone with the requisite experience is eligible to apply. If you're 37, you won't be paid any more or any less than someone who is 53, as long as you both qualify for the job.

As a result of this leniency towards age, many older workers who are coming from 10 or 20 years in the private sector can begin a full second career in government. In addition, veterans who have completed a full 20-year career in the military can begin a second career as civilian employees of the government. That's much harder to do in the private sector.

GOVERNMENT WORK ALLOWS MORE FLEXIBLE JOB QUALIFICATIONS

How many times have you seen a job advertisement ask for X years of experience or a specific type of college degree? Such qualifications are standard for most private-sector jobs.

In the government, however, the process of qualifying for jobs is much more flexible. Often, a vacancy announcement will indicate that X years of experience can be substituted for X years of college education, or even for a college degree. Because it is a public-sector employer paying salaries with public funds, the government has made a point—supported by laws and legislation—to protect the rights and career aspirations of all Americans. As a result, very few government positions require a specific type of college degree. Not even senior-level positions require a specific degree, and in many cases, they require no degree at all. In practice, this means that a person with no degree can become a top-level manager overseeing the work of Ph.Ds.

As long as you present your qualifications effectively on the application forms that you submit, you can qualify for many government jobs that might be out of reach in the private sector. The key, of course, is presenting your qualifications effectively. You'll learn that in the following chapters.

THE PRIVATE SECTOR VALUES "SUPERSTAR" EMPLOYEES, MORE SO THAN THE PUBLIC SECTOR

Working in a government bureaucracy is not about acting alone. Nor is it about taking chances based on sudden hunches, in hopes of taking center stage and getting applauded for your intuition and initiative. Unlike private companies, there are very few "superstars" in the Federal government. Instead, there are endless committee meetings to keep people "in the loop." Government work is not about being an all-star or a lone wolf. It's more about building a set of working relationships with professionals throughout government service, and using these contacts to advance your organization's agenda.

If you are someone who needs attention and recognition, you may well be better off in the private sector. If you don't mind working behind the scenes and don't care who gets the credit as long as the job gets done, you may do very well in a government career.

THE PRIVATE SECTOR OFFERS FASTER, GREATER REWARDS TO ITS EXECUTIVE WORKERS THAN THE PUBLIC SECTOR

Do you want to make a lot of money—and make it quickly? Depending on how important this is to you, the private sector may be the better place.

Top executives in the private sector make as much as five times more than public-sector executives who are managing programs of comparable size. Commissions, stock options, golden parachutes—none of these are available to civil service workers.

Deciding On the Best Job for You

There is no easy formula for comparing civil service jobs to those in the private sector. There are no numbers that result in a right or wrong answer to the question of where you should work. There are only advantages and disadvantages to consider, each of which has its own importance to your particular situation. Many of the advantages are practical: salary, health-care, vacation, and pension benefits. Conversely, many of the disadvantages are more a matter of atmosphere, context, and your own personality.

The smart way to make the decision is to be absolutely honest about your needs, your family's needs, what motivates you, and even what drives you crazy. Ask yourself these tough questions:

- How much money is "enough"?
- How much job risk is tolerable?
- How much money does your family need?
- How much risk can your family tolerate?
- What are the health-benefit needs of you and your family?
- How well do you handle change?
- Do you require constant change?
- What type of work environment do you prefer? Slow-paced vs. fast-paced, etc.
- How well do you work with other people?
- Can you be a team player or must you be the "star"?
- How much frustration can you tolerate, in exchange for how much security?

You will have to choose which factors make the most sense for you and your personal situation. You'll also have to rely on a certain level of instinct and decide which "feels right" to you—or at least feels better.

LAUNCHING YOUR FEDERAL GOVERNMENT JOB SEARCH

The Federal government is so huge and complicated that it may be difficult to envision yourself as a Federal employee. You're familiar with civil service in the local area: You know your town or city's police and fire personnel, at least by sight, and you've probably had dealings with borough officials. You may even be somewhat familiar with civil service on the county level; perhaps you've had jury duty and have toured the county's court and jail system.

But the *Federal* government? Since we seldom think of Charlie, our letter carrier, as a Federal employee, trying to "break into Washington" may summon up the picture of ourselves knocking on the door of the White House.

But the Federal government has innumerable offices throughout the country. Look in your county phone book for the government listings. The Veterans Administration, Social Security Administration, various divisions of the Armed Forces, Justice Department, Internal Revenue Service, Small Business Department, Department of Transportation, and others all likely have offices surprisingly close to where you live right now. And everyone in those offices is a Federal employee. You could be, too.

General Job Categories and Programs Available at the Federal Level

As we said in the last chapter, the Federal government is the country's largest employer. That means it has room for almost every imaginable occupation. It also has an enormous variety of special programs to encompass many different hiring situations. A quick look will show you just how many:

- **Professional occupations** require knowledge of a field that is usually gained through education or training equivalent to a bachelor's degree or higher, with major study in or pertinent to the specialized field—e.g., engineer, accountant, biologist, chemist.
- **Administrative occupations** usually require progressively responsible experience. More than a college education is required, although professional training and study may be involved—e.g., personnel specialist, administrative officer.
- **Technical occupations** involve training and experience—e.g., computer programmer, telecommunications specialist, electronics technician.
- **Clerical occupations** generally involve structured work in support of office, business, or fiscal operations—e.g., clerk-typist, mail and file clerk.
- **Skilled trades** involve manual work that usually requires a "journeyman" status in fields such as plumbing, HVAC technician, electricians, carpenters, and machinists.

PART-TIME PROGRAMS

Part-time positions—that is, 16 to 32 hours per week—are available in agencies throughout the Federal government. Flex time, job sharing, and nontraditional workday and workweek scheduling is also available in some positions. Inquire at personnel offices in agencies where you feel you may want to apply.

13

STUDENT PROGRAMS

The Federal government has a number of programs in place specifically designed to provide employment for students. These programs include:

- **Summer employment** for high school, college, law, medical, and dental students is available. Applications are accepted for summer employment from December through April 15, and the jobs usually run from mid-May through September 30. Hiring is done by individual agencies. Some restrictions limit summer employment in the same agency where the applicant's parent also may be employed.
- **The Federal student career program** is a work/study option for high school, vocational, or technical school, and college students enrolled in school at least half-time. This program offers employment in positions directly related to the student's course of study. Positions in this program can lead to permanent employment upon a student's graduation. Students interested in this option should contact their high school counselors, college employment coordinators, or the agency where they would like to work.
- **Student temporary employment** offers a part-time opportunity for students. These positions are not necessarily related to the professional careers for which these students are preparing themselves. This employment must end when a student is no longer enrolled in school at least half-time. The procedure for identifying and qualifying for this program is similar to the Federal student career experience.
- **The Presidential Management Interns (PMI) program** is targeted at graduate students in the last year of their advanced studies who intend to make a career in public service. Only graduate students who expect to receive their degrees by the next June should apply. These students enter the two-year PMI program at the GS-9 level and perform high-level work in their chosen fields. At the end of the two years, PMIs may continue in regular Federal employment at the GS-12 level. Students interested in this program must be nominated by the dean of the college or university or by the chairman of their department or graduate program.

VETERANS PROGRAMS

U.S. Military veterans are entitled to special consideration in Federal hiring. In some cases, veterans are entitled to positions that are not open to the general public. In other cases, extra points are added to their exam scores, giving them a competitive advantage. The Veterans Employment Coordinator at the agency where you want to apply can give you additional information.

PROGRAMS FOR PERSONS WITH DISABILITIES

Persons with disabilities should contact the Selective Placement Coordinator at the agency of interest to explore special placement assistance that is available to candidates with physical, cognitive, or emotional disabilities. By law, the Federal government—just as the private sector must—will make "reasonable workplace accommodations" for persons with disabilities; this means that the employer may adjust the duties of the job, the location where it's performed, or the methods in which it's performed.

PROGRAMS FOR RESIDENTS OUTSIDE THE CONTINENTAL U.S.

Alaska, Guam, Hawaii, Puerto Rico, and the Virgin Islands offer very limited Federal employment possibilities. Local residents will receive first consideration for employment in these areas. Other candidates will be considered only when there are no qualified residents available.

How to Find Federal Jobs That Are Right for You

Matching your experience and background to a Federal job is perhaps one of the most difficult aspects of getting Federal work. Part of this difficulty results from the fact that you have to find the vacancies yourself. You can't simply send in a resume or application and say, "Hey, Washington—here's what I can do. Who wants to hire me?"

There's no centralized personnel department for the Federal government. Years ago, the Office of Personnel Management (OPM) used to serve that function. However, with so many agencies and so many applicants, OPM would take months to identify candidates and send their applications to the agency with the opening. Agencies complained that it was almost impossible for them to hire the people they needed, *when* they needed them. Finally, OPM gave up its authority in this area and now each Federal agency does its own hiring. The result, however, doesn't make it easier for applicants, for a number of reasons, many of which are discussed below.

YOU MUST LOOK BEYOND THE TITLE

Say you want to become a Federal employee. You're open to a number of position types, but because of your background you look for jobs with titles similar to your current title. If you limit yourself to that, you might miss other openings for which you qualify. Instead of looking at a title and thinking, "I don't have the experience to do that," pick titles that make you think, "Gee, that sounds interesting." Then read the qualifications. You just might be eligible.

Also, some titles can be very deceptive. When looking for a Federal position, for example, an administrative assistant rightfully may think the position of "secretary" could be appropriate, then discovers it's for a high-ranking executive (think "Secretary of State"). Or, a recent graduate might see impressive-sounding titles such as "Agriculture Science Research Technician" or "Airway Transportation Systems Specialist" and immediately assume these are higher-ranked jobs for people with years of experience. A look at the salary, however, shows that these jobs start under $22,000—obviously positions for the newer employee. A few extra seconds of investigation can help you decipher the title to get a closer look at the job.

Additionally, don't dismiss Federal work in general because the government just wouldn't hire "someone like you." The government needs more than just accountants, soldiers, mechanics, clerks, nuclear scientists, and so on. On a single recent day, there were openings for a graphic illustrator, a sports specialist, an archaeologist, a horticulturist, a manager for a community club, an outdoor-recreation planner, a leisure-travel arranger, and a religious education specialist. What's even more surprising than the variety is that all these jobs were for the same agency—the Army!

KEEP CHECKING THE ANNOUNCEMENTS

You must apply for a particular position in a particular agency, because you're really applying for a specific vacancy, not just a job title. Most agencies don't refer to past applications. They don't "keep your resume on file," which many private-sector companies do. Think of it like this: You're not just applying for, say, an accounting position. When accountant Pat Smith retires, it's Pat Smith's vacancy you're applying for. What this means in terms of legwork is a constant monitoring of openings.

For every opening, agencies must publish an announcement of the vacancy, if they're going to fill it. This means you must constantly watch the job vacancy announcements for the agency you're interested in—or keep track of vacancies for several agencies if you're focused more on the kind of job rather than the agency where you perform it.

APPLY SEPARATELY FOR EACH VACANCY

Each time you spot an appropriate vacancy, you usually have to fill out an application form. You can't ask Agency X to refer to the application you sent in last month to Agency Y—even though that application might have taken days to fill out and was two dozen pages long. Except for a few closely related jobs that might be open within the same agency, each position requires its own application.

TAILOR YOUR APPLICATION OR RESUME TO THE JOB

While you would do this in the private sector as well, there is simply no comparison to the depth of "tailoring" that's needed to get Federal employment. The two-dozen-page application mentioned above is not an exaggeration. Your application should mirror the language of the vacancy announcement, then provide details that prove you have the knowledge, skills, and abilities (abbreviated KSAs) to fill the opening. You learn more about KSAs in Chapter 3.

WATCH OUT FOR CIVIL SERVICE JOB-HELP SCAMS

About now you may be asking yourself, "Can't anyone help me? Aren't there Federal-Employment Agencies?" And the answer is—beware! The government does not sign itself up with employment agencies the way a private-sector company might, so avoid any "employment agency" which promises that the government or a particular agency is its client and that it can help you—for a hefty fee—get the job you want.

Everything you need to get Federal work can be had directly from the government and it's readily available if you're willing to spend the time and do the legwork to find it. All the information is free, the forms and directions are free, the process of applying is free. A person or agency that suggests otherwise is stealing from you as directly as a pickpocket. Also beware a person or agency that guarantees you a job, or guarantees you a higher score, or says that there are "hidden" vacancies not listed in the announcements, but which *they* can reveal to you.

REMEMBER, YOU CAN DO IT YOURSELF

What's *legitimate* help? Your *Civil Service Handbook* and other guides to the topic are not only legitimate, they're often your best buy—giving you "the most bang for your buck." These guides can help you save time and effort, plus give you valuable proven tips you might not have discovered otherwise. There are also personal coaches who will hold your hand step by step through the search-and-application process. They, too, are legitimate but sometimes provide simply the same information that's in a guide like this, only at higher cost because of the personalized, one-on-one nature of their service.

With the advent of the Internet also comes brand-new legitimate help—search engines that automatically match up key words in your experience or education with keywords in current vacancies. Some of the free government sites will do this. There are also private sites that provide this matching, as well as a range of other services, for varying prices—a monthly subscription cost in some cases, a flat fee per each service in others.

If you're interested in this type of help, however, try to stay with sites that appear as links on official government Web pages. These will be the most reputable. And check carefully. Some online sites have names that imply they're "official government sites" by tagging "U.S." or "American" or the like onto the site title—then burying the fee down where the information you want most is located. Private sites say right up front that they're a private source of information.

And speaking of sources of information leads to the next question on any job seeker's list: Since you can apply only for a specific opening, where do you find announcements about actual job vacancies?

Making Contact: How and Where to Track Down Actual Job Vacancies

Although the difficulty involved may convince you otherwise, the Federal government *wants* you to work for it and, therefore, has many ways you can find out what openings are available in what agencies. The following sections discuss the many sources for Federal employment information and job bank listings.

DIRECT CONTACT

If you know which agency or agencies you want to work for, you may contact them directly to learn what vacancies exist and how to apply for them. At some agencies, you may be able to prepare an application that will be kept on file for future vacancies. Other agencies accept applications only for current or projected openings. Ask, so you'll know whether the agency's openings need constant monitoring.

If a Federal agency has an office in your area, you may find its telephone number under "U.S. Government" in the blue pages of the phone book. If the agency has no office in your area, place a call to information in the District of Columbia, (202) 555-1212, and ask for the telephone number of the personnel office or employment office of the agency you want to reach. Calls to government offices must be made during business hours, so prepare your questions ahead of time to hold down your phone bill.

To get you started, Appendix A, "Important Civil Service Employment Contacts," lists phone numbers, addresses, and Web sites for the major Federal agencies.

AUTOMATED PHONE CONTACT

Under the blue-page listing for "U.S. Government," there should also be numbers for the U.S. Office of Personnel Management or the nearest Federal Job Information Center. These numbers can give you automated job information about your own area or may direct you to a location where you can pick up printed materials or conduct a detailed search on a computer touch screen. Automated telephone systems can be accessed 24 hours a day by touch-tone phone. Because you may be on for quite a while searching job categories and geographical areas, you may want to place your call while less-expensive evening, night, or weekend phone rates apply. A complete listing of local numbers for Automated Telephone Systems appears in, "Important Civil Service Employment Contacts," on page 207.

Another source of automated telephone information is the *Career America Connection*. This system provides current worldwide Federal job announcements, salary and employee-benefits information, special recruitment messages, and so on. The system can also record your name and mailing address so you can be sent vacancy announcements and forms through the mail. This service can be contacted using the following telephone number:

Career America Connection
(912) 757-3000
TDD Service (912) 744-2299

FAX ON DEMAND

Yet another way to receive information is through *FEDFAX*. This fax-on-demand service allows you to receive information on a variety of employment-related topics, as well as forms, by fax. The automated service may be accessed 24 hours a day, 7 days a week, by calling any of the following telephone numbers from a touch-tone phone or a fax machine:

Atlanta: (404) 331-5267

Denver: (303)969-7764

Detroit: (313) 226-2593

San Francisco: (415) 744-7002

Washington, D.C.: (202) 606-2600

STATE EMPLOYMENT OFFICES

Some state employment offices carry Federal job listings in print or on microfiche. Others maintain touch-screen computers, which have the listings of available Federal jobs within those states. To see what services *your* state employment office offers, call it directly or check with your public library.

TOUCH-SCREEN COMPUTER KIOSKS

Federal Job Information Touch-Screen Computers are located throughout the United States. These kiosks (small, open-sided buildings, like a newsstand) provide current Federal job opportunities available worldwide, online information, and more. The kiosks are generally open during normal business hours, Monday through Friday. Appendix A, "Important Civil Service Employment Contacts," contains a complete listing of locations for these kiosks across the United States.

THE INTERNET

The Internet is perhaps the single most valuable source of Federal job information. Information on Federal jobs available in your neighborhood is as easily accessed as information on jobs across the country—or around the world. You can also download application forms, check salaries and benefits, even research the geographic areas where particular jobs are located.

The Net greatly reduces your legwork; now you can "let your fingers do the walking."

In "Webliography of Federal Employment Web Sites," on page 213, you'll find listings of sites enormously useful in getting Federal employment. Not all of them are official government sites. But even the private ones contain much helpful information and practical tips—for free.

The Anatomy of a Federal Job Announcement: What to Look For and How to Use It

Job announcements in the private sector are short and simple. A classified ad, whether in the paper or online, states that the ABC company wants to hire someone for an XYZ position. The requirements are summed up in a few words or, at most, a few sentences. An address or phone number is given to mail, e-mail, or fax your resume. You send in your cover letter and one- or two-page resume and that's it—you've successfully applied for the job. Your resume generally goes to ABC's Human Resources Department and, if it passes the initial screening, is forwarded to the actual department with the opening.

In the Federal government, however, this process is more complicated. Most Federal vacancy announcements are between four and eight pages in length, single-spaced. That's just the job *announcement,* not the application document you submit for the job. The announcement may include descriptions of the position's duties and responsibilities, qualifications, experience desired, KSAs desired (Knowledge, Skills, and Abilities), whether competitive testing is required, and so on.

The key to surviving the application process and to being seriously considered (and thus, hired) begins with your understanding the job vacancy announcement. The vacancy announcement is filled with details that *MUST* be on your application or instructions that *MUST* be followed to keep your resume out of the trash bin. The announcement is also filled with clues that, if found and understood, tell you what *SHOULD* be on your application to get you called in for an interview.

THE "MUSTS"

You must make absolutely certain that you include each of the following items on your application:

- **The job's vacancy announcement number.** You already know that to qualify for a Federal job, you must apply for an announced vacancy: a *specific* position with its own vacancy announcement number. This number must be put on your application; otherwise, the screening panel won't know which position you want to be considered for. Without this number—whether you apply by form or resume—your application is likely to be thrown out. The screening panel will *not* sift through all the available jobs to match up other hints from your application to the current vacancies: "Oh, he must have meant Job #XXXX." It won't happen.

- **The job's title, job classification series, and grade-level number.** When you refer to the vacancy in your application, in any correspondence or communication, even in a phone conversation, you must refer to the position you want by its official job title, job classification series, and grade-level number. For example, *Computer Specialist, GS-334-11,* means that the job title is "Computer Specialist," its classification series is "334," and its pay-grade level is GS-11. GS refers to positions covered by the General Schedule; they go all the way up to GS-13, 14, and 15 management positions; SES in this number refers to the higher-rated Senior Executive Service positions, which range from SES-1 to SES-5 in terms of the salaries they pay.

- **The application deadline.** While the deadline date does not have to be entered on your application, it absolutely must be met. Check the announcement for the date. Some Federal jobs are "open until filled" and some are "continuously open," but this usually isn't the case. Most Federal announcements will have a two- to four-week application period. Also, how to meet the deadline is different from announcement to announcement. Some require that the deadline date be the *postmark date;* others require that the deadline date be when applications must be *received.* Read carefully. Most announcements look the same, but they don't all read the same. If you submit your application after the closing date, it will not be considered.

- **The application procedure.** Most Federal vacancies can be applied for by one of several methods—Form SF-171, Form OF-612, resume, or computer-scannable resume. However, some vacancies must be applied for in only one way, or a page limit will be given for the usually longer-is-better form or resume. Again, read carefully. Each announcement is explicit about what is required.

THE "SHOULDS"

Once you have the mandatory details straight, also check the announcement for hints on what should be on your form or resume. Here's a list of strong possibilities:

- **Language that mirrors the job announcement language.** The Federal announcements are lengthy and detailed. Agencies know what they're looking for. Your application should echo the job announcement's language to show the agency that *you* are *exactly* what they're looking for. Obviously, this doesn't mean to either quote directly from the announcement or to falsify background, experience, or abilities—but do keep the announcement at hand when crafting your application or resume. Focus on what's important to the hiring agency.
- **KSAs or "ranking factors."** An application or resume is sometimes not required to include a description of the applicant's KSAs (Knowledge, Skills, and Abilities) to be considered for a job— but it really should. If more than one applicant passes the initial screening, the KSAs are used to rank the qualified applicants. An application with no or inadequate KSAs will drop to the bottom of the list.

Selected Jobs in Federal Employment

If you haven't yet taken a good look at Federal job announcements, do so now. The following section shows you what an announcement may look like. Representative jobs have been selected: clerk-typist, police officer, accounting technician, computer specialist, personnel management specialist, contracting specialist, budget analyst, electrical worker, and welder. The pay levels range from entry-level positions to those requiring additional experience and qualifications.

Note that each announcement is set up just a bit differently than the others, so when you look for job vacancies for yourself, read those announcements carefully. Also note how specific each announcement is. It explains exactly what the duties of the position are; what the applicant must have in terms of experience and background; whether education, work experience, or volunteer experience may be substituted for any of the requirements; whether there are additional factors involved, such as taking a competitive exam or needing a security clearance; and so on. KSAs—Knowledge, Skills, and Abilities— are increasingly important as the job level goes up. In essence, KSAs are the fruit of your experience— what you learned to do.

SELECTED SERIES IN THE FEDERAL SERVICE AND JOB ANNOUNCEMENTS

Vacancy announcement information has been taken from actual vacancy announcements. The information given is abbreviated and the vacancies may not be currently available.

EXAMPLES OF GENERAL SCHEDULE OCCUPATIONS

Clerk-Typist Series (GS-0322)

Primary duties in this series involve typing letters, memoranda, and reports, using manual or electric typewriters. There is a performance test for this series, and many job announcements require a specific typing speed as verified by that test. Those employed as clerk-typists may also perform general clerical work. The clerical duties cannot include those that require specialized experience or training.

Example of Vacancy Announcement: Clerk-Typist (GS-4)

(U.S. Government Printing Office, Office of Personnel, Employment Branch)

Major Duties: Acting as a receptionist. Receiving, logging in, and making appropriate distribution of applications for employment. Preparing Standard Form 52's for separation actions and confirming requested release date with appropriate supervisor. Typing a variety of correspondence, memoranda, letters, and reports as requested. Documenting and assembling information from files, telephone calls, visitors, and other appropriate sources for use by the office.

Qualification Requirements: To qualify you must be certified to type 40 words per minute, and must have taken and passed the Clerical Examination, and meet one of the minimum qualification requirements listed below.

GS-4 Grade Level: At least 52 weeks of progressively responsible clerical, office duties, such as acting as a receptionist for the Employment Branch and responding to requests for information on various personnel topics, etc.

OR

Possess two years of education above high school level. This education must have been obtained in an accredited business, secretarial or technical school, junior college, college or university. One year of full-time quarter hours, or the equivalent in a college or university, or at least 20 hours of classroom instructions per week for approximately 36 weeks in business, secretarial, or technical school.

Other Information: You must be a United States citizen to apply.

Police (GS-0083)

The work of Federal police officers ranges from passive to very active involvement in law enforcement and protective activities. Police are trained to deal with misdemeanors and felonies. They carry firearms or other weapons, wear uniforms and badges, and use military style ranks (private, sergeant, lieutenant, etc.). They are often required to familiarize themselves with authorized weapons and demonstrate skill in using them. Federal police officers are involved in patrol duties, "control desk" activities, or detective work. They receive training in police academies or other training facilities. Titles include *Police Officer* or *Detective*.

Example of Vacancy Announcement: Police Officer (GS-5)

(Department of Veterans Affairs)

Principal Duties: The incumbent enforces Federal, state and local criminal codes and Department of Veterans Affairs regulations.

Incumbent will be responsible for response to reports of a crime in progress or calls for police assistance. He/She will conduct and prepare full reports of all investigations by questioning and taking statements from victims, witness, and complainants.

Qualification Requirements: You must be a citizen of the United States.

English Language Proficiency—If you are appointed to a direct patient-care position, you must be proficient in spoken and written English as required by 38 US 4105 (c).

GS-5 Grade Level: One year of specialized experience comparable to the next lowest level if in Federal service.

<u>Specialized Experience:</u> At least one year of specialized experience, comparable to the next lowest level if in Federal Service, which provided a knowledge of basic laws and regulations, law enforcement operations, practices, and techniques and involved responsibility for maintaining order and protecting life and property. Examples of creditable service include work on a police force, through service as a military police officer; or performing criminal investigative duties.

<u>Substitution of Education for Experience:</u>

<u>GS-5:</u> Successful completion of a full four-year course of study leading to a bachelor's degree in Police Science or a comparable degree program related to the work of the position is full qualifying.

Successful completion of a general, state, county, or municipal police academy or comparable training course that included at least 40 classroom hours of instruction in police department procedures and methods, and local law and regulations, may be substituted for a maximum of three months of specialized experience.

<u>Basis of Rating:</u> There is no written test. You will be rated based on the extent, quality, and currency of your education, experience, and training relevant to the duties of the position. Such ratings will be based on your statements in the application and on any additional information obtained by our office.

Accounting Technician Series (GS-0525)

Included in this series are account maintenance clerical and accounting technician support positions. These positions require a basic understanding of accounting systems, policies, and procedures in performing or supervising the examination, verification, and maintenance of accounts and accounting data. Positions that perform technical audit functions, develop or install revised accounting procedures, or perform similar quasi-professional accounting work are also included.

Positions require knowledge of existing accounting procedures, standard accounting codes, classifications, and terminology. Also required are an understanding of agency accounting policies, procedures, and requirements, and the ability to apply various accounting methods, forms, and techniques, but less than the broad understanding and theoretical knowledge of accounting acquired through professional education and training. Duties include classifying accounting transactions, maintaining and reconciling accounts, closing accounts and preparing reports and statements, analyzing accounting data, and examining accounts.

Basic titles in this series are *Accounts Maintenance Clerk* and *Accounting Technician*.

Example of Vacancy Announcement: Accounting Technician (GS-05)

(Defense Finance and Accounting Service—Indianapolis Center)

<u>Duties/Responsibilities:</u> Examines, verifies, and maintains account and accounting data, using knowledge of accounting systems, codes, classifications, and terminology. Representative tasks include reviewing commitment and obligation documents and collection vouchers for completeness and accuracy, reconciling monthly listings of accounts, initiating correspondence or personal contact to clear accounts and compute charges.

<u>Qualification Requirements:</u>

<u>Special Experience:</u> One year of specialized experience as a GS-04 in the Federal service, or comparable in difficulty and responsibility to GS-04 if outside the Federal service; or related experience which provided a knowledge of the subject-matter field in which the duties are to be performed. Examples of positions for which such experience may have been acquired are voucher examiners, budget clerks, cash clerks, military pay clerks, or any other position in the GS-500 group.

Educational Requirements:

Substitution of Education for Experience: Four years of successfully completed education above high school level in any field which high school graduation or the equivalent is a prerequisite may be substituted for the experience required.

Computer Specialist (GS-0334)

Computer Specialists are responsible for analyzing, managing, supervising, or performing work necessary to plan, design, develop, acquire, document, test, implement, integrate, maintain, or modify systems for solving problems or accomplishing work processes by using computers. Those in positions included in this series are responsible for helping others accomplish their work. They must know how digital computers process data, and know how to evaluate and organize work processes and problems for computer solution. Computer Specialists often support subject-matter users by developing or designing computer applications and in selecting, or assisting in selecting, computer equipment.

Example of Vacancy Announcement: Computer Specialist (GS-13)
(Department of Health and Human Services, Food and Drug Administration)

Major Duties: The incumbent manages the automated information system(s) that support(s) the product, device, establishment submissions and/or licenses regulated by the organization. The incumbent is the primary point of contact for integration and testing of regulatory management information system. Specific duties include:

- Establish and maintain integration and testing laboratory;

- Manage testing team;

- Coordinate and conduct user acceptance testing;

- Provide guidance for software quality assurance and certify the application deliverables;

- Perform fact finding studies in support of hardware and software selections, analyzing potential procurement in terms of system costs, considerations, and requirements;

- Analyze and resolve problems in the use of the network system and database architecture.

Qualifications: No general experience is required. Candidates must have had at least 52 weeks of specialized experience equivalent to the GS-12 level in the Federal service.

Specialized Experience: is experience which is directly related to the work of the positions such as: Experience that demonstrated accomplishment of computer project assignments that required a wide range of knowledge of computer requirements and techniques pertinent to the position to be filled.

Knowledge, Skills and Abilities Required:

Evaluation Method: Candidates found basically qualified will be further evaluated by determining the extent to which their work or related experience, education, training, awards, etc., indicated their possession of the knowledge, skills, and abilities (KSAs) described below.

1. Ability to manage and perform integration and testing of Oracle database applications in Windows NT and Open VMS environment. Knowledge of software engineering quality control, software testing techniques and Internet/Intranet application testing.

2. Knowledge of Oracle database and application development tools: Oracle DBMS 7.x or above, Forms 3.0, SQR, Developer 2000, Designer 2000, SQL * Plus, PL/SQL, SQL *Net.

3. Knowledge of information technology systems, including network and desktop hardware and software, communications, and programming languages.

4. Ability to meet and deal with all levels of management and customer base.

Personnel Management Series (GS-0201)

Positions in this series are responsible for directing or assisting in a personnel management program, or advising on, supervising, performing or providing staff leadership and technical guidance for work which involves two or more specialized personnel functions. Those in personnel management may also be concerned with performing specialized personnel management work not covered by other series in the Personnel Management and Industrial Relations Group (GS-0200). Personnel management involves the acquisition, retention, motivation, development, and use of the human resources of an organization.

Example of Vacancy Announcement: Personnel Management Specialist (GS-12/13)

(Health and Human Services, National Institutes of Health, Office of Research Services)

Duties: The incumbent serves as senior Personnel Management Specialist and participates in the development of Human Resources Management (HRM) policies consistent with new and changing ORS program requirements and in the planning and implementation of other major HRM projects such as programs and activities. The incumbent has responsibility for competitive examining under the Office of Personnel Management's (OPM) Delegated Examining Authority (DEU). As such, the incumbent will perform basic qualifications assessment of job candidates, determine rating of basically qualified job candidates and proper ranking, and assess veteran's preferences, etc.

The incumbent also will be assigned a program area and provide management advisory services and perform staffing, placement, classification, position management, and pay management for program areas assigned. Provides expert advice and assistance to human resource staff, job applicants, and program and management officials on a variety of complex issues such as recruitment/staffing, compensation, position descriptions, and crediting plans. The incumbent will advise on classification principles and practices which address issues of sound position management, effective organizational structure and employee promotional potential. Serves as an expert and senior staff resource person in the area of personnel staffing. Advises management on laws, rules, regulations, and policies formulated at the OPM, DHHS, and NIH levels which apply to Human Resource Management.

Knowledge, Skills, and Abilities (KSAs):

1. Knowledge of the rules, policies, and procedures pertaining to the operations of a U.S. Office of Personnel Management (OPM) delegated management unit.

2. Knowledge of classification principles, regulations, policies, and practices including positions in both the general schedule and wage-grade pay plans.

3. Knowledge of staffing principles, regulations, policies, and practices.

4. Skill in written communication.

Contracting Series (GS-1102)

Those who work in occupations that are included in this series manage, supervise, perform, or develop policies and procedures for professional work involving the procurement of supplies, services, construction, or research and development. They use formal advertising or negotiation procedures and evaluate contract price proposals. They administer contracts, from initiation to termination and close out. Positions in the Contracting Series require knowledge of the legislation, regulations, and methods used in contracting, and of business and industry practices, sources of supply, cost factors, and requirement characteristics.

Example of Vacancy Announcement: Contract Specialist (GS-7)

(National Park Service, Omaha, Nebraska)

Duties: The incumbent serves as a contract specialist and performs the full range of contracting duties, or provides assistance to a higher ranking contract officer. Is independently responsible for the pre-award, award, administration, and close out of standard contracts for supplies, services, or construction. Works with program managers to develop and administer interagency and cooperative agreements. Performs other administrative and related duties.

Qualification Requirements: Applicants will not be required to take a written examination, but will be rated on the extent and quality of their education and/or experience according to information provided in their application forms. To be rated eligible, applicants must meet the Basic Requirements and ONE of the additional requirements described below.

Basic Requirements:

A. A four-year course of study leading to a bachelor's degree with a major in any field.

OR

B. At least 24 semester hours in any combination of the following fields: accounting, business, finance, law, contracts, purchasing, economics, industrial management, marketing, quantitative methods, or organization and management, OR a passing score on an examination or examinations considered by the Director, Office of Personnel Management to demonstrate skill, knowledge, or abilities comparable to that of an individual who has completed at least 24 semester hours (or the equivalent) of study in any of these academic disciplines, PLUS appropriate experience or additional education.

Additional Qualifications for Contracting Specialist: GS-7

Specialized Experience: Applicants must have at least one year of experience performing work of the type listed in the following examples: developing, preparing, and presenting terms and conditions in bids or proposals related to the award of contracts; or negotiating and awarding contracts, contract modifications, and subcontracts; or in legal practice involving the analysis of procurement policies and procedures; or administering the terms and conditions of contracts, including such aspects as preparing contract modifications, evaluation of performance under the contract, and contract termination; or analyzing proposed prices or costs, including such aspects as evaluating technical and audit reports, forecasting price trends, evaluating economic factors, estimating production efficiencies, and evaluating methods of allocating costs through various types of overhead and general administrative expense.

OR

Education: Applicant must have one year (18 semester hours) of graduate education or law school which equipped them with the knowledge, skills, and abilities to successfully perform the duties of this position. This education should be in one of, or a combination of, the following: acquisition management, business administration, contracting or procurement, economics, finance, industrial management, law, management and organization, marketing, public administration, purchasing, quantitative methods, or another field related to the position.

Budget Analysis Series (GS-0560)

Work in this series includes formulation of budget and cost estimates to support plans, programs, and activities. They present and defend budget estimates before fund reviewing and granting authorities, and review and evaluate budget requests. Responsibilities also include administration and review of requests for apportionments and allotments; review, control, and reporting of obligations and expenditures; and development, determination, and interpretation of budgetary policies and practices.

Example of Vacancy Announcement: Budget Analyst (GS-13)

(Navy, Naval Supply Systems Command)

Duties/Responsibilities: The incumbent is responsible to the program managers for all areas of financial support that includes budget formulation, budget presentation and justification, budget execution, contract review and monitoring, financial management and financial security.

Selective Placement Factor: Minimum of two years specialized experience in Sensitive Compartmented Information Programs and security requirements involved in finance execution and administration of such Programs.

(MUST MEET THIS FACTOR TO BE CONSIDERED)

Qualification Requirements: Qualification requirements are derived from the Office of Personnel Management's Qualification Standards handbook. Experience must indicate how it has equipped the applicant with the particular knowledge, skills, and abilities to perform successfully the duties of the position described above. Education may be substituted for experience. All education and experience must be met by closing date to be considered.

Candidates must possess a minimum of one year of specialized experience equivalent to the next lower grade level. Specialized experience is experience that is directly related to the position to be filled and which has equipped the candidate with the particular knowledge, skills, and abilities to successfully perform the duties of the position.

Knowledge, Skills, and Abilities: Eligible applicants meeting the minimum qualification requirements for this position will be further evaluated based on their possession of the essential knowledge, skills, and abilities necessary for the successful job performance. This rating process will determine those who will be referred to the selecting official (i.e., the best qualified). Please describe fully but concisely how your experience supports each of the following job elements. At the end of the discussion of each job element, please provide a cross reference (by paragraph number) to your application (OF 612, SF 171 or other records).

Ranking Factors: (These are not mandatory to be considered for a position, but will be used to determine who are the highest qualified candidates among those who meet the selective placement factor.)

1. Knowledge of DoD Planning, Programming and Budget System

2. Knowledge of financial/business management functions

3. Knowledge of DoD and Navy budgeting and programming policies

4. Knowledge of and application of spreadsheet applications

5. Ability to analyze and evaluate financial data

6. Ability to be a team member

7. Ability to communicate orally and in writing.

Security Clearance: A Top Secret security clearance with access is a requirement for employment; must meet DCID 1/14 requirements for continued employment; polygraph required.

EXAMPLES OF FEDERAL WAGE SYSTEM (WS) OCCUPATIONS

Electrical Worker (WG-2805, Grade 8)

Workers at this grade level make repairs that involve removing, replacing, tightening, splicing, soldering, and insulating defective wiring, controls, equipment, and fixtures such as broken and bare wiring, burned out switches and relays, loose connections and fittings, damaged light fixtures, and poorly operating thermostats. They follow work orders, oral instructions, and wiring diagrams that describe the nature of the repair or installation to be made, the layout and placement of circuitry, fixtures, and controls, and the types of wiring, parts, and equipment installed.

Electrical workers must possess a knowledge of where fixtures, wiring, and controls, such as light switches, circuit breakers, fuses, relays, and outlets are installed and how to operate them. They must be able to read and follow wiring diagrams, and have the skill necessary to measure, cut, and bend wire and conduit to specified lengths and angles. They must have the ability to use hand and portable power tools, and a limited variety of test equipment.

Example of Vacancy Announcement: Electrical Worker (WG-8)

(Marine Corp Air Ground Combat Center)

Major Duties: The incumbent will make repairs to electric systems by locating worn or damaged wiring components, using visual checks and test equipment; will remove, replace, tighten, adjust or solder defective wiring, controls, relay switches, motors, and fixtures. Installs conduit boxes and other fittings pertaining to raceways for electrical circuits by cutting, threading, bending, and fitting. Installs conductors in conduits and raceways, completing systems by connecting fixtures, switches and other components.

Performs preventive maintenance inspections on electrical and dynamic equipment; cleans, lubricates, and adjusts using inspection guides and making written reports of deficiencies. The incumbent will perform installation, modification, repairs; troubleshoots new and existing electrical/electronic systems, components circuits, lines, troubleshooting industrial solid-state electronic and electronic controlled computer circuits and systems, uninterrupted power sources, intrusion alarm systems, boiler controls, fire alarms, heating, ventilating, diesel generators, battery chargers, motors, motor controls, cranes, lighting system, electric tools, appliances, distribution panels, galley and laundry equipment shop tools and electronic controlled clock circuits. Incumbent will perform other related duties as assigned.

Qualifications Required: Applicant(s) will be required to complete Declaration for Federal Employment (OF-306) prior to offer of employment. Must be able to lift/carry up to 40 pounds.

Knowledges, Skills, and Abilities Required: In addition to the basic qualifications requirements, eligible applicants will be further evaluated against the following ranking factors to determine highly qualified candidates.

1. Ability to do the work of the position without more than normal supervision (Screen-out).

2. Knowledge of electrical equipment.

3. Knowledge of the theory and instructions used in shop and trade practices.

4. Knowledge of technical practices (theoretical, precise, and artistic).

5. Ability to use electrical drawings.

6. Ability to use and maintain hand tools (electrical).

7. Ability to troubleshoot electrical systems and use electrical test equipment.

Credit will be given for appropriate unpaid experience or volunteer work such as in community, cultural, social services, and professional association activities, on the same basis as for paid experience, provided it is directly related to the job for which you are applying. Therefore, you may report such experience in one or more of the experience blocks at the end of your employment history if you feel that it represents qualifying experience for the position for which you are applying. To receive proper credit, you must show the actual time (such as the number of hours per week) spent in such activities.

Welder, Grades 8 and 10

Grade 8 welding workers carry out standard, previously done welding operations, by applying a variety of electric resistance welding methods and equipment, or one or more manual welding processes. Grade 10 welders use accepted trade methods and a variety of manual welding processes. Grade 10 Welders, as compared to Grade 8 welders, apply knowledge of a wider range of manual welding processes and make more difficult welds. Grade 10 welders determine the work to be done and what steps are needed to accomplish it.

Example of Vacancy Announcement: Welder (WG-10)

(Department of Transportation, U.S. Coast Guard)

<u>Duties:</u> This position involves the set up and adjustment of flame cutting equipment, electric arc welding, brazing, spot welding, inert gas welding, machine cutting equipment, power shears, brake, rolls, punches, dies and other hand tools used in the welding trade and the forming of sheet metal. The incumbent welds horizontal, flat and overhead; welds on various metals and alloys of different thickness used in the fabrication and repair of machinery castings, boilers, buoys, structures, boats, ships, and their associated equipment; and fabricates sheet metal cabinets, panels, heating and air conditioning duct, transitions and fittings. Applicants must be able to lift material and equipment that weighs over 50 pounds.

<u>Qualification Requirements:</u> Although no specific amounts of education or experience are required, applicants must be able to perform journeyman-level welding without more than normal supervision.

<u>Credit for Volunteer Service:</u> Credit will be given for appropriate unpaid experience or volunteer work on the same basis as for paid experience, provided it is directly related to the job for which you are applying. To receive proper credit, you must show the actual time spent in such activities.

Making Your Way Through the Application Maze

You've already heard so many references to different forms and resumes—SF-171, OF-612, Federal Resume, computer scannable resume, Resumix, KSAs, Ranking Factors—that you may want to just give up. If you're not accustomed to writing in your current job, or if writing intimidates you, you may be even more tempted. "I'm a talker, not a writer," you may be thinking. "Interview me!"

Unfortunately for talkers, at this stage of the process, effective written presentation of your background and experience is critical. Unless you can prove some kind of disability that prevents you from preparing a written application, you must conform to the set procedures. And although it feels otherwise, fear is not considered a disabling factor.

Here are a few tips that will hopefully get you past your fear and through the maze of forms and procedures:

1. *You don't need to do everything.* Some of the forms and resumes constantly being mentioned are simply alternative ways of applying. You really only need two things: The first is a Form SF-171 *or* a Form OF-612 *or* a Federal Resume *or* a computer scannable resume. (Each of these is explained more in the next chapter.) The second thing you really need is a list of your KSAs. That's all. Each one should be detailed, true, but that's far better than needing all of them.

2. *You can choose to do what's most comfortable.* Most jobs do not require you to use a particular form, so use the one you're most comfortable with. To discover which one that is, be willing to experiment. You may be afraid of the SF-171's length, for example, only to find out the detailed questions are like someone taking your hand and walking you step-by-step through the application, making sure you forget nothing. See what works for you.

3. *Everyone else feels as intimidated as you.* No one looks at an SF-171—either to write it up or read the filled-in form—and says, "What luck! And there was nothing good on television tonight, either!" Every applicant is nervous; every applicant is doing something unfamiliar. Think of your fear as a leveling factor and just get on with it.

4. *Filling out the form is half the battle.* So many people never get past the application, you're immediately ahead of many competitors just by sitting down and filling it out. Patient persistence often wins over talent and luck. Plus, quitting now only exchanges possible rejection for certain rejection. For that's what you're doing if you yield to fear—rejecting yourself.

5. *Chapter 3 of this book gives you line-by-line help filling out the form.* Your fastest guide to getting help with your application is right in your hands—in the next chapter.

And remember that when you're culling information from the vacancy announcement and adding all the necessary detail to your application, you must be familiar with the government's hiring terminology. The "Glossary of Civil Service Hiring Terminology" on page 223 of this book has a complete listing of the most common terms you'll encounter, and how the government agencies use those terms.

Examinations for Federal Civil Service Jobs

You made it through the application filling-out, you made it through the first step of the screening process, you made it through the second step. Is it time to polish your shoes for the interview?

Not yet. Many of the positions also require the results of competitive testing. The test must be passed, and test grades also become part of the factors that determine how you compare to other competitors.

There are generally two types of competitive tests: *assembled exams* and *unassembled exams*. An assembled exam means that all the applicants assemble at the same time to take the test—whether it's a written test or a physical test of performance. An unassembled exam actually means there's no exam at all. The applicant is judged on the education and experience presented in the application; proof of achievement is usually required (diplomas, training certificates, etc.).

A written test is usually a paper-and-pen, multiple-choice format. The format of the performance test depends on the physical tasks that need to be measured. You'll receive a notice in the mail telling you of the test date and where it is to be held. If the test or the test location presents a problem to applicants with disabilities, they should call personnel at once to make other arrangements. "Federal Occupations That Require Examinations," on page 215, contains a listing of more than 220 exam-dependent occupations and their grades, and the type of exam required for each position.

The results of the test also come in the mail, giving you your test score (70 is passing) and your place on the list of eligibles when ranked with the other applicants.

Remember that not every Federal job applicant has to take a competitive exam. Some positions are by appointment rather than testing. And some groups of people *may* be eligible for appointment; in other words, they *may* be exempted from the requirement. These groups include the following:

- **Disabled veterans**—who are 30 percent or more disabled
- **Persons with severe disabilities**—who have either physical or mental impairments
- **Peace Corps or VISTA volunteers**—who have left the service within the past year
- **Foreign Service employees***—who have been, whether presently or formerly, appointed under the Foreign Service Act of 1946
- **Overseas Federal employees or family members***—who seek appointments within three years of their return to the U.S.
- **National Guard technicians***—who have been involuntarily separated from service within the last year

* There may be restrictions on certain members of these groups. See the hiring agency for details.

PUTTING TOGETHER YOUR FEDERAL JOB APPLICATION

Finding the right job with the Federal government is a big step—but it's only the first of many. The Federal government application and hiring procedures are very different from those of the private sector. You need to know how to "read" the Federal Job Announcement—to pull out all of the information you'll need in order to craft the best application. Then, you must find and correctly complete the right application form.

The Federal job application is the "make or break point" of aspiring Federal employees, the place where dreams either *remain* dreams, or become reality. Some people never even get past the forms and give up before they apply; others don't put enough effort into their applications and never get called.

There's no getting around it: The process is difficult, but it is *not* impossible. It may just take more time and patience than you had anticipated.

Giving Yourself the Edge in the Federal Hiring Process

Remember that you can't approach the Federal-employment hiring process the same way you would the private sector. To begin, you have to hustle more in the beginning—to track down job openings, to apply separately for each one, and to tailor your application or resume to the listed requirements. In a way, it's not like applying to one employer but to dozens—as many agencies and departments as you are interested in.

Above all, you must follow procedure—no matter how brilliant or qualified you may be. In other words, even though you haven't yet been hired, it's time to start thinking like a bureaucrat: Fill out the entire application, answer all the questions, recognize that *more* paperwork is *better* paperwork.

If you approach your Federal job search the same way you approach the job search in the private sector, you can be hurt by several different points of ignorance. For example, you might assume—because it's true elsewhere—that brevity is the heart of a good presentation. When searching for a job with the government, however, this is the not the case. You might also assume that if anything crucial were missing from your application package, the hiring agency would call and ask for it. Another wrong assumption. If an agency does not have the required information to process your application, you could be taken out of consideration—without knowing it. In other words, what you don't know *can* hurt you.

Information is key to your success. Find out as much as you can beforehand about the particular job, the agency, the application process, etc. Then give the agency as much information as you can in return. It's really a very influential factor. In your search, patience and persistence are as important as any of the special qualifications you may bring to the job.

Finally, think of the application as an example of the kind of work you normally do, a way to show the screening panel the neatness, accuracy, and thoroughness you normally bring to the job every day.

Federal Application Forms

With your selected job vacancy announcement in hand, you now begin the process of filling out an application form. There is a wide variety of applications you may use to apply for a job with the Federal government. So which do you use?

Basically, you only need two forms: First, you will need what is called an entry document, which can be an SF-171, an OF-612, a Federal Resume, *or* a computer scannable resume. Second, you will need a set of KSAs.

Let's look at each of these in turn.

THE SF-171

This is the "Everest" of Federal-employment forms—the one that has traditionally intimidated applicants on a regular basis. A completed SF-171 form can be quite long. A good one can run anywhere from 7 to 15 pages. (There's an example of one later in this chapter.) And the form is tedious to fill out. You have to provide details about your academic and professional career that you may not have thought about for years. But if you don't provide these details, or at least respond to these questions in some way, chances are that a personnel clerk may review your SF-171, see that items are left blank, and throw it out. Then, no matter how qualified you may be, your application will receive no further consideration.

As a result, you should fill in *all* the blanks. If you don't know the answer to a question on the form, write "N/A." But make sure you write *something* in the every blank.

One final piece of advice: Remember to sign the form. In fact, Federal personnel specialists advise that you sign it in *blue* ink, rather than black. On a quick glance, black ink may look like a photocopy. Since your application must contain an *original* signature, it could get thrown out by mistake.

THE OF-612

This form, developed during the mid-1990s, was part of a well-intended effort by the U.S. Office of Personnel Management to simplify the Federal hiring process by having an alternative form. The OF-612 is less cluttered visually and doesn't squeeze in two columns of questions on the very first page the way the SF-171 does. It also skips a few of the SF-171's questions, such as availability, military service, and others. Simply put, OF-612 looks less intimidating and more user-friendly, which is probably what the OPM wanted in an alternative form.

Unfortunately, in trying to simplify the Federal hiring process, they wound up making it more complicated because they did not drop the old form when they instituted the new one. Instead of just having one simpler form, OPM gave people a choice, and choices are always confusing. Which form should applicants fill out? Is one form better than the other? Do two forms mean they need to fill out both? And finally, many applicants think that because the OF-612 form is only two pages long and looks easier to write and to read, that their responses should be shorter.

That makes sense, but it's not true. When the OF-612 comes to the questions on describing your past work duties and describing your other qualifications, you should provide the same detail as you would on an SF-171. Don't hesitate to attach your own sheets of paper to the application so that you have room to explain in full. As with all Federal job application documents, you'll do better if you write more, rather than less. Invariably, Federal screening panels choose the strongest set of paperwork. As far as these screening panels are concerned, a good candidate equals a good set of paperwork. If you keep this in mind, you'll think more like the people who actually have a vote about your application, and that's a useful thing to do. Their vote is your ticket to a Federal job. Try to put yourself in their shoes.

THE FEDERAL RESUME

Yet another alternative way of applying, the Federal Resume is probably the least understood, because it often gets confused with a private-sector resume. Unlike a private-sector resume, which is usually no more than one or two pages, a Federal Resume can be as long or short as you want it to be. Some Federal Resumes are as long as an SF-171.

In fact, the only significant difference between this type of resume and an SF-171 is that the Federal Resume is generated by you and therefore doesn't have the form's printed lines and boxes all over the page. In addition, some of the personal information requested on the SF-171 isn't needed on a Federal Resume: your date and place of birth, questions about whether you've ever been arrested, how many hours a week you're willing to work, and more. In short, a good Federal Resume provides as much information about the details of your work history as an SF-171 does. The higher the level of the position you are applying for, the more detailed your Federal Resume should probably be. Federal Resumes that run 6 to 12 pages are acceptable. In the private sector, job candidates would never turn in a 12-page resume unless they were applying for an upper-level academic or research position and had dozens of publications to their credit.

Warning: Don't be misled by the word "resume" on the vacancy announcement. The "resume" you're being asked to submit is a Federal Resume.

If the "How to Apply" section of a vacancy announcement states that you can submit "a resume, SF-171, or OF-612," the kind of resume you should submit is the *Federal Resume.* If you read the vacancy announcement carefully, you will often see a list of details that your resume needs to provide: names and phone numbers of your present and past job supervisors, salaries you earned in these positions, and similar information. On a private sector resume, this information is not expected. However, on a Federal Resume you are usually asked and expected to provide this information and more.

THE COMPUTER SCANNABLE RESUME, OR RESUMIX™

The computer scannable resume and Resumix™ are one in the same. Resumix™ is simply the name of the company that invented this form. This is an application document that several Federal agencies have started to use.

Unlike the SF-171 or OF-612 (which are reviewed by actual people), the computer scannable resume is fed into the database of a mainframe computer system. An artificial intelligence program then scans your material, looking for certain key words and phrases. As a result, in writing this kind of resume, you need to mirror the language contained in the vacancy announcement you are responding to, since that is the key to this process.

You also need to produce a document which is physically capable of being scanned—or, in some cases, e-mailed. Forget the different fonts and stylistic creativity that you hope make your private-sector resume stand out in the pile. Here are some simple tips to follow:

- Do not underline for emphasis.
- Do not use bold or italics for emphasis.
- Do not use forward or backward slashes, such as "supervised each employee in drawing up his/her professional goals."
- Do not use fancy or unusual fonts. Simple typefaces are recommended, such as Courier, Arial, or Times New Roman. No part of any letter must touch any part of any other letter.
- Do not use very small or very large type sizes. The standard is 10 pt. or 12 pt.
- As with every computer document, do not bend, fold, staple, tape, or mutilate your resume in any way.

The hiring agency that allows a Resumix™ may ask that you cover only specific points on it, so that it may end up being rather short (compared to an SF-171). However, in those cases, the agency will also give you a *supplemental data sheet* with a list of questions, to be submitted as a separate document. The supplemental data sheet solicits the other information usually asked for on the SF-171—such as your lowest acceptable pay grade, willingness to accept temporary or part-time work, military experience, and so on. All this is in addition to the computer scannable resume and in addition to the KSAs.

THE KSAs OR RANKING FACTORS

Almost every Federal vacancy lists criteria that the hiring agency feels is essential for strong job performance. These criteria are called different names by different Federal agencies. Some agencies call these "ranking factors," "selection criteria," or "rating factors." Some agencies actually call them "KSAs."

KSA stands for "Knowledge, Skill, Ability"—because these are the general criteria an agency expects a successful candidate to possess in order to do the job. Some typical KSAs are "Ability to communicate orally and in writing," or "Knowledge of the Federal budgeting system," or "Skill in negotiating contracts with vendors and suppliers." Usually there are four to six of these KSA factors for each vacancy announcement. Many KSAs repeat from one vacancy announcement to another, so if you're applying for eight different positions as an Accounting Technician, say, you'll probably find that all eight vacancy announcements are fairly similar and that the KSAs you wrote for the first one can be used again almost verbatim for the others.

You must respond in writing separately—apart from your entry document—to these KSAs in order to be selected for an interview. As a general rule of thumb, if you are applying for a position at the GS-5 level or below, a half-page response is usually sufficient. But if you are applying at the GS-7 level or above, you should submit a full-page written response to each factor, detailing examples of times when you used the type of Knowledge, Skill, or Ability referred to in the vacancy announcement.

These KSAs are quite important in the final selection process. Don't ignore or neglect them, as they are usually the difference between a decent application and a winning one.

WHICH FORM DO I CHOOSE?

On occasion, a hiring agency will state in the job announcement the format that it prefers you use. So, of course, in that instance, you will use the requested form. However, most agencies accept all of them and will say so in the announcement. From your point of view, it probably makes no difference. The questions that have been dropped from the SF-171 are relatively short anyway. In all cases you should focus on describing your past duties and responsibilities; detailing the Knowledge, Skills, and Abilities you developed; and quantifying or in some other way explicitly explaining what you did and the results.

Crafting Your Application to Match Career Area and Agency Standards

The Federal government uses a two-stage screening process in selecting candidates to be interviewed and, ultimately, hired. The first stage involves the SF-171, OF-612, Federal Resume, or computer scannable resume that has been asked for in the vacancy announcement. In the first stage, these documents are screened by a Federal personnel clerk to weed out those that are unacceptable or incomplete, then they're screened by a panel of Federal mid- to senior-level managers to see who is eligible to compete for the vacancy at the level that was announced. So, for example, your application as a GS-13 Budget Analyst might be complete in all its parts, but the panel may determine that you have only enough experience for a GS-11 level—which is not the advertised opening. At that point, your application will be out of the running.

If it makes it through the panel, you face the second step in the screening process where the panel then compares you directly to all the other applicants that have made it that far. The panel does this by using your KSAs to rank the "survivors." So you see how providing a wealth of detail on your application helps. You don't get a second chance to explain yourself; there is no "back-up plan." Both the application and the KSAs must be as complete as possible from the very beginning.

To develop an effective and competitive SF-171, OF-612, Federal Resume, or computer scannable resume for a Federal position, you will need to keep the following points in mind:

- **Remember to describe your professional experience, in detail.** You will have to provide more details than any private-sector job application ever requested. Some of the questions may seem obvious or repetitious. Complete them anyway.
- **Do more than re-describe your official job duties and job description.** Most competent employees do a lot more than their job descriptions, because most official job descriptions don't capture the true complexity of the work that has to be done. Unfortunately, instead of writing about what they *really* do in their jobs, many people just repeat the official job description.
- **Give yourself credit.** You've earned it with your good work. But you've got to let people know. Federal screening panels are quite literal in the way they review and score your application. They give you points for what is relevant in your paperwork. And remember, they *don't* give you any points for what is not included. So don't feel bashful! You don't have to sound conceited, but you *do* have to point out your accomplishments.
- **Use your Federal Resume, SF-171, OF-612, KSAs, and scannable resumes to narrate your professional "victories."** One good way to point out your accomplishments is to describe these professional "victories." These could be times when you've dealt effectively with problems, special projects, and troubleshooting assignments, or times when you've really demonstrated your value to the organizations for which you've worked. Properly described, these stories are like money in the bank. They make you and your abilities come alive to the screening panel and have impact, rather than being disguised by the verbiage of official job descriptions.
- **Highlight your professional skills by using an "action/ result" presentation.** Show your skills actually being used. Most actions have a result, especially if your actions were effective. Don't shortchange yourself. If things you have done have generated bottom-line results for your employers, then say so. Did your innovative idea save them money? Did your initiative and persistence make them money? Say so—and how much. Describe what happened. There's nothing more convincing to a skeptical screening panel than to see the word "Result" appear again and again throughout your application. It lets them know that *you* know where the bottom line is—and how to get there. *That's* what they are looking for in an employee.
- **Stop scaring yourself.** Writing an effective SF-171 or set of KSAs depends on your attitude, more than on your writing skills. Filling out these forms is unpleasant, but don't let that discourage you. The task is certainly within your abilities. And remember, the application is not a test. There are no "right/wrong" answers. There are only other competitors like yourself, who find the process just as difficult as you do. If you compete with these competitors effectively, you stand a good chance of winning.

And remember: *Someone's* going to be selected for these positions—it might as well be *you.*

"Before" and "After" Examples of Federal Job Applications

What does a good 171 or KSA look like? The easiest way to learn how to write a good Federal job application is to see the difference between some "bad" examples from several different fields—contrasted against actual job-winning entries. Note that the "bad" examples won't really seem dreadful, just rather ordinary when seen next to the "good" entries.

DESCRIPTIONS OF MAJOR DUTIES

Bad:

Coordinated complex civil cases. Developed detailed reviews and analyses. Researched and prepared comprehensive legal memoranda.

Now see how much detail has been added to the job-winning version:

Good:

Coordinated complex civil cases with various departments or divisions within FDIC. Developed detailed reviews and analyses, in preparation for counseling client representatives to improve their request for legal services.

Researched and prepared comprehensive legal memoranda for clients, drawing on my extensive knowledge and experience litigating various issues under the FDI Act, FIRREA, the FDIC Improvement Act, commercial law, real estate law, and the Bankruptcy Code.

Here is another example:

Bad:

Served as a contracting officer and contract administrator. Performed pre-award, award, and contract administration duties. Headed evaluation teams reviewing potential contractors. Prepared lease agreements.

The added details in the following show how the applicant's duties were much more responsible and varied:

Good:

Served as contracting officer and contract administrator for multi-million-dollar supplies and services, construction, and architectural and engineering contracts. Possessed a contracting officer's warrant. Performed pre-award, award, and contract administration duties. Prepared *Commerce Business Daily* synopses and advertisements, developed and reviewed technical specifications, and issued solicitations and Requests for Proposals (RFPs). Headed evaluation teams reviewing potential contractors' financial data. Prepared lease agreements for properties where contractors performed construction work.

DESCRIPTIONS OF ADVANCED TRAINING

Bad:

FBI/RTC Bank Failure School (December 7–10, 1993); Basic Examination School for Attorneys (January 1998).

Good:

FBI/RTC Bank Failure School (December 7–10, 1993). This was a highly intensive course focusing on the aspects of fraud involving financial institutions, covering such topics as Fraud Detection and Investigation, Forensic Accounting Approach, Prosecution of Financial Institution Fraud Cases, and The Importance of CPAs to Bank Examiners and Criminal Investigations.

Basic Examination School for Attorneys (January 1998). This was a week-long concentrated course focusing on fundamentals of bank supervision, basic report analysis, bank accrual accounting, loan classifications, and financial analysis.

DESCRIPTIONS OF KSAs OR RANKING FACTORS (FOR AN UPPER-LEVEL POSITION)

Bad:

Knowledge of materiel life cycle management functions, programs and systems used to provide logistical support: Gained valuable understanding of military facilities planning while serving as Acting Chief of the Facilities Management Office. Responsible for issuing policy pertaining to the total acquisition life cycle baseline parameters. Strong working knowledge of PPBES. Broad experience writing, revising, and implementing policy.

Obviously the applicant didn't know that, at this job level, he or she should include a full page for each KSA, explaining how and when the knowledge, skills, or ability was demonstrated. The paragraph above works as a bare-bones outline for the detailed job-winning entry below.

Good:

Knowledge of materiel life cycle management functions, programs and systems used to provide logistical support.

My current job includes a very substantial degree of life cycle management responsibility. For example, I currently run the policy operation of Acquisition Life Cycle management. In this capacity, the information related to guidance addressing Army's Acquisition Program Baselines (APBs) for Army Acquisition Category (ACAT) I, II and some representative III programs. Examples of my strong working knowledge in this area include the following:

Analyze the content of the APBs and ensure that APBs adequately address program requirements.

Result:

I recently issued APB policy which now requires APBs to address "total life cycle costs" which by definition includes operating and support (O&S) costs.

Keep Army and OSD leadership informed regarding how the Army executes their cost, schedule and performance parameters within their respective APBs.

Result:

Maintain close ties and frequent contacts with officials at all levels in the Army and DoD as well as the respective PEOs and PMs and Command Groups. Any known logistical support requirements would also be captured within the respective APBs.

I have gained substantial working knowledge and hands-on experience through interacting with officials in the Comptroller and Acquisition communities related to acquisition life cycle subject matter contained within APBs, SARs and DAES reports, as well as through managing these processes.

Result:

My effort to include O&S costs within APBs is unique. To this point, the other Military Services have not yet followed suit but will likely do so soon, since it is DoD policy to make Program Managers responsible for "total life cycle management." If and when this happens, these Program Managers would have total "cradle-to-grave" program responsibility—as well as operational control of the budget dollars to make sure that this level of responsibility is discharged fully and effectively.

The job-winning applicants might well have phrased their experience, background, and abilities as in the "bad" examples. If these had been private-sector resumes, that might have been enough. But the procedure is very different applying for a Federal job.

Samples of Completed Application Forms

Now let's see the results when this kind of attention to detail is applied to the entire form. Following are full-length, filled-in samples of actual job-winning application tools: a filled-in SF-171, a filled-in OF-612, a Federal Resume, a Resumix™ or computer scannable resume, and a KSA list.

A COMPLETED SF-171

Application for Federal Employment–SF 171

Read the instructions before you complete this application. *Type or print clearly in dark ink*

Form Approved
OMB No. 3206-0012

GENERAL INFORMATION

1 What kind of job are you applying for? Give title and announcement no. (if any)

2 Social Security Number
000-00-0000

3 Sex
[X] Male   [ ] Female

4 Birth Date *(Month, Day, Year)*
2-4-53

5 Birthplace *(City and State or County)*
XXXXXXXX,

6 Name *(Last, First, Middle)*
XXXX, XXXXXXX

Mailing address *(include apartment number, if any)*
000000 XXXXXX Street

City	State	ZIP Code
Mission Viejo	CA	92692

7 Other names ever used *(e.g., maiden name, nickname, etc.)*
N/A

8 Home Phone
Area Code 714   Number 000-0000

9 Work Phone
Area Code 714   Number 000-0000   Extension

10 Were you employed as a civilian by the Federal Government? If "NO", go to item 11. If "YES", mark each type of job you held with an "X".

[ ] Temporary   [ ] Career Conditional   [X] Career   [ ] Excepted

What is your highest grade, classification series and job title?
GG-905-15/6, Counsel

Dates at highest grade: FROM 6/96 TO present

AVAILABILITY

11 When can you start work? *(Month and year)*
Within 2-4 weeks from notification

12 What is the lowest pay you will accept? *(You will not be considered for jobs which pay less than you indicate.)*
Pay $ _____ per _____ OR Grade 15/6

13 In what geographic area(s) are you willing to work?
Per announcement; no geographic restriction

14 Are you willing to work:

	YES	NO
A. 40 hours per week *(full time)*?	X	
B. 25-30 hours per week *(part time)*?		X
C. 17-24 hours per week *(part time)*?		X
D. 16 or fewer hours per week *(part time)*?		X
E. An intermittent job *(on call/seasonal)*?		X
F. Weekends, shifts, or rotating shifts?		X

15 Are you willing to take a temporary job lasting:

	YES	NO
A. 5-12 months *(sometimes longer)*?		X
B. 1-4 months?		X
C. Less than 1 month?		X

16 Are you willing to travel away from home for:

	YES	NO
A. 1-5 nights each month?	X	
B. 6-10 nights each month?	X	
C. 11 or more nights each month?	X	

MILITARY SERVICE AND VETERAN PREFERENCE

17 Have you served in the United States Military Service? If your only active duty was training in the Reserves or National Guard, answer "NO". If "NO" go to item 22.

YES	NO
	X

18 Did you or will you retire above the rank of major or lieutenant commander

FOR USE OF EXAMINING OFFICE ONLY

Date entered register

Form reviewed:
Form approved:

Option	Grade	Earned Rating	Veteran Preference	Augmented Rating
			[ ] No Preference Claimed	
			[ ] 5 Points *(Tentative)*	
			[ ] 10 Pts. *(30% Or More Comp. Dis.)*	
			[ ] 10 Pts. *(Less Than 30% Comp. Dis)*	
			[ ] Other 10 Points	
			[ ] Disallowed	[ ] Being Investigated

FOR USE OF APPOINTING OFFICE ONLY

Preference has been verified through proof that the separation was under honorable conditions, and other proof as required.

[ ] 5 Point   [ ] 10-Point—30% or More Compensable Disability   [ ] 10-Point—Less Than 30% Compensable Disability   [ ] 10-Point—Other

Signature and Title

Agency   Date

MILITARY SERVICE AND VETERAN PREFERENCE

19 Were you discharged from the military service under honorable conditions? *(If your discharge was changed to "honorable" or "general" by a Discharge Review Board answer "YES". If you received a clemency discharge, answer "NO".)*

YES	NO

Discharge Date *(Month, Day, Year)*   Type of Discharge

20 List the dates (Month, Day, Year), and branch for all active duty military service.
From   To   Branch of Service

21 If all your active military duty was after October 14, 1976, list the full names and dates of all campaign badges or expeditionary medals you received or were entitled to receive.

22 Read the instructions that came with this form before completing this item. When you have determined your eligibility for veteran preference from the instructions, place an "X" in the box next to your veteran preference claim.

[X] NO PREFERENCE

[ ] 5-POINT PREFERENCE—You must show proof when you are hired

10 POINT PREFERENCE—If you claim 10-point preference, place an "X" in the box below next to the basis for your claim. To receive 10-point preference you must also complete a Standard Form 15, Application for 10-point Veteran Preference, which is available from any Federal Job Information Center. ATTACH THE COMPLETED SF 15 AND REQUESTED PROOF TO THIS APPLICATION.

[ ] Non-compensably disabled Purple Heart recipient

[ ] Compensably disabled, less than 30 percent

[ ] Spouse, widow(er), or mother of a deceased or disabled veteran.

[ ] Compensably disabled, 30 percent or more.

THE FEDERAL GOVERNMENT IS AN EQUAL OPPORTUNITY EMPLOYER
PREVIOUS EDITION USABLE UNTIL 12-31-90

NSN 7540-00-935-7150   171-110   Standard Form 171 (Rev. 6-88)
U.S. Office of Personnel Management
FPM Chapter 295

WORK EXPERIENCE If you have no work experience write "NONE" in A below and go to 25 on page 3

23 May we ask you present employer about your character, qualifications and work record? A "NO" will not affect our review of your qualifications. If you answer "NO" and we need to contact your present employer before we can offer you a job, we will contact you first ....

	YES	NO
		X

24 WORK EXPERIENCE

A			
Name and address of employer's organization (include ZIP Code, if known) Federal Deposit Insurance Corporation (FDIC) 4 Park Plaza Irvine, CA 92714	Dates employed (give month and year) From: 1/96 To: present Salary or earnings Starting $ GS-15 per year Ending $ GS-15 per year	Average number of hours per week 40 Place of employment City Irvine, State CA	
Exact title of your job **COUNSEL,** **CLIENT SERVICE GROUP**	Your immediate supervisor Name XXXX XXXXXX Area Code 714 Telephone Number 000-0000	Number and job titles of any employees you supervise(d) N/A	
Kind of business or organization (manufacturing, accounting, social service, etc.) US Government	If Federal Employment (civilian or military) list services, grade or rank and the date of your last promotion GG-905-15/6, 6/96	Your reason for wanting to leave Career advancement; office is being closed.	

Description of work: Describe your specific duties, responsibilities and accomplishments in this job. If you describe more than one type of work (for example, carpentry and painting or personnel and budget), write the appropriate percentage of time you spent doing each.

OVERVIEW
- **Client Services Group Attorney** for the Major Asset Group.
- **Provide in-depth legal advice and counsel** to senior management on litigation and bankruptcy strategies affecting the disposition of assets from the Client's $1.1 Billion asset portfolio.

KEY ACTIVITIES

Coordinate complex civil cases with various departments or divisions within FDIC. Developed detailed reviews and analyses, in preparation for counseling Client representatives to improve the Client's requests for legal services. Research and prepare comprehensive legal memoranda for Clients, drawing on my extensive knowledge and experience litigating various issues under the FDI Act, FIRREA, the FDIC Improvement Act, commercial law, real estate law and the Bankruptcy Code.

RESULT:
- Initiated major civil fraud investigation of FDIC judgment debtor, who fraudulently transferred assets in anticipation of entry of FDIC's judgments, including use of asset freeze provisions pursuant to Crime Control Act.
- Successfully coordinated FDIC's efforts to obtain $11 Million restitution order in U.S.A. v. Charles W. Knapp case.
- Initiated and coordinated FDIC's efforts to collect on reserved fraud claims involving $10 Million golf course formerly owned by Great American Bank and its wholly owned subsidiary.
- Researched and developed best foreclosure practices for environmentally contaminated real estate for Client's use in Western Service Center in Irvine.

EVALUATION OF PERFORMANCE

"Has demonstrated a very high degree of analytical ability. Particularly, Mr. Xxxx has been involved in providing background information and assistance to the Washington DC Appellate Litigation Section regarding the ACC/Lincoln Savings Securities Litigation and the RTC v. Keating, et. al. Mr. Xxxx's contributions have been relied upon by the Appellate Section in their representation of the FDIC."
(from Evaluation, 1996)

For Agency Use (skill codes, etc.)

Standard Form 171-A—*Continuation Sheet for SF 171*

•Attach all SF 171-A's to your application at the top of page 3.

1. Name (Last, First, Middle Initial)	2. Social Security Number
XXXX, XXXXX	000-00-0000

3. Job Title or Announcement Number You Are Applying For	4. Date Completed

ADDITIONAL WORK EXPERIENCE BLOCKS IF NEEDED

B Name and address of employer's organization (include ZIP Code, if known)

Resolution Trust Corporation (RTC)
4000 MacArthur Boulevard - 5th floor
Newport Beach, CA 92660-2516

Dates employed *(give month and year)*	
From: 6/92	To: 12/95

Number of hours per week: 40

Salary or earnings	
Starting $ 70,656	per year
Ending $ 82,209	per year

Place of Employment
City: Newport Beach,
State: CA

Exact title of your job	Your immediate supervisor	Number and job titles of any employees you supervised
COUNSEL / SECTION CHIEF, PROF'L LIABILITY SECTION	Name XXXXXXXX Area Code 202 Telephone Number 000-0000	14: legal / support staff

Kind of business or organization *(marketing, accounting, social service, etc.)*	If Federal Employment (civilian or military) list series grade rank and the date of your last promotion	Your reason for wanting to leave.
US Government	GG-905-15/4 3/95	Office was closed; career advancement

Description of work: Describe your specific duties, responsibilities and accomplishments in this job. If you describe more than one type of work (for example, carpentry and painting or personnel and budget), write the appropriate percentage of time you spent doing each.

OVERVIEW

<u>MANAGERIAL</u>: **Directed and managed a 14-person staff**, including five attorneys and a support staff of nine paralegals and legal technicians. Assigned, managed, and evaluated the staff's work performance. Planned and coordinated work assignments within both the PLS unit and the Investigations Department.

<u>TECHNICAL</u>: **Reviewed and recommended the initiation of litigation** against directors, officers, shareholders, other insiders, employees, borrowers, accountants, attorneys, or other persons employed by failed financial institutions or any affiliate, underwriters, or any party causing a loss to a failed financial institution.

KEY ACTIVITIES   <u>MANAGERIAL</u>

Employed proactive and consultative management techniques to motivate and unify professional staff to achieve RTC's PLS program objectives. Developed methods to increase cross-communication between PLS and the Investigations Department. Conducted extensive in-house meetings with staff to determine the staff's training needs and to identify various ways to increase staff morale and productivity.

<u>RESULT</u>:
- Created a cohesive, unified working group of professional staff from what had been a fragmented and demoralized staff following RTC's reorganization in 1992.

- Significantly improved working relationship and communication between PLS and RTC's Investigations Department which later served as a model for national policy statement on the Roles and Responsibilities between the two departments.

- Successfully downsized PLS for RTC's 12/31/95 sunset without adverse actions from affected employees.

- Advocated and developed a national civil fraud training program including written materials to improve RTC's national civil fraud program.

For Agency Use (skill codes. etc.

XXXXXX XXXX
SSN 569-76-5020

#24-B, continued – KEY ACTIVITIES:

MANAGERIAL

Developed outreach initiatives to generate a greater degree of active participation by women-owned and minority law firms in PLS cases.

RESULT: • Recognized by RTC's Minority and Woman's Program Office for efforts to increase the participation of minority and women law firms in PLS cases.

EVALUATION OF PERFORMANCE

"A highly effective manager. Mr. Xxxx has organized the work of his section effectively and manages the work skillfully notwithstanding the high level of controversial high profile matters that cross his desk on a daily basis. He has been instrumental in establishing and fostering excellent working arrangements with the US Department of Justice and the US Attorney's Office. He has a natural maturity and confidence and has been a strong contributor to the California Legal Division Management Team." (from Evaluation, 1995)

TECHNICAL

Investigated 62 failed thrifts and prosecuted civil claims from 34 thrift institutions. Advised and conferred with immediate supervisors regarding significant developments affecting legal cases and/ or personnel matters.

RESULT: • Generated cash recoveries of $88,149,523, as of 12/31/95.

• Maintained a 5-to-1 recovery to cost ratio. The total cost of collection, exclusive of in-house salaries and overhead, was $16,172,374.

• Issued more than 577 administrative subpoenas prior to initiation of Authority to Sue Memos developing thorough factual and financial investigations of potential targets.

• Authored comprehensive memo for Assistant General Counsel analyzing the potential impact that the Senate's proposed D'Oench reform legislation would have on future parallel proceeding cases such as Lincoln Savings & Loan.

Cooperated with U. S. Attorneys Office in San Diego in civil forfeiture of 2,000 acres of undeveloped land involved in a sham joint venture between a subsidiary of HomeFed Bank and a developer.

RESULT: • The forfeiture has resulted in cash recoveries of $13.6 million and the elimination of contractual obligations of at least $9.8 million.

SEE NEXT PAGE

XXXXX XXXXX
SSN 000-00-0000

#24-B, continued – KEY ACTIVITIES:

TECHNICAL

In addition to duties as PLS Section Chief, **I continued to work on the resolution of Lincoln Savings & Loan's outstanding professional liability matters,** which were not finished when I began my tenure in California with PLS in June of 1992.

RESULT:
- Generated civil settlements totaling approximately $295 Million.

- Generated cash recoveries totaling in excess of $248 Million, and nondischargeable judgments totaling approximately $1.4 Billion.

- Successfully argued an entry of summary judgment against Keating for an amount in excess of $4.3 Billion.

- Successfully argued for Federal criminal convictions of Keating on 77 federal felony counts; and of his son, Charles H. Keating, on 64 felony counts for bank fraud, wire fraud, securities fraud, bankruptcy fraud, and racketeering.

- Successfully obtained Federal criminal indictments against eight Keating confederates and resulting felony pleas by Judy Wischer, Ray Fidel, Andrew Ligget, Robert Wurzelbacher, Mark Sauter, Bruce Dickson, Robin Symes, and Ernie Garcia.

- Obtained criminal forfeitures, including Charles H. Keating's for $122 Million, in excess of $265 Million.

EVALUATION OF PERFORMANCE

"Has outstanding analytical and problem solving skills that he has applied to virtually every kind of legal problem arising from failed financial institutions.
"His high level of cognition and his ability to analyze difficult legal scenarios are evident on a day-to-day basis. A dedicated professional...consistently performs at a high level. Very creative and original in his work."
(from Evaluation, 1995)

Standard Form 171—*Continuation Sheet for SF 171*

•Attach all SF 171-A's to your application at the top of page 3.

1. Name (Last, First, Middle Initial)	2. Social Security Number
XXXX, XXXXXX	000-00-0000

3. Job Title or Announcement Number You Are Applying For	4. Date Completed

ADDITIONAL WORK EXPERIENCE BLOCKS IF NEEDED

C Name and address of employer's organization (include ZIP Code, if known)	Dates employed (*give month and year*)	Number of hours per week
Resolution Trust Corporation (RTC) 2910 North 44th Street Phoenix, AZ 85018	From: 2/90 To: 6/92	40

	Salary or earnings	Place of Employment
	Starting $ 53,112 per year	City Phoenix,
	Ending $ 64,073 per year	State AZ

Exact title of your job	Your immediate supervisor			Number and job titles of any employees you supervised
COUNSEL / SECTION CHIEF	Name XXXXXXX	Area Code 202	Telephone Number 000-0000	41: legal / support staff

Kind of business or organization (*marketing, accounting, social service, etc.*)	If Federal Employment (civilian or military) list series grade rank and the date of your last promotion	Your reason for wanting to leave.
US. Government	GG-905-14/3 5/92	Office was being closed; career advancement

Description of work: Describe your specific duties, responsibilities and accomplishments in this job. If you describe more than one type of work (for example, carpentry and painting or personnel and budget), write the appropriate percentage of time you spent doing each.

OVERVIEW   <u>MANAGERIAL:</u> **Section Chief, Legal Division**, Central Western Consolidated Office, Phoenix, Arizona (CWCO) for Lincoln Savings and Loan and Great American Bank. **Supervised and managed a 41-person staff,** including 7 attorneys and paralegals from the Coastal Consolidated Office (CCO) as part of a transition of the legal management of Great American Bank from CWCO to CCO.

<u>TECHNICAL:</u> **Reviewed a wide range of cases and made recommendations** regarding the wisdom and suitability of initiating, continuing, or settling cases involving complex litigation concerning issues of national interest. **Served as Acting Managing Senior Attorney** in the absence of the Managing Senior Attorney and the Deputy Managing Senior Attorney.

KEY ACTIVITIES   <u>MANAGERIAL</u>

Supervised and managed a staff of 34 professionals, including CWCO staff attorneys, financial institution in-house attorneys, and support personnel. In addition, as of April 1, 1992, I also supervised and managed another 7 attorneys and paralegals from the CCO as part of an assignment to complete the orderly transition of legal management of Great American Bank from CWCO to CCO.

Assigned, directed, and evaluated the work performance of all staff members. In addition, developed and coordinated plans for the accomplishment of work assigned to my Section. Directed and reviewed the work of the attorneys, paralegals and support staff assigned to my section.

Litigation Manager for the RTC Legal Division within CWCO. supervised legal and cost-effective aspects of more than 5,000 litigation cases.

Maintained extensive inter-organizational liaison, ensuring that high-level managers were kept informed of all significant developments. Conferred with and advised the Managing Senior Attorney, the Deputy Managing Senior Attorney, and all CWCO Section Chiefs regarding the application of the RTC's litigation policy to a broad spectrum of legal matters.

SEE NEXT PAGE

	For Agency Use (skill codes. etc.

XXXX XXXXXX
SSN 000-00-0000

#24-C, continued – KEY ACTIVITIES:

TECHNICAL

Participated in and contributed to negotiations and settlements of complex asset dispositions and major litigation involving issues of national interest by providing legal advice and legal strategies to RTC legal and business executives. **Participated in the formulation strategy, trial preparation, and settlements** of the RTC's Civil Racketeering (RICO) Lawsuit against Charles Keating, Jr. and other Lincoln Savings and Loan directors, officers, accountants and lawyers, including various insurance carriers with policies affected thereby.

RESULT: • Worked successfully with outside counsel, and with the RTC's Acting General Counsel and the Assistant General Counsel (PLS), in negotiating approximately $295 Million in pretrial settlements which included the largest (to date) pretrial settlements with a national law firm and a big six accounting firm by the RTC/FDIC.

• Successfully argued an entry of summary judgment against Keating for an amount in excess of $4.3 Billion.

• Successfully argued for Federal criminal convictions of Keating on 77 federal felony counts; and of his son, Charles H. Keating, on 64 felony counts for bank fraud, wire fraud, securities fraud, bankruptcy fraud, and racketeering.

Negotiated with representatives from the government of Kuwait regarding the sale of the Phoenician and Crescent Hotels which were part of the Keating/Lincoln S&L holdings.

RESULT: • Developed the strategy which enhanced RTC's negotiating position by restructuring the ownership of the hotels, placing RTC in a position to repudiate the Shareholders' Agreement. This strategy resulted in the sale of the RTC's 55 % interest in the hotels for a sum which exceeded the Kuwait government's offer prior to the Gulf War by 159%.

Prepared with outside counsel what became known as the Drexel Task Force questionnaire, based upon our knowledge of Keating and Milken's junk bond transactions at Lincoln.

RESULT: • The questionnaire was used to gather evidence to support the RTC's claims against Drexel, Milken, and others from thrifts within the RTC's control around the country.

Negotiated favorable settlements with 35 subcontractors and the general contractor in the McCarthy case which involved the foreclosure of a $18.5 Million mechanics lien against the Phoenician Hotel.

RESULT: • Settlements with 35 subcontractors were negotiated for approximately 79% of their claimed lien amount, exclusive of attorneys' fees and interest. The settlement with the general contractor represented approximately 57 % of the amount it claimed under its lien, exclusive of other subcontractors' claims, attorneys' fees and interest.

SEE NEXT PAGE

XXXXX XXXXXXX
SSN 000-00-0000

#24-C, continued – KEY ACTIVITIES:

TECHNICAL

Developed a Litigation Claims Procedure Manual which was used by RTC in-house and outside counsel.

RESULT: • By using standard forms and pleadings for routine, recurring claims issues, our unit successfully eliminated the need for duplicative yet expensive legal research and pleading preparation associated with many FIRREA claims issues.

Compiled a standard forms pleading book.

RESULT: • By using standard pleadings and briefs for routine RTC matters, our unit reduced outside counsel expense substantially.

Supervised and managed the review of 1,087 contracts, issued legal opinions as to the advisability of repudiation, and prepared 260 repudiation cases for the client, as part of Great American Bank's liquidation.

Organized, supervised, and managed the RTC Legal Division Fraud Task Force's investigation of Western Savings & Loan Association.

RESULT: • This investigation led to the RTC's filing of a civil RICO complaint against Western's former officers, directors, accountants, attorneys, and accommodation parties.

• To date, the RTC and FDIC have recovered over $87 Million, at an approximate cost of $9.5 Million.

• In addition to the RTC's civil RICO action against Western's former insiders, professionals and accommodation parties, the Arizona and Los Angeles U.S. attorneys have indicted four of Western's former insiders or accommodation parties. One has plead guilty to, and three have been convicted of, various federal criminal bank fraud charges.

EVALUATION OF PERFORMANCE

"He balances competing goals and interests deftly. Energetic and resourceful. Notwithstanding the enormity of the workload, complexity of the issues, and rapidity of the pace, his staff is well-motivated and loyal, and morale is high. A highly effective manager.

"Possesses superb substantive legal skills. As one of our most experienced trial lawyers on staff, Mr. Xxxx serves as litigation coordinator for our office. His personal involvement in the day-to-day management of the highly successful Lincoln Savings/Charles Keating, Jr. racketeering litigation is but one example of Mr. Xxxx's consistently exceptional performance.

"Mr. Xxxx enjoys an excellent working relationship with members of the Legal Department staff and our client alike. He has earned the respect of others at all levels within the RTC, as well as outside the agency. An extremely valuable employee."

(Evaluation, 1992)

← ──────── **ATTACH ANY ADDITIONAL FORMS AND SHEETS HERE**

EDUCATION

25 Did you graduate from high school? If you have a GED high school equivalency or will graduate within the next nine months, answer "YES".

YES X ▶ If "Yes", give month and year graduated or received GED equivalency: 6/71
If "NO", give the highest grade you

26 Write the name and location (*city and state*) of the last high school you attended or where you obtained your GED high school equivalency.

Westside H.S. - Omaha, NE

27 Have you ever attended college or graduate school   YES **X** ▶ If "YES", continue with **28**
NO   ▶ IF "NO", go to **31**.

28 NAME AND LOCATION (city, state and ZIP Code) OF COLLEGE OR UNIVERSITY. If you expect to graduate within nine months, give the *month* and *year* you expect to receive your degree:

Name	City	State	ZIP Code	From	To	Semester	Quarter	TYPE OF DEGREE (e.g. B.A., M.A.)	MONTH AND YEAR OF DEGREE
1) Creighton University School of Law	Omaha	NE	68012	9/75	5/78	75		J.D.	5/78
2) University of Nebraska	Lincoln	NE	68501	9/71	5/75	135		B.A.	5/75
3)									

Column group headers: MONTH AND YEAR ATTENDED (From/To); NUMBER OF CREDIT HOURS COMPLETED (Semester/Quarter)

29 CHIEF UNDERGRADUATE SUBJECTS
Show major on the first line

	NUMBER OF CREDIT HOURS COMPLETED Semester	Quarter
1) English	50	
2) History	15	
3) Philosophy	15	

30 CHIEF GRADUATE SUBJECTS
Show major on the first line

	NUMBER OF CREDIT HOURS COMPLETED Semester	Quarter
1) Law	75	
2)		
3)		

31 If you have completed any other courses or training related to the kind of jobs you are applying for (*trade, vocational, Armed Forces, business*) give information below

NAME AND LOCATION (city, state and ZIP Code) OF SCHOOL	From	To	CLASS-ROOM HOURS	SUBJECT(S)	TRAINING COMPLETED YES	NO
School Name 1) National Institute fore Trial Advocacy - NITA City Notre Dame State Indiana ZIP Code 46556	6/96	6/96	74	Trial Advocacy Building Trial Skills	X	
School Name 2) Hastings College of the Law City San Francisco State CA ZIP Code 94018	8/79	8/79	40	Civil and Criminal Trial Advocacy	X	

Column group header: MONTH AND YEAR ATTENDED (From/To)

SPECIAL SKILLS, ACCOMPLISHMENTS AND AWARDS

32 Give the title and year of any honors, awards or fellowships you have received. List your special qualifications, skills or accomplishments that may help you get a job. Some examples are: skills with computers or other machines; most important publications (do not submit copies); public speaking and writing experience; membership in professional or scientific

PLEASE SEE ATTACHED SHEET

33 How many words per minute can you:

TYPE? TAKE DICTATION?
25   N/A
Agencies may test your skills before hiring you.

34 List job-related licenses or certificates that you have, such as: registered nurse; lawyer; radio operator; driver's; pilot's; etc.

LICENSE OR CERTIFICATE	DATE OF LATEST LICENSE OR CERTIFICATE	STATE OR OTHER LICENSING AGENCY
1) Attorney	1978-present	Nebraska
2) Attorney	1986-present	Iowa

35 So you speak or read a language other than English (include sign language)? Applicants for jobs that require a language other than English may be given an interview conducted solely in that language.

YES **X** ▶ If "YES", list each language and place an "X" in each column that applies to you.
NO   ▶ If "NO", go to **36**.

LANGUAGE(S)	CAN PREPARE AND GIVE LECTURES Fluently	With Difficulty	CAN SPEAK AND UNDERSTAND Fluently	Passably	CAN TRANSLATE ARTICLES Into English	From English	CAN READ ARTICLES FOR OWN USE Easily	With Difficulty
1) French		X		X		X		X
2)								

REFERENCES

36 List three people who are not related to you and are not supervisors you listed under **24** who know your qualifications and fitness for the kind of job for which you are applying.

FULL NAME OF REFERENCE	TELEPHONE NUMBER(S) (include Area Code)	PRESENT BUSINESS OR HOME ADDRESS (Number, street and city)	STATE	ZIP CODE
1) XXXXXX	404-000-0000	285 XXXXXX Street Atlanta	GA	30303
2) XXXXXX	202-000-0000	1717 XXXX Street – Room 000 Washington	DC	20434
3) XXXXXX (US District Court Judge, retired)	619-000-0000	101 West XXXXXX– Suite 1700 San Diego	CA	92101

Page 3

XXXX, XXXXXX
SSN 568-76-5020

#31, continued: ADVANCED TRAINING

FBI / RTC Bank Failure School   December 7-10, 1993
This was a highly intensive course focusing on the aspects of fraud involving financial institutions.
Topics covered included:
Fraud Detection and Investigation
Forensic Accounting Approach
Prosecution of Financial Institution Fraud Cases
The Importance of CPAs to Bank Examiners and Criminal Investigations

Basic Examination School for Attorneys   January 1988
This was a week-long concentrated course focusing on:
Fundamentals of bank supervision
Basic report analysis
Bank accrual accounting
Loan classifications
Financial analysis

#32, continued: HONORS AND AWARDS

August 6, 1995: Special Act or Service Award
Recognizing my efforts in developing, supervising, and implementing RTC's civil fraud program.

July 10, 1994: Performance Award & Special Act or Service Award
Recognizing my leadership in RTC/DOJ joint civil forfeiture which recovered $13.6 Million in cash,
and eliminated contractual obligations of at least $9.8 Million.

November 3, 1991: Special Act or Service Award
Recognizing my role in developing successful "repudiation" of Shareholder Agreement strategy and
employing it in negotiating favorable sale of RTC's interest in Phoenician Hotel.

LICENSES

Attorney:	1978-present	U.S. District Court, Nebraska
	1987-present	U.S. Court of Appeals, Eighth Circuit
	1988-present	U.S. District Court, Southern District, Iowa
	1988-present	U.S. District Court, Northern District, Iowa

BACKGROUND INFORMATION—*You must answer each question in this section before we can process your application.*

	YES	NO
37 Are you a citizen of the United States? *(In most cases you must be a U.S. citizen to be hired. You will be required to submit proof of identity and citizenship at the time you are hired.)* If "NO", give the country or countries you are a citizen of:		X

> **NOTE: It is important that you give complete and truthful answers to questions 38 through 44.** If you answer "YES" to any of them, provide your explanation(s) in Item 45. **Include** convictions resulting from a plea of nolo contendere (no contest). **Omit:** 1) traffic fines of $100.00 or less; 2) any violation of law committed before your 16th birthday; 3) any violation of law committed before your 18th birthday, if finally decided in juvenile court or under a Youth Offender law; 4) any conviction set aside under the Federal Youth Corrections Act or similar State law; 5) any conviction whose record was expunged under Federal law. We will consider the date, facts, and circumstances of each event you list. In most cases you can still be considered for Federal jobs. However, **if you fail to tell the truth or fail to list all relevant** events or circumstances, this may be grounds for not hiring you, for firing you after you begin work, or for criminal prosecution (18 USC 1001).

	YES	NO
38 During the last **10 years**, were you **fired from any job** for any reason, did you **quit after being told that you would be fired,** or did you leave by mutual agreement because of specific problems?		X
39 Have you **ever** been convicted of, or forfeited collateral for **any felony violation?** *(Generally, a felony is defined as any violation of law punishable by imprisonment of longer than one year, except for violations called misdemeanors under State law which are punishable by imprisonment of two years or less.)*		X
40 Have you **ever** been convicted of, or forfeited collateral for **any firearms or explosives violation?**		X
41 Are you **now** under charges for **any** violation of law?		X
42 During the last 10 years have you forfeited collateral, been convicted, been imprisoned, been on probation, or been on parole? Do not include violations reported in 39, 40, or 41, above.		X
43 Have you **ever** been convicted by a military **court-martial?** If no military service, answer "NO"		X
44 Are you **delinquent** on any Federal debt? *(Include delinquencies arising from Federal taxes, loans, overpayment of benefits, and other debts t the U.S. Government plus defaults on Federally guaranteed or insured loans such as student and home mortgage loans.)*		X

45 If "YES" in: **38** - Explain for each job the problem(s) and your reason(s) for leaving. Give the employer's name and address.
      39 through 43 - Explain each violation. Give place of occurrence and name/address of police or court involved.
      44 - Explain the type, length and amount of the delinquency or default, and steps you are taking to correct errors or repay the debt. Give any identification number associated with the debt and the address of the Federal agency involved.
    NOTE: If you need more space, use a sheet of paper, and include the item number.

Item No.	Date (Mo./Yr.)	Explanation	Mailing Address
			Name of Employer, Police, Court or Federal Agency City State ZIP Code
			Name of Employer, Police, Court or Federal Agency City State ZIP Code

	YES	NO
46 Do you receive, or have you ever applied for retirement pay, pension, or other pay based on military, Federal civilian, or District of Columbia Government service?		X
47 Do any of your relatives work for the United States Government or the United States Armed Forces? Include: father; mother; husband; wife; son; daughter; brother; sister; uncle; aunt; first cousin; nephew; niece; father-in-law; son-in-law; daughter-in-law; brother-in-law; sister-in-law; stepmother; stepson; stepdaughter; stepbrother; stepsister; half brother; and half sister		X

Name	Relationship	Department, Agency or Branch of Armed Forces

SIGNATURE, CERTIFICATION, AND RELEASE OF INFORMATION

YOU MUST SIGN THIS APPLICATION. Read the following carefully before you sign.

- A false statement on any part of your application may be grounds for not hiring you, or for firing you after you begin work. Also, you may be punished by fine or imprisonment (U.S. Code, title 18, section 1001).
- If you are a male born after December 31, 1959 you must be registered with the Selective Service System or have a valid exemption in order to be eligible for Federal employment. You will be required to certify as to your status at the time of appointment.
- **I understand** that any information I give may be investigated as allowed by law or Presidential order.
- **I consent** to the release of information about my ability and fitness for Federal employment by *employers, schools, law enforcement agencies and other individuals and organizations,* to *investigators, personnel staffing specialists, and other authorized employees of the Federal Government.*
- **I certify** that, to the best of my knowledge and belief, **all** of my statements are true, correct, complete, and made in good faith.

48 SIGNATURE *(Sign each application in dark ink)*   **49** DATE SIGNED *(Month, day, year)*

*U.S. Government Printing Office: 1991 -281-782-20310

A COMPLETED OF-612

OPTIONAL APPLICATION FOR FEDERAL EMPLOYMENT - OF 612

You may apply for jobs with a resume, this form, or any other format. If your resume or application does not provide all the information requested on this form and in the job vacancy announcement, you may lose consideration for a job.

1 Job title in announcement **Computer Specialist, Supervisory**	2 Grade(s) applying for **GS-0334-14/15**	3 Announcement number **99-63-AP**

4 Last name XXXXXXX	First and Middle names XXXXXX	5 Social Security Number **000-00-0000**

6 Mailing address
000 Stillwater Place

7 Phone Numbers (include area code)

Daytime (703) 000-0000

City XXXXXXX	State MD	ZIP Code 00000	Evening (301) 000-0000

WORK EXPERIENCE

8 Describe your paid and nonpaid work experience related to the job for which you are applying. Do **not** attach job descriptions.

1) Job title (if Federal, include series and grade)
COMPUTER SPECIALIST, GS-0334-13

From (MM/YY) 8/96	To (MM/YY) present	Salary $71,565	per year	Hours per week 40

Employer's name and address Defense Information System Agency (DISA) 00000 XXXXXXX Square; XXXX, VA 00000	Supervisor's name and phone number John XXXXX 703-000-0000

Describe your duties and accomplishments

OVERVIEW
- **Computer Specialist** in the Defense Message System (DMS)Operations Branch on the staff of the DMS Global Service Manager. DMS is a computer-based (X.400/X.500) worldwide Department of Defense-wide Area Network messaging system that will replace the obsolete Automated Digital Network (AUTODIN) now in place. The mission of the Branch is to exercise day-to-day management control of, and provide staff level operational direction over, deployed elements of the DMS.

- **Personally responsible** for ensuring that reliable, efficient, effective, and economic DMS operations meet the customer's requirements.

KEY ACTIVITIES

Oversee and manage the global system of Regional Operations and Security Centers (ROSC).
- RESULT • Visited ROSC-C to assist in bring the center to full operational status prior to the start of IOT&E.
- Coordinated the requirements and assessments of the three ROSC to prepare the final format of the Continuity of Operation Plan for the DMS portion of the ROSC's worldwide structure.

Develop policy and directives which provide a framework for processes and procedures in the execution of system implementation as well as operational tasks.
- RESULT • Developed, coordinated, and established the ALLDMSSTA general message in order to establish an electronic means of formally disseminating policy and procedure changes.
- Drawing on program management and cryptologic background, assessed (in concert with D4) the requirements for instituting a viable maintenance management program.

SEE NEXT PAGE

XXXXXX XXXXX. — SSN: 000-00-00000

<u>#1, continued, WORK EXPERIENCE</u>

Monitor the implementation of all hardware and software changes/enhancements to the DMS components and infrastructure.
> <u>RESULT</u> • Formally approved all Field Engineering Notes for distribution and implementation during IOT&E using newly established software distribution procedures, a process that proved to be highly organized and successful.

Conduct operational performance evaluations and ensure overall compliance with technical criteria to maintain the DMS performance above management thresholds.

Maintain liaison with representatives of the Joint Staff, military departments, and other government agencies. Represent the Branch at meetings and conferences with higher echelons.

Obtain, direct, and coordinate necessary technical support when problem resolution requires expertise beyond that of on-site personnel.
> <u>RESULT</u> • Worked closely with the DISA PAC and DISA EUR Regional Service Management staff and the WESTHEM Columbus RCC to develop and implement an interim problem reporting mechanism pending arrival of the DMS Contractor products.

Function as the task monitor for cognizant portions of the DMS that are staffed under contract support and ensure contractor personnel and contract deliverables are in full compliance with requirements as detailed in the contract.

Provide operations input to the implementation design validation process.

<u>EVALUATION OF PERFORMANCE:</u>
"A self-starter who uses initiative to research exiting activities associated with system and network management tools and capabilities to ensure DMS will be able to readily migrate to a fully integrated system." (from Evaluation, 1996)

2) Job title (if Federal, include series and grade)
TELECOMMUNICATIONS SPECIALIST, GS-0391-13

From (MM/YY) 5/95	To (MM/YY) 8/96	Salary $63,442	per year	Hours per week 40

Employer's name and address Space and Naval Warfare (SPAWAR) Systems Command 2451 Crystal Drive; Arlington, VA 22245-5200	Supervisor's name and phone number CDR XXXXXX 703-000-0000

Describe your duties and accomplishments

OVERVIEW • **Project Manager** for computer/communication systems deployments of the Nova and MMS (Multi-level Mail Server), which were designated as Navy Defense Messaging System transitional components, and provided for the upgrade of automated messaging services while allowing the Naval Telecommunications System to transition from legacy platforms to the Defense Messaging System (DMS) target X.400 and X.500 architecture and components.

KEY ACTIVITIES

Managed and evaluated the execution of contractor performance for acquisition, installation, maintenance, and software support services. Directed and approved contractor efforts in the development of computer integrated logistic support planning (ILSP) and developed and coordinated site survey and system installation schedules.
RESULT • Mediated and resolved numerous difficulties, discrepancies, disagreements between and/or among installation support activities (engineering field activities, contractors, and others).

Provided technical information and direction relative to DMS transitional components which interfaced to host computers.

Reviewed and evaluated computer/communications systems architecture and wiring plans and diagrams. As part of the review process, also developed and submitted detail wiring schematics and diagrams which described errors and corrections.
RESULT • Used knowledge of Naval Telecommunication System architecture, interface techniques, and capabilities to provide input to the formulation of a system architecture and connectivity between Navy, Marine, Coast Guard, and other DoD and civil agency components where the object was to provide a seamless transition to the target X.400/X.500 DMS architecture.

Primary liaison with various organizational DMS coordinators in order to ensure timely update of requirements and fielding priorities. Represented the Division at internal or external committees, working groups, and meetings.
RESULT • Prepared and presented a variety of well-received point papers and briefings to provide information, recommendations, and defense of program positions or actions to be executed.
• Established working relationships across organizational boundaries which were essential to process improvement in the delivery of quality customer services.

SEE NEXT PAGE

50612-101   NSN 7540-01351-9178   Optional Form 612 (September 1994)
U.S. Office of Personnel Management

XXXXXX XXXXX.— SSN: 000-00-00000

<u>#2, continued, WORK EXPERIENCE</u>

Provided administrative management for project implementation tracking and monitoring.

As a member of the Software Configuration Control Board, evaluated and recommended adoption or disapproval of software changes and proposals which were relevant to the Nova, MMS, and related systems.

    <u>RESULT</u> • Made significant contributions to SPAWAR in the economy, efficiency, and service in the implementation of transitional system platforms (Nova, PCMT, GATEGUARD, and MMS).

<u>EVALUATION OF PERFORMANCE:</u>

"....a model employee who has proven during this period his value to the organization. He has taken the changes driven by organizational restructuring and realignment in stride and has actively promoted the goals and objectives of SPAWAR." (from Evaluation, 1996)

9 May we contact your current supervisor

YES [X]   NO [   ]   If we need to contact your current supervisor before making an offer, we will contact you first.

EDUCATION

10 Mark highest level completed   Some HS [   ]   HS/GED [   ]   Associate [   ]   Bachelor [   ]   Master [X]   Doctoral [   ]

11 Last high school (HS) or GED school. Give the school's name, City, State, ZIP Code (if known), and year diploma or GED received.

Eastern High School, Washington DC

12 Colleges and universities attended. Do **not** attach a copy with your transcript unless requested.

Name		Total Credits Earned		Major(s)	Degree - Year
		Semester	Quarter		(if any) Received
Name University of the District of Columbia				Electronic Technology	A.S., 1979
City Washington	State DC	ZIP Code			
Name National-Louis University				Managment	B.S., 1995
City McLean	State VA	ZIP Code 22102			
Name Eastern Michigan University				Information Security	M.S., 1997
City Ypsilanti	State MI	ZIP Code 48197			

OTHER QUALIFICATIONS

13 **Job-related** training courses (give title and year). Job-related skills (other languages, computer software/hardware, tools, machinery, typing speed, etc.). **Job-related** certificates and licenses (current only). **Job-related** honors, awards, and special accomplishments (publications, memberships in professional/honor societies, leadership activities, public speaking, and performance awards). Give dates, but do **not** send documents unless requested.

PLEASE SEE ATTACHED

GENERAL

14 Are you a U.S. citizen?   YES [X]   NO [   ]   Give the country of your citizenship

15 Do you claim veteran's preference?   NO [   ]   YES [X]   Mark your claim of 5 or 10 points below

5 points [X]   Attach your DD214 or other proof.   1   0 points [   ]   Attach an Application for 10-Point Veterans' Preference (SF-15) and proof required.

16 Were you ever a Federal civilian employee?   NO [   ]   YES [X]   For highest civilian grade give:

Series	Grade	From (MM/YY)	To (mm/YY)
0391/0334	13	10/90	present

17 Are you eligible for reinstatement based on career or career-conditional Federal status?   NO [X]   YES [   ]   If requested, attach SF 50 proof.

18 I certify that, to the best of my knowledge and belief, all of the information on and attached to this application is true, correct, complete and made in good faith. **I understand** that false or fraudulent information on or attached to this application may be grounds for not hiring me or for firing me after I begin work, and may be punishable by fine or imprisonment. **I understand** that any information I give may be investigated.

SIGNATURE   DATE SIGNED

XXXXXX XXXXX. — SSN: 000-00-00000

#13 — OTHER QUALIFICATIONS

Successfully completed numerous courses on COMSEC and computer equipment and systems. Classes of COMSEC equipment and systems on which trained include general purpose data, voice, specialized tactical, bulk, and broadcast. Specific details will be provided on request.

1) George Washington University
       Fiber-Optic Technology for Communications, 2.16 CEUs   28 Jun 90
       Application of T-Carrier to Private Networking, 3.60 CEUs   27 Jul 90
       Data Communication Standards: Interfaces and Protocols for Open Systems
            Network Architectures, 2.16 CEUs   14 Sep 90

2) Data-Tech Institute
       Intensive Introduction to T1/T3 Networking, 1.50 CEUs   10 Aug 90

3) Naval Electronic Systems Security Engineering Center
       Contracting Officer's Technical Representative (COTR's) Course   23 Aug 89

4) Office of Personnel Management
       Instructor Training Workshop   14 May 82
       Project Management: Planning, Scheduling, and Control   14 Feb 92

5) Human Resources Office, NW NMCNCR
       Supervisory Development I   16 May 86
       Supervisory Development II   20 Aug 86

6) Management Concepts Incorporated
       Statement of Work / Specification Preparation   1 Jul 87

7) Human Resources Office, Washington NY
       Managing Conflict   19 Apr 90
       How To Negotiate   11 May 90
       Value Engineering   06 Aug 92

8) Naval Computer & Telecommunication Command
       Acquisition Streamlining   15 Mar 91
       Total Quality Leadership Awareness   15 Apr 92

9) Department of Navy Program Information Center
       Planning, Programming and Budgeting System (PEBS) Course   30 Sep 92

10) National Defense University, Information Resources Management College
       Information Engineering   28 May 93

SEE NEXT PAGE

XXXXXX, Alfred L. — SSN: XXXXXX

<u>#13, continued</u> — <u>OTHER QUALIFICATIONS</u>

11) Defense Information Systems Agency
      Defense Data Network Seminar   26 Aug 93

12) Naval Computer & Telecommunication Command
      X.400/X.500 DMS/MSP Training (J.G. Van Dyke)   10 Mar 95

13) National Security Agency
      Information Systems Security Engineering Course   12 May 95

<u>AWARDS:</u>

Graduated with honors, B.S. Management, 1995

Honors Student Award, MLS Information Security, 1997

Letter of Appreciation for Technical Professionalism from Commanding Officer NAS Memphis, 1980

Sustained Superior Performance Awards: 1982, 1983

Outstanding Performance Awards: 1992, 1993, 1994, 1995, 1996

A COMPLETED FEDERAL RESUME

XXXX XXXXXXX
Announcement number:

XXXXX XXXXXXXX

000000 Alex Guerrero Circle
El Paso, Texas 79936

Home / Fax: (915) 000-0000
Email: xxxxxx@xxx.com
Office: xxxxxxxxxx
Email:xxxxx@xxx.org
U.S. citizen
Highest security clearance held: TOP SECRET (1985-90)
Highest Federal civilian grade: GG-1102-12
Date of last promotion : December, 1996

GOAL   Announcement Number:
Position title:

PROFILE   **Current responsibility:**
Contracting Officer
Border Environment Cooperation Commission
Assigned to facility in Juarez, Mexico

Proven experience managing budgets for contracts ranging in value up to
$200 million. Experience supervising up to 5 employees.

Primary focal point for the award of several multi-million dollar construction,
architectural and engineering, and management services contracts.

Strategic liaison responsibility. Frequently interact with high-ranking city,
county, and state officials, as well as consultants and the general public to provide
funding and construction of border projects in Mexico and the United States.

Served as Equal Employment Opportunity Counselor. Also served on
Qualification Review Boards to rank applicants for Federal positions.

Designed and implemented operating policies and procedures. Automated
library operations and recorded retrieval procedures. Participated in establishment
of computerized accounting program for non-appropriated funds.

Accomplished communicator. Principal point-of-contact and lead negotiator
during contract deliberations.

Strong written communication skills. Developed and wrote Agency-wide
operating standards.

CURRENT TITLE: CONTRACTING OFFICER
Border Environment Cooperation Commission (BECC)   Juarez, Mexico 32470
GRADE: N/A   **SALARY:** $57,000   **HOURS:** 40/week
DATE: January 1998-present   **SUPERVISOR:** XXXXXX

Direct, monitor, and personally oversee the award of architectural and engineering and other management services contracts for the BECC, a quasi-government agency.

RESULT   Responsible for the development of water/waste water and sanitation master plans, cost and price analysis, development of pre-negotiation memorandums and projects' negotiations, and assembling documentation required to certify projects for construction funds. Selected to fill in for the incumbent Technical Assistance Program Manager during her travel or absence.

Serve as lead negotiator and facilitator for the evaluation team. Responsible for coordinating all business development and contract administration activities for the organization. Direct proposal efforts, lead negotiation teams and chair status meetings with all disciplines involved in complex, high-dollar development projects.

RESULT   Expertly guiding principals through the contracting process, successfully directed contracting efforts (cradle to grave) for multi-year, multi-million dollar projects.

Supervise and coordinate the work of subordinate staff of U.S. and Mexican nationals, managing planning efforts, devising organizational structures to support quality control, task management, technical operations and administrative functions.

RESULT   Establish work schedules, assign tasks, advise subordinates on proper techniques and procedures and prepare annual performance reviews.

Review Mexico's contracting law and procedures and the United Nations Model Law on Procurement in order to develop Agency specific procurement standards. Because the BECC was created under a North American Free Trade Agreement (NAFTA) side-agreement and is a bi-national agency, funded by both the United States and Mexican governments and the U.S. Environmental Protection Agency (USEPA), the BECC is not required to conform to Federal Acquisition Regulations (FAR). As a result, no such procurement regulations were in place.

RESULT   Developed procurement standards and procedures for this relatively new Agency.
IMPACT   These procedures are written in a clear, concise and detailed manner and contain information that is vital to the efficient and effective administration of the procurement program. These procedures were instrumental in securing new contracts with the corporate community and launched the procurement program.

Prepare reviews for the agency's Legal Counsel on contract clauses and other legal issues. Review financial feasibility of projects. Examine environmental and sustainability aspects, as well as criteria required to qualify for construction funding. Where possible, work is coordinated with graduate studies in the MPA program at the University of Texas at El Paso (UTEP).

RESULT   Successfully handled two protests for disqualification of proposals during the evaluation stage.
IMPACT   This early resolution of the problem prevented a more serious challenge.

Point-of-Contact for management study and internal needs assessment.

RESULT   Coordinate project tracking systems, electronic and hard copy record keeping, general operating procedures, manual writing, and accounting/budgeting processes.
IMPACT   Until my intervention there were few standards or operational practices in place. Recipient, "Excellent" job performance rating.

XXXX XXXXXXX
Announcement number:

TITLE: Contract Specialist (NOTE: hired as GS-1102-7 Intern; promoted to GS-9/11/12)
U.S. Section, International Boundary and Water Commission   El Paso, TX 79902-1441
GRADE: GG-1102-12   **SALARY:** $45,000   **HOURS:** 40/week
DATE: 12/90-1/98   **SUPERVISOR:** XXXXXX

Served as contracting officer and contract administrator for multi-million dollar supplies and
services, construction, and architectural and engineering contracts. Possessed a contracting
officer's warrant. Performed pre-award, award, and contract administration duties.

RESULT   Prepared *Commerce Business Daily* synopses and advertisements, developed and
reviewed technical specifications, and issued solicitations and Requests For
Proposals (RFPs). Headed evaluation teams reviewing potential contractors'
financial data. Prepared lease agreements for properties where contractors
performed construction work.

Performed price and costs analyses, conducted contract negotiations, monitored expenditures,
and developed legal interpretations. Presided over bid openings and site visits.

Set priorities and demonstrated effective leadership. Since contracting does not leave much
room for variance, it was my responsibility to ensure that rules were strictly adhered to.

RESULT   Established good working relationships with diverse groups of individuals in
order to effectively solicit compliance with regulatory requirements.

IMPACT   Anticipated questions and provided necessary information and guidance.

Instituted policy and procedures for Acquisition Division in areas of Ethics, Imprest Funds,
and Memorandums of Understanding for grants and cooperative agreements with Federal
agencies.

RESULT   Developed technical expertise in all phases of the contracting cycle from per-
award through negotiations and contract administration.

IMPACT   Led staff members through the process of changing and updating old habits and
implementing required procedures.

Coordinated with technical and engineering staff, end users, and senior executives within the
client organizations and Federal contract managers to ensure timely compliance with all terms of
the contracts and the Federal Acquisition Regulations (FAR).

RESULT   Worked with diverse individuals to create cohesive plans and strategies,
incorporating the often-divergent objectives of many disciplines. Oversaw several
projects of national interest.

IMPACT   In the operation and maintenance of the Nogales International Wastewater
Treatment Plant, made the determination that it would be more cost effective to
contract the work out to a private firm than to have the government continue its
operation of the plant. As a result of contracting out, the government was able to
realize a cost savings over a five year period.

Main point-of-contact, internally and externally, ensuring that client organizations were satisfied
and that contractors delivered goods/services in accordance with Statements-of-Work documents.

Served as Equal Employment Opportunity (EEO) Counselor. Provided supervisors and
managers with detailed explanations of applicable EEO laws and regulations prohibiting
discrimination. Participated in EEO workshops.

RESULT   Often called upon to provide assistance in matters involving disciplinary actions,
grievances, EEO complaints and illegal separations.

IMPACT   Used tact to provide practical advisory services in potentially volatile situations.

Facilitated affirmative action hiring, providing advice and support for manager involved. explaining Federal regulations to assist them in devising effective job search strategies.
RESULT   Gained the support of management and employees throughout the organization.
IMPACT   As a result, was able to resolve all issues presented to me at the local level without the need for expensive and disruptive litigation.
Recipient of several "Excellent" job performance ratings during this period.

TITLE: Records Officer (Mail and File Assistant)
U.S. Section, International Boundary and Water Commission   El Paso, TX 79902-1441
GRADE: GG-307-07   **SALARY:** $25,000   **HOURS:** 40/week
DATE: 6/85-6/90   **SUPERVISOR:** XXXXXX
Chief, Headquarters Communications and Records Branch with TOP SECRET security clearance and purview over 12 field offices throughout the U.S. and Mexico border region.
RESULT   Exercised primary responsibility for the Agency's records management, mail management, correspondence management, library (legal and technical) operations, Freedom of Information and Privacy Act programs, and public relations program.
Conducted assistance visits to field offices to conduct operational audits in records management. Wrote reports of my findings and made recommendations. Taught classes in records management, records disposition, correspondence management, mail management, micrographics management, directives management, copier use and ADP management.
RESULT   Wrote the Agency's Freedom of Information Act regulations, and rewrote the records disposition and correspondence manuals.
Initiated a records control program for Privacy Act records.
RESULT   Established a directives system, and initiated a micrographics program. Computerized the library's operations as well as its records retrieval procedures.
IMPACT   My ideas were adopted, implemented, and maintained. When completed, these new or revised documents and procedures went a long way in reducing turnaround time, enabling our staff members to make renewed progress toward mission goals.
Supervised and directed the activities of subordinate staff.
RESULT   Managed planning and designed organizational structures capable of supporting strong quality control, task management, technical and administrative functions.
IMPACT   Established work schedules, assigned tasks, advised subordinates on proper techniques and procedures and prepared annual performance reviews.
Recipient, several "Excellent" job performance ratings during this period.

TITLE: Administrative Clerk
Loan Servicing Department, Small Business Administration   El Paso, TX 79935
GRADE: GS-301-4   **SALARY:** $16,800   **HOURS:** 40/week
DATE: 5/84-6/85   **SUPERVISOR:** XXXXXXX
Planned, organized, and coordinated administrative activities of the office.
RESULT   Completed special projects that involved contact with administrative and management staff at all levels within the Agency.
IMPACT   Given greater responsibilities than the job called for while in this position.
NOTE: *Accepted this position in order to return to Federal service.*

XXXX XXXXXXX
Announcement number:

TITLE: Homemaker
xxxxxx Alex Guerrero Circle   xxxxxx, Texas 00000
GRADE: N/A   **SALARY:** N/A   **HOURS:** N/A
DATE: 5/83-5/84   **SUPERVISOR:** N/A

Stayed home to care for newborn child. Responsible for child care, home operations, budgeting and family support.

TITLE: Administrative Officer
Administration Division, Department of the Army   WSMR, NM 88022
GRADE: GS-341-9   **SALARY:** $21,000   **HOURS:** 40/week
DATE: 9/81-5/83   **SUPERVISOR:** XXXXXX

Administrative management for Morale Support Activities Division's budget, procurement of supplies, publicity, personnel and manpower, and property and facilities management. **Monitored expenditures and developed annual budget forecasts.** Established five-year budget plans. Funding was provided through either non-appropriated (self earning) or appropriated means. Served as principal conduit for all information flow to the Director.
    RESULT   Applied accounting techniques which determined if activities were profitable, identified ways of improving activities' income, and determined the need for supplemental funding through appropriated means.
    IMPACT   Computerized accounting program for non-appropriated funds resulted in savings to the government.
            Recipient, Letter of Appreciation (1982).
Main point-of-contact for all budget issues for the Division, providing interpretation of accounting statements to supervisor, activity managers, and the Colonel. Worked with both appropriated and non-appropriated funds. Performed audits of private organizations at the Missile Range to assure their financial soundness and their compliance with regulatory requirements.
    RESULT   Implemented mandated financial data format changes for private organizations.
    IMPACT   Earned the trust and cooperation of all private organizations serviced and brought them into compliance with regulatory requirements.
            Recipient, Special Act Award for working with private organization (1982).
Supervised and directed the work of five staff members (3 civilians and 2 military). Managed planning efforts, devised organizational structures to support quality control, task management, technical operations and administrative functions.
    RESULT   Established work schedules, assigned tasks, advised subordinates on proper techniques and procedures and prepared annual performance reviews.

TITLE: Management Assistant
Administration Division, Department of the Army   WSMR, NM 88002
GRADE: GS-344-7   **SALARY:** $16,000   **HOURS:** 40/week
DATE: 8/79-9/81   **SUPERVISOR:** XXXXXX

Assisted in the analysis and assessment of management issues for the Administrative Management Branch.

    RESULT   Suggested solutions to administrative and management problems. Collected data, reviewed and analyzed information. Interviewed managers and employees while observing their operations, taking into account the nature of the organization, the relationship it had with other organizations, its internal organization and culture.

    IMPACT   Reported findings and recommendations to client organization, often in writing. In addition, made oral recommendations. Assisted in implementation of suggestions.

Taught classes in records management, records disposition, correspondence management, mail management, micrographics and directives management, copier use and ADP management.

    RESULT   Recipient, Letter of Appreciation for instructing military personnel in records management (1980).

Conducted audits, and wrote reports of findings with recommendations. Allocated timeframes to offices to correct deficiencies and did follow-up visits where appropriate. Held secret security clearance. Acted in behalf of supervisor during her absence.

    RESULT   Led individuals to change what they were doing incorrectly in order to conform to regulatory requirements.

    IMPACT   Facility was upgraded to exceed all records management requirements.

EDUCATION

Bachelor of Business Administration (B.B.A.)
University of Texas at El Paso, 1993

Masters of Public Administration candidate (M.P.A. degree due: May 1999)
University of Texas at El Paso

PROFESSIONAL ORGANIZATIONS

National Institute of Government Purchasing (NIGP)
National and Local Chapters

RELATED SKILLS

Computer literate in Windows, WordPerfect, MS Word and Works, Lotus (Quattro Pro), and database management software, the Internet, intranets, and on-line services.

LANGUAGE SKILLS

Fluent in spoken and written Spanish

A COMPUTER SCANNABLE RESUME OR RESUMIX™

XXXXXXXXX
SSN 000-00-0000

XXXXXX XXXXX
SSN 000-00-0000
0000 Spain Drive
Stafford, Virginia 00000
Home: (540) 000-0000
Work: (703) 000-0000
DSN: 000-0000
E-mail: xxxx@xxx.xxx

SUMMARY OF SKILLS
Military Satellite Communications
Manager, Defense Satellite Communications System (DSCS)
Proven Staff Leadership
Task Manager
Lead Evaluator
Contractor Supervision
Liaison and representation
Technical Troubleshooting
Spacecraft Reconfiguration
Data Integration
Operating Parameters
Control and Coordination
Operational Assessments
Contingency Planning
Specialized Engineering
Contingency Communications
Earth Terminals Optimization
System Reliability
Maintainability Standards
Control Concepts
System Capabilities
Interface Requirements
Requirements Analysis
Project Coordination
High-level Briefings
Frequency Modulation
Digital Baseband Equipment
Common-user Communications
Modeling and Simulation
Network Management
Information Security
Communications Link Configurations
System Optimization
Detection of Degradations

XXXXXXXXX
SSN 000-00-0000

EXPERIENCE:
January 1991 to present. 40-50 hours/week.
Telecommunications Manager.
TOP SECRET / SCI security clearance
Defense Information Systems Agency (DISA)
Supervisor: XXXXXXX
Pay-grade: GS-391-14
Functional leader within DOD for the DSCS Operational Control System. Integrate complex data and conclusions from various functional areas to formulate policy and develop procedures for operating DSCS to serve DOD and other Federal agencies. Recruited by DSCS Operations Branch (DOT) at DCA/DISA. Promoted to GS-0391-14 as of 10-19-92 due
to "accretion of duties" and assigned as Deputy/Assistant to the Senior Satellite Communications System Manager; served as primary in his absence. Assumed all management duties effective October 1998 during his transition to retirement. Acting in that capacity to date. Supervise management of DSCS and technical direction of DSCS Operations Control Centers. Manage satellite communication payloads and network coordination. Establish parameters of satellite service. Exercise managerial authority regarding access to DSCS. Prepare and issue Telecommunications Service Requests (TSR). Develop implementation directives for the O&M commands. Coordinate execution of these directives. Develop objectives, policies and procedures for the Joint Staff concerning current and projected DSCS operations. Provide liaison and representation regarding operational requirements in the planning, development, programming, budgeting, acquisition and deployment of DSCS space and ground equipment and related operational control systems. Extensive use of DCAD 800-70-1 and 310-65-1 for TSR services, as governed by MOP 37. Evaluate all requests for DSCS access; prepare DISA's recommendations to the Joint Staff for its approval/disapproval and subsequent entry into the Integrated Consolidated SATCOM Data Base (ICDB). Serve as DNSO representative on ICDB-related matters. Extensive interaction with, and instruction of, DISA and other Defense and Intelligence Community managers, frequently including decision-makers with limited knowledge of satellite technology. Provide recommendations for communications link configurations that optimize the use of DSCS satellite resources. Plan satellite cut-overs and frequency plans to optimize loading of operational satellites.
RESULTS PRODUCED: Key player in ensuring highly efficient utilization of assets. Instrumental in developing and implementing a reconstitution effort during unexpected transponder failures. Planned and implemented error-free satellite Telecommunications Service Requests. Develop and maintain policies, procedures, concepts of operation, parameters and standards for DSCS, including ECCM and the use of partial satellites. Develop, produce, and publish operational and control concepts for DSCS in DISAC 800-70-1. Develop new and modified concepts and configurations in support of ongoing missions. Extensive troubleshooting in the following areas: limited bandwidth, restricted available power from satellite transponders, antenna patterns and earth terminal characteristics, shortage of specific filters or multiplexers, front-line coordination with field sites, creating cut-over plans. Provide inputs for updated edition of DCAC 800-70-1. Initiated change of ENR codes for all strategic satellite terminals in use worldwide.

1989 to 1991. 40-50 hours/week. **MilNet Manager.**
Defense Data Network, Operations
Supervisor: XXXXXXXX
Assigned to DDN Operations as DDN MilNetManger. Operational manager of the DOD global MilNet. Provided direction in network design and implementation from user level to nodal points, including fielding of NACs and CISCO routers.

1987 to 1989. 40 hours/week. **Integrated Test Facility Manager.**
Defense Data Network
Supervisor: LTC XXXX
Managed the Defense Data Network (DDN) Integrated Test Facility (ITF) in Reston, VA.
Responsible for baseline development of BLACKER encryption device. Was detailed into position as Branch Chief upon transfer of LTC XXXX.

1985 to 1987. 50-60 hours/week. **Head, Communications Department.**
NAVELEXDETPAX, Patuxent River, MD.
Supervisor: XXXXXXX
Managed four (4) Telecommuncation Facilities (2 Strategic Genser, 1 Tactical, 1 SCIF) providing Air, Land and Sea Test & Evaluation Platforms. Conducted performance evaluations at all participating test facilities.

SECURITY CLEARANCE:
TOP SECRET / SCI

EDUCATION
Graduate, Southwest XXXX XXXXX Public High School, April 1961

ADVANCED PROFESSIONAL TRAINING
Customer Service Orientation (40 hour course), 1995
DSCS DOSS/DASA Course (80 hour course), 1991
DSCS Network Engineering Course (40 hour course), 1991
Orientation to Contracting (16 hour course), 1987
COTR Training (40 hour course), 1985
Leadership Management Education and Training, 1981
Satellite Controller Course (three month course), 1978
Radioman "B" School, (six month course),1971
Teletype Maintenance and Operation, 1966
Radioman "A" School (seven month course), 1962

AWARDS AND HONORS
Joint Service Commendation Medal
Vietnam Service Medal, with two Bronze Stars
Recipient of continuous "Outstanding" performance appraisals throughout my tenure at DISA.

KSAs OR RANKING FACTORS

XXXXXXX

xxxxx

EVALUATION FACTORS

1. **ABILITY TO SELECT, DEVELOP, AND SUPERVISE A SUBORDINATE STAFF, WHICH INCLUDED THE ABILITY TO ACTIVELY PURSUE MANAGEMENT GOALS AND SUPPORT THE EQUAL OPPORTUNITY PROGRAM.**

I believe my ability to lead and facilitate the work of others has been demonstrably evident throughout my career. For example, on numerous occasions I have interacted with staffs that I have led by (1) providing a clear sense of direction and (2) setting my expected performance levels at a level that is commensurate with these organizations' objectives, thereby (3) motivating my staff toward a higher level of goal accomplishments.

In addition, I have promoted quality performance through effective use of the agency's performance management system and I have established performance standards, appraised subordinate staffs' accomplishments, and acted to reward or counsel them, as their performance indicated was appropriate. I also have made it my practice to assess my employees' developmental needs and provide opportunities to help maximize their skills, capabilities, and ongoing professional development.

I welcome and value cultural diversity and I use these and other differences as one more tool to foster an environment where people can work together cooperatively, while achieving organizational goals. In all of my leadership roles, I have worked to promote commitment, pride, trust and group identity, and I have sought to prevent situations that could have resulted in unpleasant confrontations.

Examples of my ability in this area include:

Recruited, supervised and led the activities of subordinate staff in five (5) separate assignments.

RESULT
- Managed planning efforts, devised organizational structures to support quality control, task management, technical and administrative functions.
- Established work schedules, assigned tasks, advised subordinates on proper techniques and procedures; prepared annual performance reviews.

Conducted local Title 10 training sessions to familiarize personnel with Army MDAPs and associated reporting requirements and to equip them to recognize potential threshold breaches when they occur.

RESULT
- Sponsored an Army developmental assignment program whereby individuals within Army competed to participate at HQ, DA. Candidates were screened from applications received from HQ, DA and PEO/PM offices. Those participating gained hands-on experience with the various Title 10 reporting requirements associated with the Armyís Major Defense Acquisition Programs (MDAPs).

SEE NEXT PAGE

XXXXXXX

XXXXX

EVALUATION FACTORS

1. **ABILITY TO SELECT, DEVELOP, AND SUPERVISE A SUBORDINATE STAFF, WHICH INCLUDED THE ABILITY TO ACTIVELY PURSUE MANAGEMENT GOALS AND SUPPORT THE EQUAL OPPORTUNITY PROGRAM.** (continued)

Served as Team Leader during major financial management exercises, making determinations regarding proper and effective procedures.

RESULT
- Designed studies, coordinated planning, developed strategy, and identified potential sources for reliable and responsive information and assigned tasks. Teamwork included the compilation and review of budget data reflecting existing operations and data from feasibility studies on proposed programs.

Participated in the development and implementation of recruiting programs to meet EEO requirements and Affirmative Action objectives.

RESULT
- Identified appropriate advertising vehicles for minority recruiting.
- Provided assistance and input in matters involving career development, training, disciplinary actions, grievances, EEO complaints and separations.

Actively recruited, interviewed, and selected individuals from or for the following positions: Computer Programmers, Budget Analyst, Program Analysts, Budget Clerks, Facilities Managers, and Engineering Technicians.

RESULT
- I have maintained a better than 50% ratio of women/minority positions within the organizations affected.
- Successfully achieved minority representation in key staff positions within both the Program Management Resource Divison and in the Directorate for Assessment and Evaluation.
- All offices in which I have worked have met or exceeded workplace diversity goals during my tenure. I believe that having diversity tools available is crucial for managers to help ensure fair and equitable treatment of employees. Also, I believe if done right, culturally diverse offices can be rewarding and conducive to a high-performing, healthy work environment.

Actively recruited and mentored individuals to fill developmental assignments within the division.

RESULT
- Managed the developmental program in such a way that their parent organizations continued to support our developmental program by staffing vacancies. I keep in touch with many of our former developmental employees and monitor their professional development and progress.

XXXXXXX
xxxxx

EVALUATION FACTORS

2.   **KNOWLEDGE OF MATERIEL LIFE CYCLE MANAGEMENT FUNCTIONS, PROGRAMS AND SYSTEMS USED TO PROVIDE LOGISTICAL SUPPORT.**

My current job includes a very substantial degree of life-cycle management responsibility.

For example, I currently run the policy operation of Acquisition Life Cycle management. In this capacity, the information related to guidance addressing Army's Acquisition Program Baselines (APBs) for Army Acquisition Category (ACAT) I, II and some representative III programs.

Examples of my strong working knowledge in this area include the following:

Analyze the content of the APBs and ensure that APBs adequately address program requirements.

RESULT   • I recently issued APB policy which now requires APBs to address "total life cycle costs" which by definition includes operating and support (O&S) costs.

Keep Army and OSD leadership informed regarding how the Army executes their cost, schedule and performance parameters within their respective APBs.

RESULT   • Maintain close ties and frequent contacts with officials at all levels in the Army and DoD as well as the respective PEOs and PMs and Command Groups.
   • Any known logistical support requirements would also be captured within the respective APBs.

I have gained substantial working knowledge and hands-on experience through interacting with officials in the Comptroller and Acquisition communities related to acquisition life cycle subject matter contained within APBs, SARs and DAES reports, as well as through managing these processes.

RESULT   • My effort to include O&S costs within APBs is unique. To this point, the other Military Services have not yet followed suit but will likely do so soon, since it is DoD policy to make Program Managers responsible for "total life cycle management".
   • If and when this happens, these Program Managers would have total "cradle-to-grave" program responsibility—as well as operational control of the budget dollars to make sure that this level of responsibility is discharged fully and effectively.

XXXXXXX
xxxxx

EVALUATION FACTORS

3.   KNOWLEDGE OF ADVANCED LIFE CYCLE MANAGEMENT PLANNING PRINCIPLES AND PRACTICES.

My strong background in the Comptrollership and Acquisition areas has given me an unusually broad set of qualifications in this area.

Examples of my knowledge in this area include the following:

Gained valuable understanding of military facilities planning while serving as Acting Chief of the Facilities Management office.

RESULT   • This experience exposed me to requirements associated with our proposed military construction, Army (MCA) projects and the MCA processor.

Currently responsible for issuing policy at HQ, DA level, pertaining to the total acquisition life cycle baseline parameters (cost, schedule and performance) for the Armyís major programs.

RESULT   • In 1996, the Army adopted the idea to include operating and support cost estimates within Acquisition Program Baselines (APBs). I began enforcing the policy in earnest several months later .

• Soon, the Army will have "total life cycle" cost data captured routinely in the APBs. This is one example of the "high-level" Army policy areas for which I am responsible (APBs, CARS, DAES, UCRs and SECDEF program certification) and in which I am intimately involved.

Strong working knowledge of PPBES, the DoD planning, programming, budgeting and execution system.

RESULT   • Oversee the submission of three budget cycle positions each year (POM, BES and PB) as they relate to the Armyís ACAT I programs.

• Prepared substantial portions of the internal operating budget (IOB) at the installation level.

Broad experience writing, revising, and implementing policy at HQ, DA level, as it relates to legal reporting requirements associated with Title 10, United States Code.

RESULT   • Review, update and issue revised policy and guidance pertaining to the required content of Major Defense Acquisition Programs (MDAPs - Section 2430), Selected Acquisition Reports (SARs - Section 2432), Nunn-McCurdy Unit Cost Reporting (UCRs - Section 2433) and Acquisition Program Baselines (APBs-Section 2435). Since Title 10 is generally DoD-wide in scope, it must not conflict with DoD policy and guidance. I work closely with the other services and DoD to ensure communication is clear.

XXXXXXX

xxxxx

EVALUATION FACTORS

4. ABILITY TO EFFECTIVELY COMMUNICATE BOTH ORALLY AND IN WRITING REGARDING THE DUTIES OF THIS POSITION.

I have had extensive experience communicating, both orally and in writing. For example, I have defended/advocated my organizations' programs to Congress, DoD, DA and industry. As a steward of government funds, I often have written to determine the disposition of un-liquidated obligations to ensure that the government's money was properly accounted for.

Examples of my ability in this critical skill area include the following:

Frequently prepare written correspondence for senior officials of the Army, DoD, and Congress.

RESULT   • Represent the Army in writing—and in person—in a variety of areas. Much of the interaction is in the form of Integrated Product Teams (IPTs) which often includes aspects of Title 10, DoD 5000 and AR 70-1, which requires substantial subject matter expertise which must be communicated either by written policy or correspondence or both. Some of these areas include:

  • Major Defense Acquisition Programs (MDAPs)- 10, USC, Section 2430.
  • Selected Acquisition Reports (SARs) - 10, USC, Section 2432.
  • Nunn-McCurdy Unit Cost Reporting (UCRs) - 10, USC, Section 2433
  • Acquisition Program Baselines (APBs) - 10, USC, Section 2435
  • Defense Acquisition Executive Summary (DAES - DoD 5000)

Extensive personal liaison with senior Army and other DoD officials.

RESULT   • Selected to brief the Secretary and Under Secretary of the Army regarding our Title 10, United States Code reporting requirements.

Issue written guidance and policy related to a broad area of responsibilities under my authority.

RESULT   • Recently issued new Title 10 policy to the Program Executive Offices (PEOs) and their Project Managers (PMs).
  • Wrote Congressional Notification Letters to the House and Senate Leaders informing them of the NM unit cost breaches, for which we subsequently sent Congress reports.

Held managerial and staff leadership positions at installation and HQ, DA levels.

RESULT   • At the installation level, was intimately involved with frequent manpower surveys and writing justifications to defend our TDA.

How to Give Yourself the Edge Filling Out a Federal Job Application

The key to filling out an eye-catching Federal job application is attitude. Just keep reminding yourself how capable you are and that what you're being asked to do is no different than what many less-qualified people were able to do. Once you have yourself pumped up with as much enthusiasm as you can get, follow these tips:

- Be sure your application or resume includes all the mandatory information requested in the job vacancy announcement.
- Leave no lines blank. Fill in "N/A" or "not applicable" to show you're responding to it.
- Write up your application or resume. Then, go back and "write" it again, using the first as an outline to expand wherever possible.
- Quantify where possible. How much money did you save the company? How many people did you supervise? How many convictions did you get? How many programs did you institute?
- Remember to respond to the KSAs, ranking factors, or selection criteria separately. For grade levels at or above GS-7, respond with a full page to each KSA.
- Sign your application in colored, not black, ink and remember to mail the original, not the copy.

TWO

Getting a Job with the U.S. Postal Service

CONTENTS

WORKING FOR THE U.S. POSTAL SERVICE

The United States Postal Service is an independent agency of the Federal government. This means that postal employees enjoy the same generous benefits as other Federal employees. These benefits include an automatic raise at least once a year, regular cost-of-living adjustments, liberal paid vacation and sick leave, life insurance, hospitalization, the opportunity to join a credit union, and the same job security of other government positions. At the same time, the operation of the Postal Service is businesslike and independent of politics. An examination system is used to fill vacancies. This system provides opportunities for those who are able and motivated to enter the Postal Service and to move within it.

What Is It Like to Work for the U.S.P.S.?

Most people are familiar with the duties of their local letter carrier (also known as a city carrier) and the post-office window clerk. Yet, very few are aware of the many different tasks required in processing mail or of the variety of occupations in the Postal Service.

THE STRUCTURE OF THE POSTAL SERVICE

While your local post office is open only for set hours during the day, the Postal Service itself works day and night. At any given moment, a steady stream of letters, packages, magazines, and papers moves through the typical large post office. City carriers have collected some of this mail from neighborhood mailboxes; other mail has been trucked in from surrounding towns or from the airport. When a truck arrives at the post office, mail handlers unload the mail. Postal clerks then sort it according to destination. After being sorted, outgoing mail is loaded into trucks for delivery to the airport or nearby towns. Local mail is left for carriers to deliver the next morning.

To keep buildings and equipment clean and in good working order, the Postal Service employs a variety of service and maintenance workers, including janitors, laborers, truck mechanics, electricians, carpenters, and painters. Some workers specialize in repairing machines that process mail.

Postal inspectors audit the operations of post offices to see that they are run efficiently, that funds are spent properly, and that postal laws and regulations are observed. They also prevent and detect crimes, such as theft, forgery, and fraud, involving use of the mail.

Postmasters and supervisors are responsible for the day-to-day operation of the post office, for hiring and promoting employees, and for setting up work schedules.

Almost 85 percent of all postal workers are in jobs directly related to processing and delivering mail. This group includes postal clerks, city carriers, mail handlers, rural carriers, and truck drivers. Postmasters and supervisors make up only 10 percent of total employment, and maintenance workers about 4 percent. The remainder—less than 2 percent—includes postal inspectors, guards, personnel workers, and secretaries.

GENERAL WORKING CONDITIONS AND EARNINGS

Most post-office buildings are clean and well-lit, but some of the older ones are not. The Postal Service is in the process of replacing and remodeling these outmoded buildings, and conditions are expected to improve.

75

Postal Service employees are paid under several separate pay schedules, depending upon the duties of the job and the knowledge, experience, or skill required. For example, there are separate schedules for production workers, such as clerks and mail handlers, for rural carriers, for postal managers, and for postal executives. In all pay schedules, except that of executives, employees receive periodic "step" increases"—up to a specified maximum if their job performance is satisfactory.

4.1 LETTER CARRIER PAY SCHEDULE—3/14/1998 (YEARLY)

Grade Level	Step A	Step B	Step C	Step D	Step E
5	$27,011	$29,895	$32,210	$34,443	$34,731
6	$28,585	$31,665	$32,859	$35,147	$35,462

Grade Level	Step F	Step G	Step H	Step I	Step J
5	$35,022	$35,309	$35,600	$35,888	$36,177
6	$35,777	$36,088	$36,404	$36,718	$37,029

Grade Level	Step K	Step L	Step M	Step N	Step O
5	$36,468	$36,755	$37,046	$37,334	$37,623
6	$37,345	$37,660	$37,973	$38,290	$38,604

4.2 MAIL HANDLER PAY SCHEDULE—3/13/1999 (YEARLY)

Grade Level	Step A	Step B	Step C	Step D	Step E
4	$23,808	$28,512	$30,721	$33,975	$34,237
5	$25,122	$30,149	$32,419	$34,618	$34,900

Grade Level	Step F	Step G	Step H	Step I	Step J
4	$34,503	$34,766	$35,029	$35,293	$35,559
5	$35,187	$35,467	$35,753	$36,039	$36,320

Grade Level	Step K	Step L	Step M	Step N	Step O
4	$35,823	$36,087	$36,350	$36,614	$36,877
5	$36,606	$36,886	$37,171	$37,455	$37,739

4.3 RURAL CARRIER EVALUATED SCHEDULE—3/13/1999
FULL-TIME ANNUAL BASIC RATES (PARTIAL SCHEDULE)

Hours Worked	Step A	Step B	Step C	Step 1	Step 2	Step 3	Step 4
12	$7,768	$8,590	$9,220	$9,859	$9,952	$10,043	$10,135
18	$11,649	$12,887	$13,832	$14,788	$14,926	$15,066	$15,203
24	$15,533	$17,178	$18,439	$19,719	$19,900	$20,082	$20,266
30	$19,415	$21,480	$23,056	$24,651	$24,878	$25,111	$25,337
40	$25,887	$28,633	$30,735	$32,862	$33,167	$33,475	$33,779
48	$33,655	$37,223	$39,955	$42,721	$43,119	$43,518	$43,914

Hours Worked	Step 5	Step 6	Step 7	Step 8	Step 9	Step 10	Step 11
12	$10,226	$10,321	$10,413	$10,503	$10,597	$10,688	$10,781
18	$15,343	$15,479	$15,618	$15,756	$15,896	$16,034	$16,172

Hours Worked	Step 5	Step 6	Step 7	Step 8	Step 9	Step 10	Step 11
24	$20,449	$20,633	$20,817	$21,000	$21,182	$21,368	$21,550
30	$25,566	$25,796	$26,026	$26,255	$26,484	$26,714	$26,945
40	$34,087	$34,392	$34,698	$35,006	$35,310	$35,618	$35,923
48	$44,313	$44,713	$45,111	$45,509	$45,907	$46,306	$46,704

4.4 FULL-TIME REGULAR APWU SALARY SCHEDULE (PS)—9/12/1998
(POSTAL CLERK; DISTRIBUTION CLERK, MACHINE; MARK-UP CLERK, AUTOMATED;
FLAT SORTING MACHINE OPERATOR; MAIL PROCESSOR)

Grade Level	Step AA	Step A	Step B	Step C	Step D	Step E	Step F	Step G
1	$22,715	$25,041	$27,128	$29,216	$32,323	$32,536	$32,750	$32,962
2	$23,000	$25,393	$27,533	$29,667	$32,837	$33,067	$33,297	$33,527
3	$23,364	$25,771	$27,964	$30,155	$33,393	$33,641	$33,893	$34,138
4	—	$25,738	$28,434	$30,688	$33,997	$34,265	$34,536	$34,805
5	—	$27,219	$30,103	$32,418	$34,651	$34,939	$35,230	$35,517
6	—	$28,793	$31,873	$33,067	$35,355	$35,670	$35,985	$36,296
7	—	$29,392	$32,545	$33,774	$36,119	$36,457	$36,794	$37,133
8	—	—	—	$34,365	$36,937	$37,304	$37,670	$38,037
9	—	—	—	$35,191	$37,829	$38,228	$38,624	$39,021
10	—	—	—	$36,062	$38,771	$39,199	$39,625	$40,054

Grade Level	Step H	Step I	Step J	Step K	Step L	Step M	Step N	Step O
1	$33,174	$33,387	$33,600	$33,813	$34,027	$34,236	$34,451	$34,663
2	$33,760	$33,988	$34,219	$34,451	$34,679	$34,912	$35,142	$35,370
3	$34,389	$34,635	$34,887	$35,134	$35,383	$35,630	$35,879	$36,126
4	$35,071	$35,340	$35,609	$35,879	$36,150	$36,418	$36,686	$36,953
5	$35,808	$36,096	$36,385	$36,676	$36,963	$37,254	$37,542	$37,831
6	$36,612	$36,926	$37,237	$37,553	$37,868	$38,181	$38,498	$38,812
7	$37,474	$37,809	$38,149	$38,485	$38,823	$39,163	$39,500	$39,837
8	$38,406	$38,771	$39,141	$39,505	$39,873	$40,239	$40,605	$40,974
9	$39,415	$39,810	$40,206	$40,605	$40,999	$41,399	$41,765	$42,191
10	$40,483	$40,909	$41,337	$41,766	$42,192	$42,621	$43,049	$43,476

Most postal workers are members of unions covered by a national agreement with the Postal Service. Therefore, the benefits described below are subject to collective bargaining and may well be different by the time you are employed by the Postal Service.

Full-time employees work an eight-hour day, five days a week. Both full-time and part-time employees who work more than 8 hours a day or 40 hours a week receive overtime pay of one-and-a-half times their hourly rate. In addition, pay is higher for those on the night shift.

Postal employees earn 13 days of annual leave (vacation) during each of their first three years of service, including prior Federal civilian and military service; 20 days of annual leave during their fourth to fifteenth year of service; and 26 days after 15 years. In addition, employees earn 13 days of paid sick leave a year regardless of length of service.

Other benefits include retirement and survivorship annuities, free group life insurance, and optional participation in health insurance programs supported in part by the Postal Service.

GENERAL QUALIFICATIONS, TRAINING, AND ADVANCEMENT

While specific Postal Service positions often have specific qualifications, some general qualifications apply to all. An applicant for a Postal Service job must pass a written examination and meet minimum age requirements. The minimum age is usually 18 years, but a high school graduate may begin work at 16 years if the job is not hazardous and does not require use of a motor vehicle. Candidates must also pass a urinalysis drug test, a personal suitability screening standard, and a medical examination.

Many Postal Service jobs do not require formal education or special training. Applicants for these jobs are hired on the basis of their examination scores. However, other jobs do have special education or experience requirements. In addition, certain positions are open only to veterans. Any special requirements will be stated on the announcement of examination.

Male applicants born after December 31, 1959, must be registered with the Selective Service System, unless they are exempt.

The Immigration Reform and Control Act of 1986 applies to postal workers. All postal workers must be citizens of the United States or must be able to prove their identity and their right to work in the United States (permanent resident alien status—Green Card).

Training of new employees is done either on the job by supervisors and other experienced employees or in local training centers. Training ranges from a few days to several months, depending on the job. For example, mail handlers and mechanics' helpers can learn their jobs in a relatively short time. Postal inspectors, on the other hand, need months of training.

Advancement opportunities are available for most postal workers because there is a management commitment to provide career development. Also, employees can get preferred assignments, such as the day shift or a more desirable delivery route, as their seniority increases. When an opening occurs, employees may submit written requests, called "bids," for assignment to the vacancy. The bidder who meets the qualifications and has the most seniority gets the job.

In addition, postal workers can advance to better-paying positions by learning new skills. Training programs are available for low-skilled workers who wish to become technicians or mechanics.

Applicants for supervisory jobs must pass an examination. Additional requirements for promotion may include special training or education, a satisfactory work record, and appropriate personal characteristics, such as leadership ability. If the leading candidates are equally qualified, length of service is also considered.

Although opportunities for promotion to supervisory positions in smaller post offices are limited, workers may apply for vacancies in a larger post office and thus increase their chances of promotion.

The Types of Jobs Available in the Postal Service

Here's a more detailed look at the type of jobs you'll find listed when you begin to search through Postal Service openings. You get a description of the duties of each of those positions; special qualifications, if any; and the working conditions, if unusual. You'll notice that many of the positions require Exam 470 to be given. A sample Exam 470, together with the answers and explanations, is given in Chapter 6, "Finding Jobs with Your State or Municipal Government."

POSTAL CLERK

Duties of the Job

People are most familiar with the window clerk who sits behind the counter in post office lobbies selling stamps or accepting parcel post. However, the majority of postal clerks are distribution clerks who sort incoming and outgoing mail in workrooms. Only in a small post office does a clerk do both kinds of work.

When mail arrives at the post office, it is dumped on long tables where distribution clerks and mail handlers separate it into groups of letters, parcel post, and magazines and newspapers. Clerks feed letters into stamp-canceling machines and cancel the rest by hand. The mail is then taken to other sections of the post office to be sorted by destination. Clerks first separate the mail into primary destination categories: mail for the local area, for each nearby state, for groups of distant states, and for some of the largest cities. This primary distribution is followed by one or more secondary distributions. For example, local mail is combined with mail coming in from other cities and is sorted according to street and number. In post offices with electronic mail-sorting machines, clerks simply push a button corresponding to the letter's destination, and the letter drops into the proper slot. These clerks are often called distrbution clerks.

Clerks who staff post office windows provide a variety of services in addition to selling stamps and money orders. They weigh packages to determine postage and check to see if their size, shape, and condition are satisfactory for mailing. Clerks also register and insure mail and answer questions about postage rates, mailing restrictions, and other postal matters. Occasionally, they may help a customer file a claim for a damaged package. In large post offices, a window clerk may provide only one or two of these services; they are often called a registry, stamp, or money order clerk.

Working Conditions

Working conditions of clerks differ according to the specific work assignments and the amount and kind of labor-saving machinery used. In small post offices, clerks must carry heavy mail sacks from one part of the building to another and sort the mail by hand. In large post offices, chutes and conveyors move the mail, and much of the sorting is done by machine. In either case, clerks are on their feet most of the time, reaching for sacks of mail, placing packages and bundles into sacks while sorting, and walking around the workroom.

Distribution clerks may become bored with the routine of sorting mail, unless they enjoy trying to improve their speed and accuracy. They also may have to work at night, because most large post offices process mail around the clock. These clerks work closely together, frequently under the tension and strain of meeting deadlines. A window clerk, on the other hand, has a greater variety of duties, frequent contact with the public, a consistent day shift, and, generally, a less strenuous job. However, window clerks must be tactful when dealing with the public, especially when answering questions or receiving complaints.

New clerks are trained on the job. Most clerks begin with simple tasks to learn regional groupings of states, cities, and zip codes. To help clerks learn these groupings, many post offices offer classroom instruction. A good memory, good coordination, and the ability to read rapidly and accurately are important. These traits are measured by performance on Exam 470.

CITY CARRIER

Duties of the Job

Most city carriers travel planned routes delivering and collecting mail. Carriers start work at the post office early in the morning, where they spend a few hours arranging their mail for delivery, readdressing letters to be forwarded, and taking care of other details.

A carrier typically covers the route on foot, toting a heavy load of mail in a satchel or pushing it in a cart. In outlying suburban areas where houses are far apart, a car or small truck is sometimes needed to deliver mail. Residential carriers cover their routes only once a day, but carriers assigned a business district may make two or more trips. Deliveries are made house to house, except in large buildings, such as apartment houses, which have all the mailboxes on the first floor.

Besides making deliveries, carriers collect COD fees and obtain signed receipts for registered and sometimes for insured mail. If a customer is not home, the carrier leaves a notice that tells where special mail is being held. Carriers also pick up letters to be mailed.

After completing their routes, carriers return to the post office with mail gathered from street collection boxes and homes. They may separate letters and parcels so that stamps can be canceled easily, and they turn in the receipts and money collected during the day.

Many carriers have more specialized duties than those just described. Some deliver only parcel post. Others collect mail from street boxes and office mail chutes.

Working Conditions

Most carriers begin work early in the morning, in some cases as early as 6 A.M. if they have routes in the business district. Carriers spend most of their time outdoors in all kinds of weather, walking from house to house with their heavy mailbags. Even those who drive must walk when making deliveries and must lift heavy sacks of parcel post when loading their vehicles.

The job, however, has advantages beyond the usual ones associated with civil service. Carriers who begin work early in the morning are through by early afternoon. They are also free to work at their own pace as long as they cover their routes within a certain period of time. Moreover, many people would rather be outside—no matter what the weather—than have to be confined inside an office or factory all day.

Applicants must have a driver's license and pass a road test if the job involves driving. They also must pass a physical examination and may be asked to show that they can lift and handle mail sacks weighing up to 70 pounds. Applicants who have had health conditions that might interfere with work must have a special review to determine their eligibility.

City carrier applicants must take Exam 470.

DISTRIBUTION CLERK, MACHINE (LETTER SORTING MACHINE OPERATOR)

Duties of the Job

Distribution clerks work indoors. Often clerks must handle sacks of mail weighing as much as 70 pounds. They sort mail and distribute it by using a complicated scheme that must be memorized. Machine distribution clerks must learn computer codes for the automated routing of mail. Clerks may be on their feet all day. They also have to stretch, reach, and throw mail. The work of the distribution clerk is more routine than that of other postal clerks; however, the starting salary is higher. Distribution clerks begin at postal pay Level 6, while other clerks and carriers begin at Level 5. Increasing automation within the postal service—together with increasing mail volume as both the population and the number of businesses grow—has made the job of the distribution clerk quite secure.

Applicants must be physically able to perform the duties described. Any physical condition that causes the applicant to be a hazard to him or herself or to others will be a disqualification for appointment.

The distant vision for clerk positions must test at least 20/30 (Snellen) in one eye (glasses are permitted). Some distribution clerk positions may be filled by the deaf.

A physical examination, drug test, and psychological interview are required before appointment. Letter sorting machine operator applicants must take Exam 470.

FLAT SORTING MACHINE OPERATOR

Duties of the Job

The work of the flat sorting machine operator is very similar to that of the letter sorting machine operator, except that the Flat Sorting Machine Operator works with large, bulky packages. Greater physical strength and stamina are required in this position.

The postal pay level at entry is Level 6, and with ever-increasing automation and mechanization of post offices, job security is virtually assured.

Flat sorting machine operator applicants must take Exam 470.

MAIL HANDLER

Duties of the Job

The mail handler loads, unloads, and moves bulk mail, and he or she performs duties incidental to the movement and processing of mail. Duties may include separation of mail sacks; facing letter mail; canceling stamps on parcel post; operating canceling machines, addressographs, and mimeographs; operating a fork-lift truck; rewrapping parcels; and so forth.

Mail handler applicants must take Exam 470. If they become eligible, they must also pass a strength and stamina test. A physical exam is required before appointment or, as noted below, sometimes even before the strength and stamina test. Anyone who has had an arm, leg, or foot amputated should not apply.

Qualifications

When eligibles are within reach of appointment, they are required to pass a test of strength and stamina. In this test, they are required to lift, shoulder, and carry two 70-pound sacks 15 feet—one at a time—and load them on a hand truck. They are required to push the truck to an area containing some 40-, 50-, and 60-pound sacks. They are required to load the sacks onto the truck. They next have to unload the truck and return the truck to its original location. Eligibles are notified when and where to report for the test of strength and stamina.

Persons with certain physical conditions must be approved by a physician before taking this test. These physical conditions include hernia or rupture, back trouble, heart trouble, pregnancy, or any other condition that makes it dangerous to the eligible to lift and carry 70-pound weights. Persons with these physical conditions are given special instructions at the time they are notified to report for the strength and stamina test.

An eligible being considered for an appointment who fails to qualify on the strength and stamina test is not tested again in the same group of hires. If the eligible fails the test a second time, his or her eligibility for the position of mail handler is canceled.

MAIL PROCESSOR

Duties of the Job

A mail processor performs the following tasks:

1. Operating mail-processing equipment, including bar code sorters and optical bar code readers;
2. Acting as minor trouble-shooter for the equipment;

3. Collating and bundling processed mail and transferring it from one work area to another;
4. Hand-processing mail that cannot be handled by the machines;
5. Loading mail into bins and onto trucks;
6. Other related tasks.

Mail processor applicants must take Exam 470.

Physical requirements for mail processors are not as stringent as those for mail handlers because the work is not as strenuous. Since the demands of the work are less, mail processors enter at postal pay Level 3, rather than at the Level 4 of mail handlers.

MARK-UP CLERK, AUTOMATED

Duties of the Job

The mark-up clerk, automated, operates an electro-mechanical machine that processes mail classified as "undeliverable as addressed." In doing this, the mark-up clerk operates the keyboard of a computer terminal to enter and extract data to several databases, including change of address, mailer's database, and address-correction file. The mark-up clerk must select the correct program and operating mode for each application, affix labels to mail either manually or with mechanical devices, and prepare forms for address-correction services. Other duties may include distribution of processed mark-ups to appropriate separations for further handling, operation of a photocopy machine, and other job-related tasks in support of primary duties.

Qualifications

An applicant for a mark-up clerk position must have had either six months of clerical or office-machine-operating experience or have completed high school or have had a full academic year (36 weeks) of business school. His or her record of experience and training must show ability to use reference materials and manuals; ability to perform effectively under pressure; ability to operate any office equipment appropriate to the position; ability to work with others; and ability to read, understand, and apply certain regulations and procedures commonly used in processing mail that is undeliverable as addressed.

A mark-up clerk must be able to read, without strain, printed material the size of typewritten characters and must have 20/40 (Snellen) vision in one eye. Glasses are permitted. In addition, the applicant must pass a computer-administered alphanumeric typing test. Candidates with high scores on the competitive exam, Exam 470, and with the requisite experience are called to the alphanumeric typing test individually as openings occur and hiring is likely. The exam is administered on a personal computer with its numeric keyboard disabled so that the candidate must use only the main keyboard. The Postal Service does not distribute sample questions for this typing test, but the instructions at the test site are very clear and ample time is allowed for preparation. The alphanumeric typing test is not a competitive test. The candidate needs only to pass to qualify.

As with general qualifications, a mark-up clerk must be 18 years old, or 16 years old if a high school graduate. However, an applicant who will reach his or her eighteenth birthday within two years from the date of the exam may take the exam and be put on the waiting list of eligibles.

RURAL CARRIER

Duties of the Job

The work of the rural carrier combines the work of the window clerk and the letter carrier, but also has special characteristics of its own. The rural carrier's day begins with sorting and loading the mail for delivery on his or her own route. Then comes a day's drive, which may be over unpaved roads and rough terrain. The rural carrier does most deliveries and pickups of outgoing mail from the postal truck. Occasionally, however, bulky packages must be delivered directly to the homeowner's door. Since rural postal patrons may be far from the nearest post office, the rural carrier also sells stamps, weighs and charges for packages to be mailed, and performs most other services performed by window clerks in post offices. At the end of the day, the rural carrier returns to the post office with outgoing mail and money collected in various transactions. The rural carrier must be able to account for the stamps, postcards, and other supplies with which he or she left in the morning and must "balance the books" each day.

A rural carrier enjoys a great deal of independence. No supervisor looks over his or her shoulder. On the other hand, there is no supervisor to turn to for advice on how to handle a new situation that may come up.

Since the rural carrier's job requires driving, the minimum age for a rural carrier is 18. He or she must have a valid driver's license, good eyesight, and the ability to hear ordinary conversation (glasses and hearing aid are permitted). In addition, the rural carrier must demonstrate physical stamina and the ability to withstand the rigors of the job.

Rural carrier applicants must take Exam 460, which is identical in every way to Exam 470.

CLERK-TYPIST

Duties of the Job

A clerk-typist types records, letters, memos, reports, and other materials from handwritten and other drafts or from a dictating machine; he or she sets up the material typed in accordance with prescribed formats and assembles it for initialing, signing, routing, and dispatch. The miscellaneous office clerical duties of the position are as follows:

1. making up file folders, keeping them in the prescribed order, and filing in them;
2. making and keeping routine office records;
3. composing routine memos and letters relating to the business of the office, such as acknowledgments and transmittals;
4. examining incoming and outgoing mail of the office, routing it to the appropriate persons, and controlling the time allowed for preparation of replies to incoming correspondence;
5. receipting and delivering salary checks and filling out various personnel forms;
6. acting as receptionist and furnishing routine information over the telephone;
7. relieving other office personnel in their absence;
8. operating office machines such as the mimeograph, comptometer, adding machine, calculator, copier, fax, and so on.

Qualifications

The applicant for a position as clerk-typist must have had one year of office experience or four years of high school business courses or 36 weeks of business or secretarial school. The applicant must also show that he or she has enough of the skills, abilities, and knowledge to read and understand instructions; perform basic arithmetic computations; maintain accurate records; prepare reports and correspondence if required; and operate office machines such as calculators, adding machines, copiers, and the like. The applicant for a clerk-typist position must pass a test of clerical abilities and a "plain copy" typing test administered on a personal computer, with a speed of 45 wpm and good accuracy.

CLERK-STENOGRAPHER

Duties of the Job

The clerk-stenographer performs all of the functions of the clerk-typist. In addition, the clerk-stenographer takes dictation, in shorthand or on a shorthand writing machine, of letters, memos, reports, and other materials given by the supervisor of the office and other employees. He or she then transcribes it on the typewriter, or word processor, setting up the material transcribed in accordance with prescribed format and assembling it for required initialing, signing, routing, and dispatch. In consideration of the extra training and skill required in the taking of dictation, the clerk-stenographer is rated at salary Level 5, rather than at the salary Level 4 of the clerk-typist.

Qualifications

The applicant for the position of clerk-stenographer must meet all the requirements of the applicant for clerk-typist in terms of education or experience and in terms of skills, abilities, and knowledge. In addition to passing the test of clerical ability and the computer-administered plain-copy typing test, the clerk-stenographer applicant must also pass a stenography test.

DATA CONVERSION OPERATOR

Duties of the Job

The newest job title in the Postal Service, data conversion operators use a computer terminal to take mail that previously could not be read by machine and prepare it for automated sorting equipment. They do this by reading typed or handwritten addresses from a letter image on the terminal screen, which has been transmitted to them from a remote encoding center. Operators then select and type essential information so that an address bar code can automatically be applied to the letter. Depending on the quality of the address information shown on the image, the data conversion operator will be prompted to key the five-number ZIP code or an abbreviated version of the street and city address. Abbreviated addresses must conform to strict encoding rules so that the abbreviation can then be expanded to a full address by the computer, enabling it to find the correct zip + 4 code. Unlike some other types of data entry, this job is not just "key what you see."

Working Conditions

Remote encoding centers offer a possibility for flexible scheduling. The basic work hours are between 3:00 P.M. and 1:00 A.M. Individual work schedules range between four and eight hours. RECs operate seven days a week. Persons filling data conversion operator positions as temporary or transitional employees will earn 1 hour of leave for every 20 hours worked but no other benefits. Career employees receive the Postal Service's full benefits package.

Qualifications

All applicants are required to pass a test of their clerical abilities with a score of 70 or better. Names are placed on a hiring list in rank order. As an applicant reaches consideration for employment, he or she will be called for a computer-based exam which is a job-simulated data entry performance test. Typing or data-entry experience is a prerequisite for this position.

Applicants must have vision of 20/40 (Snellen) in one eye and the ability to read without strain printed material the size of typewritten characters. Corrective lenses are permitted. The ability to distinguish basic colors and shades is desirable. Applicants under consideration for employment are subject to urinalysis drug screening.

CLEANER, CUSTODIAN, CUSTODIAL LABORER

Duties of the Job

Workers who serve as cleaners, custodians, or custodial laborers are charged with the maintenance of postal buildings. Their duties include routine cleaning, periodic heavy cleaning, and routine maintenance, such as replacing light bulbs. They are also responsible for noticing when specialized maintenance or repair work is called for and for following through to make sure that whatever must be done is done at the proper time.

While the work of custodial laborers, cleaners, and custodians is not generally noticed by the public, their work is vital to the operation of post offices and to the health and safety of postal workers and patrons.

Qualifications

The positions of cleaner, custodian, and custodial laborer are open *only* to veterans of the United States Armed Services. Applications from nonveterans will be rejected. While these positions are at the low end of the postal pay scale, they do afford the veteran an opportunity to earn a steady wage and to enjoy the same fringe benefits and security of all other postal employees. The person who starts his or her career with the Postal Service as a cleaner, custodian, or custodial laborer can advance to positions of greater responsibility within the custodial service or can prepare for examinations for other positions with the Postal Service. These include both more specialized jobs within building maintenance or completely different jobs such as mail handler, letter clerk, and others.

People who already work for the Postal Service in any capacity need not wait for an exam that is open to the public to be announced. After being employed at their present position for a year, they may ask to take an exam at any time. Although this request may or may not be granted, this one special advantage makes the Veterans-only feature of this position valuable. A veteran who wants a postal career can break in at the bottom and rise rapidly.

There are no educational or experience requirements for these positions and no age restrictions. Applicants must, of course, have the physical health and stamina required for the job. They must also qualify on a one-and-a-half-hour examination that tests their ability to follow directions.

GARAGEMAN-DRIVER, TRACTOR-TRAILER OPERATOR, MOTOR VEHICLE OPERATOR

Duties of the Job

What all these jobs have in common is driving various Postal Service vehicles on the highway and within the lots and properties of the Postal Service.

"Garagemen" (open to both men and women) are responsible for seeing that each vehicle is in the proper place at the proper time and that each vehicle is roadworthy before it is released. They must keep accurate records of all activity as it affects each vehicle and must follow through on whatever movement or maintenance is required.

Tractor-trailer operators drive huge mail rigs from city to city along superhighways, delivering large quantities of mail as quickly as possible within the bounds of safety. The work of a Postal Service tractor-trailer operator is really no different from the work of a tractor-trailer operator for private industry.

Motor vehicle operators drive various other Postal Service vehicles as needed, both within and between towns and cities. They pick up and deliver bulk quantities of mail at postal installations, mailing concerns, railroad mail facilities, and airports.

The exam for all these positions is designed to test powers of observation, ability to express oneself, accuracy in record keeping, familiarity with road signs, and ability to follow instructions. The exam is in two parts of 40 questions each. You will have 60 minutes to answer each part. The test requires concentration and careful attention to details. The sample questions that the Postal Service sends to applicants when notifying them of the test date provide a good idea of what to expect from the exam itself.

Qualifications

Since all these positions require a Commercial Driver's License (CDL), people appointed to them must be experienced drivers over the age of 21. In addition, applicants must have good eyesight and hearing and be in excellent health and physical condition. A physical exam, drug testing, and strength and stamina tests are part of the hiring process. Candidates must also take training on the specific type of vehicle they are required to drive.

To qualify for motor vehicle operator, persons must have a Class A or Class B commercial license and at least two years of driving experience, one of which must have been driving a five-ton truck. Applicants for tractor-trailer operator must have a Class A commercial license and at least one year of experience driving a tractor-trailer. All applicants for these positions must have safe driving records.

POSTAL POLICE OFFICER

Duties of the Job

A postal police officer is essentially a security guard at post offices and at other postal installations and facilities. The postal police officer may work inside postal buildings or out of doors at loading docks and in parking lots. A postal police officer may be armed.

Qualifications

An applicant for the position of postal police officer must be at least 20 years of age, but, unless a veteran, cannot be appointed until reaching the age of 21. The postal police officer must be physically able to perform the duties of the job, must have weight in proportion to height, must have good color vision and good distant vision (no weaker than 20/40 in one eye and 20/50 in the other eye correctable to 20/20), and must have keen hearing. Emotional and mental stability is essential for the armed officer, and drug testing and a psychological interview are part of the qualification process. The candidate must demonstrate the ability to deal with the public in a courteous and tactful manner; to work in stress situations; to collect, assemble, and act on pertinent facts; to prepare clear and accurate records; to deal effectively with individuals and groups; and to express him or herself in both oral and written communications. A background investigation will be made on all otherwise qualified candidates.

In order to be considered, each applicant must pass a written qualifying exam with a score of 70 or better out of a possible 100. Accepted candidates must complete and pass a rigorous eight week training program at the Federal Law Enforcement Training Center at Glynco, Georgia, before assignment to duty.

MAINTENANCE POSITIONS (17 TITLES)

Buildings And Equipment

Duties of the Job

Activities of the Postal Service take place in several facilities—not only post offices but also warehouses, processing centers, repair shops, garages, and office buildings. These buildings require the same maintenance services as nonpostal buildings.

Housed within these postal facilities is a variety of machinery and equipment, all requiring maintenance and service.

Rather than hiring maintenance workers from the private sector, the postal service retains a full staff of maintenance workers to care for its facilities and equipment.

Applicants for positions in the following titles must all qualify on the same exam, Exam M/N 931. The maintenance titles are:

- Area Maintenance Specialist
- Area Maintenance Technician
- Building Equipment Mechanic
- Building Maintenance Custodian
- Carpenter
- Machinist
- Maintenance Electrician
- Maintenance Mechanic 4
- Maintenance Mechanic 5
- Mason
- Painter
- Plumber
- Welder

Electronic Equipment

Duties of the Job

More and more postal operations are being handled automatically by highly sophisticated electronic equipment. The variety of sorting, stamping, coding, and routing machines is expanding rapidly. As more post offices join the switch to automation, the sheer number of these machines is also growing dramatically. Needless to say, all this electronic equipment requires regular maintenance and repair as needed.

The Postal Service retains its own teams of electronic technicians to care for its electronic equipment. These electronic technicians are hired at two levels, Electronic Technician 9 and Electronic Technician 10. The duties and responsibilities are similar, but there are some differences. The exam is Test M/N 932.

Maintenance Mechanic, Overhaul Specialist

These last two titles represent specialized, higher-level positions within the building and equipment maintenance areas. In this group are the titles Maintenance Mechanic 7 and Overhaul Specialist 8. Exam M/N 933 covers the KSAs (Knowledge, Skills, and Abilities) necessary for performance of these jobs. As with other maintenance positions, not all KSAs are needed for performance of duties in both job titles; only questions that measure relevant KSAs for the job enter into score calculations.

Qualifications

The examinations in the M/N series test a number of KSAs (Knowledge, Skills, and Abilities) that are required in the various maintenance positions. There is much overlap, but the three exams do not all test precisely the same KSAs. Further, not all positions within a group require all of the KSAs tested by any one exam. Only questions measuring the relevant KSAs are scored for any particular position.

The three exams in the M/N series are the M/N 931, the M/N 932, and the M/N 933. These exams test the following knowledge, skills, and abilities:

- *Knowledge of basic mechanics* refers to the theory of operation, terminology, usage, and characteristics of basic mechanical principles as they apply to such things as gears, pulleys, cams, pawls, power transmissions, linkages, fasteners, chains, sprockets, and belts; and includes hoisting, rigging, roping, pneumatics, and hydraulic devices.
- *Knowledge of basic electricity* refers to the theory, terminology, usage, and characteristics of basic electrical principles such as Ohm's Law, Kirchhoff's Law, and magnetism, as they apply to such things as AC/DC circuitry and hardware, relays, switches, and circuit breakers.
- *Knowledge of basic electronics* refers to the theory, terminology, usage, and characteristics of basic electronic principles concerning such things as solid-state devices, vacuum tubes, coils, capacitors, resistors, and basic logic circuitry.
- *Knowledge of digital electronics* refers to the terminology, characteristics, symbology, and operation of digital components, as used in such things as logic gates, registers, adders, counters, memories, encoders, and decoders.
- *Knowledge of safety procedures and equipment* refers to the knowledge of industrial hazards (e.g., mechanical, chemical, electrical, and electronic hazards) and knowledge of the procedures and techniques established to avoid injuries to self and others, such as lock-out devices, protective clothing, and waste disposal techniques.
- *Knowledge of basic computer concepts* refers to the terminology, usage, and characteristics of digital memory storage/processing devices, such as internal memory, input-output peripherals, and familiarity with programming concepts.
- *Knowledge of lubrication materials and procedures* refers to the terminology, characteristics, storage, preparation, disposal, and usage techniques involved with lubrication materials such as oils, greases, and other types of lubricants.
- *Knowledge of refrigeration* refers to the theory terminology, usage, and characteristics of refrigeration principles as they apply to such things as the refrigeration cycle, compressors, condensers, receivers, evaporators, metering devices, and refrigerant oils.
- *Knowledge of heating, ventilation, and air-conditioning (HVAC) equipment operation* refers to the knowledge of equipment operation such as safety considerations, start-up, shut-down, and mechanical/electrical operating characteristics of HVAC equipment (e.g., chillers, direct-expansion units, window units, heating equipment). This does not include the knowledge of refrigeration.
- *Ability to perform basic mathematical computations* refers to the ability to perform basic calculations such as addition, subtraction, multiplication, and division with whole numbers, fractions, and decimals.
- *Ability to perform more complex mathematics* refers to the ability to perform calculations, such as basic algebra, geometry, scientific notation, and number conversions, as applied to mechanical, electrical, and electronic applications.
- *Ability to apply theoretical knowledge to practical applications* refers to mechanical, electrical, and electronic maintenance applications, such as inspection, trouble-shooting equipment repair and modification, preventive maintenance, and installation of electrical equipment.

- *Ability to detect patterns* refers to the ability to observe and analyze qualitative factors, such as number progressions, spatial relationships, and auditory and visual patterns. This includes combining information and determining how a given set of numbers, objects, or sounds are related to each other.
- *Ability to use written reference materials* refers to the ability to locate, read, and comprehend text material, such as handbooks, manuals, bulletins, directives, checklists, and route sheets.
- *Ability to follow instructions* refers to the ability to comprehend and execute written and oral instructions, such as work orders, checklists, route sheets, and verbal directions and instructions.
- *Ability to use hand tools* refers to knowledge of, and proficiency with, various hand tools. This ability involves the safe and efficient use and maintenance of such tools as screwdrivers, wrenches, hammers, pliers, chisels, punches, taps, dies, rules, gauges, and alignment tools.
- *Ability to use portable power tools* refers to the knowledge of, and proficiency with, various power tools. This ability involves the safe and efficient use and maintenance of power tools, such as drills, saws, sanders, and grinders.
- *Ability to use technical drawings* refers to the ability to read and comprehend technical materials, such as diagrams, schematics, flow charts, and blueprints.
- *Ability to use test equipment* refers to the knowledge of, and proficiency with, various types of mechanical, electrical, and electronic test equipment, such as VOMS, oscilloscopes, circuit tracers, amprobes, and tachometers.
- *Ability to solder* refers to the knowledge of the appropriate soldering techniques, and the ability to apply them safely and effectively.

SUPERVISORY POSITIONS

Supervisory positions are never filled by open competitive examinations. In order to become a supervisor, you must first prove yourself as a worker in the department or function that you would like to supervise. The person who wishes to grow into a supervisory position must first prove his or her reliability, efficiency, and initiative on the job over a period of time. Then, that person must take a test of supervisory aptitude to demonstrate promise of success in a supervisory role. The test of supervisory aptitude includes questions on understanding human behavior, judgment in social situations, and judgment in business situations.

Postal Inspector

Near the top of the postal pay schedule is the position of postal inspector. Postal inspectors are law enforcement officers within the Postal Service. They perform varied, highly responsible duties that lead to the detection, prosecution, and conviction of people committing mail fraud and other crimes related to the Postal Service. Their work is exciting, difficult, dangerous, and well paid. No one may become a postal inspector without previous Postal Service experience. All postal inspectors have risen from the ranks of postal employees. In addition, postal inspectors have passed a four-hour examination consisting of 118 questions, mostly reading-comprehension and vocabulary, and have undergone and passed a rigorous 11-week training program.

Finding Out About Postal Service Job Openings

For almost 90 percent of the job openings, U.S. Postal Service hiring is very localized. This means you must apply directly at the post-office branch or branches where you would consider working. Look on that branch's bulletin board for announcements about how to apply. There you'll find information on Craft or Bargaining Unit job openings (jobs requiring a test exam) for that local office, positions such as clerk, carrier, mail handler, mail processor, custodian, etc.

These job vacancies are also posted in local newspapers and are available from District Offices. You can find the District Office closest to you by calling the U.S.P.S. Local Employment Hot Line at 800-276-5627.

Several local post offices have pages on the United States Postal Service Web site, which can be found at www.usps.gov. Some of these local offices list their job openings on this national site. Some also have a job hot line which can be used to learn about vacancies in that location. Here are the telephone numbers for these job hot lines:

Salt Lake City, Utah	801-974-2209
Washington, D.C.	202-636-1537
Northern Virginia	703-698-6561
Imperial Valley/San Diego, California	619-674-0577
Riverside/San Bernardino, California	909-335-4339
Long Island, New York	516-582-7530

If you go to the U.S.P.S. Web site, you'll see a link to "National Job Listings." These are for management, supervisory, administrative, professional, and technical positions only, which do not require a test; applicants are evaluated in other ways. There are also Telephone Job Lines for these national listings.

People not currently employed by the Postal Service should call the number for the general public: 800-JOB-USPS. Current postal employees seeking information about other jobs within the Postal Service should call 800-NATL-VAC.

Applying for Postal Service Jobs

After finding a job you're interested in, go to the local post office where you hope to work and check the bulletin board. There, you'll find information on how to obtain an application and apply for the written test. The test, called the Battery 470 Entrance Exam, is required for most post office jobs and is offered approximately every three years.

THE FACTS ABOUT POSTAL SERVICE EXAMINATIONS

If you've been out of school for any length of time (and even if you're still in school), you may feel some hesitancy about taking a written test. Try not to be nervous. The most common exams used by the U.S.P.S. are not like school tests, which focus on a single subject—such as math—and even a single category within that subject—such as algebra. The U.S.P.S. measures only those practical abilities you need to do the job. Think of it more as a test of "postal street smarts."

The Principal Exams Used by the U.S.P.S.

THE BATTERY 470/460 ENTRANCE EXAM

The Battery 470/460 Exam is required for eight common post office jobs: city carriers, rural carriers, clerks, flat sorting machine clerks, mail handlers, mark-up clerks, mail processors, and machine distribution clerks. When people say they want or are going to take "*the*" Postal Exam, 470 is usually what they're referring to.

The 470/460 Exam is offered approximately every three years. Hiring is done through the local district offices; there are about 85 district offices throughout the country. Exact dates for exams vary by the local area and by the area's job vacancies. The 460 Exam is identical to 470 except for its number; it is used to test applicants for rural carrier positions. From here on, every mention of the 470 Exam includes the 460 as well.

If you already looked at the long sample 470 Exam in Part IV, your immediate reaction might have been "That's not like any test I've ever taken." True, the 470 is not your standard multiple-choice test, so the questions and answers may not seem to make sense at first glance. But once you understand what the exam is measuring and how the questions are formatted, the whole test will become much clearer.

What the 470 Exam Measures

The 470 Exam measures your general vocabulary and reading level. In addition, it checks special aptitudes needed by specific postal positions. These aptitudes include the ability to check and compare addresses, to memorize addresses, to recognize patterns, and to follow oral directions. The ability to check and memorize addresses is important for reading and sorting mail. No doubt you can do this already, as the skill is very basic. However, the exam tests how *quickly* you can do it, while still being accurate. The ability to recognize patterns is important for understanding the sorting, routing, and marking procedures used by the post office. The ability to follow oral directions is important for responding at once to directions, essential in an environment where large sacks of letters and packages are being constantly moved. It also gives an indication of your trainability. This special aptitude does not mean the *willingness* to follow oral directions. Many times we're willing, but there's a time lapse between hearing the instruction, understanding it, and translating that into action. In a way, this part of the test measures that mental "time lapse."

How the 470 Exam Is Set Up

Just the sight of the 470 can be intimidating. That's because, instead of the paragraphs or math problems you're used to seeing on tests, the 470 uses pairs of addresses, or addresses in grids, or long strings of numbers. Those are simply the things you'll be seeing every day during actual work at the post office.

Address Checking—In this part of the exam, there won't be questions, just pairs of addresses set in columns:

1.	1781 W 20th St	1781 W 20th St
2.	4608 N Maple Ave	4806 N Maple Ave
3.	1202 Gracie Blvd	1202 Gracie Blvd
4.	Centerville NJ 07014	Centervale NJ 07014
5.	2207 Gresham St	2207 Gresham Ave

You respond to each pair by indicating on the answer sheet whether there's a difference between the two or they're the same.

There are 95 questions in this part, 95 pairs of addresses, and you have only six minutes to check them for differences. Essentially, this is a test of speed. But accuracy is also crucial. Realistically, then, you're not expected to finish. Work as fast as you can without sacrificing accuracy.

Address Memorization—First you'll be given a table like the one below. In each of five boxes there will be five addresses, for a total of 25 addresses. Some of the addresses are number ranges (4700-5599 Turner), some are names without numbers (Porter). You'll receive five minutes to memorize the location of the 25 addresses—which box is each in?

A	B	C	D	E
4700-5599 Turner	6800-6999 Turner	5600-6499 Turner	6500-6799 Turner	4400-4699 Turner
Lismore	Kelford	Joel	Tatum	Ruskin
5600–6499 West	6500–6799 West	6800–6999 West	4400–4699 West	4700–5599 West
Hesper	Musella	Sardis	Porter	Nathan
4400–4699 Blake	5600–6499 Blake	6500–6799 Blake	4700–5599 Blake	6800–6999 Blake

The questions will simply be single addresses:

1. Musella
2. 4700-5599 Blake
3. 4700-5599 Turner
4. Tatum
5. 4400-4699 Blake
6. Hesper
7. Kelford

Your answer sheet will show five choices, A through E, representing the five boxes above. For each question, you select the box that the address is in, without looking at the boxes. The first answer is B, because Musella is in Box B. The second answer is D, because 4700-5599 Blake is in Box D. And so on.

You'll be allowed three practice sessions that are not scored. This will help familiarize you with the test setup, as well as further your memorization of the locations. In the actual, scored part of the test, you'll have five minutes and 88 questions. Again, this is a test of speed as well as accuracy and you're not expected to finish all 88 questions.

Number Series—Each question will be a string of numbers. You are asked to find the pattern in the series and to predict the next two numbers. The answers will be five sets of two numbers each. You pick the one that follows the pattern.

1. 1 2 3 4 5 6 7 .... (A) 1 2   (B) 5 6   (C) 8 9   (D) 4 5   (E) 7 8
2. 15 14 13 12 11 10 9 .... (A) 2 1   (B) 17 16   (C) 8 9   (D) 8 7   (E) 9
3. 20 20 21 21 22 22 23 ...... (A) 23 23   (B) 23 24   (C) 19 19   (D) 22 23   (E) 21 23
4. 17 3 17 4 17 5 17 .... (A) 6 17   (B) 6 7   (C) 17 6   (D) 5 6   (E) 17 7
5. 1 2 4 5 7 8 10 .... (A) 11 12   (B) 12 14   (C) 10 13   (D) 12 13   (E) 11 13

In the first question, each number in the series is increased by 1. The series would continue 8 9, making the correct answer C. In the second question, each number in the series is decreased by one. The series would continue 8 7, making the answer D. The third question begins to get a bit more complicated as it involves two steps—first each number is repeated, then it's increased by 1. The series would continue by repeating 23, then adding 1 to it to make 24. So the correct answer is 23 24, or letter B.

You'll have 20 minutes to complete 24 questions.

Following Oral Directions—Since the test-taking environment can't duplicate the hustle and bustle of a mail facility—"Watch that bag!"—your ability to follow oral directions is measured by having you listen to instructions from the proctor. As each instruction is read, you are to do what is asked and to mark your answer sheet in the appropriate way. The instructions will be said only once.

The work booklet will show questions like the following:

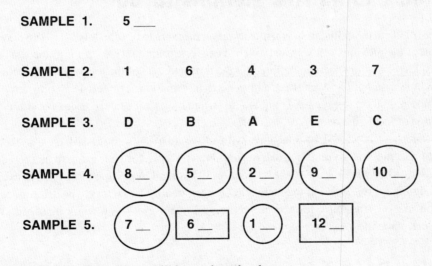

SAMPLE 1.   5 ___

SAMPLE 2.   1   6   4   3   7

SAMPLE 3.   D   B   A   E   C

SAMPLE 4.   8 __   5 __   2 __   9 __   10 __

SAMPLE 5.   7 __   6 __   1 __   12 __

Meanwhile, instructions like these will be read out loud to you:

"Line 1 has a number and a blank space beside it. In the blank space write A, as in ace. Then, on the answer sheet, find number 5 and darken the letter you just wrote on the line.

"Look at line 2. Draw a line under the third number. Now look at the answer sheet, find the number under which you just drew a line, and darken B, as in boy.

"Look at the letters in line 3. Draw a line under the third letter in the line. Now on your answer sheet, find number 9 and darken the letter under which you drew a line."

The test examiner will pause briefly after each instruction to give you time to mark your booklet and answer sheet. You'll listen to these oral instructions for about 25 minutes (depending on how fast the proctor reads). In that time you'll have to perform 20 to 25 actions.

CAUTION: For the first three questions given above, you would have marked your answer sheet 4B, 5A, and 9A. So instead of filling in the answer sheet from number 1 to number 2 to number 3 in consecutive order, you'll be skipping around according to the instructions. You may not even use all of the spaces, depending on the particular test given that day. Be prepared for this unusual format and don't let it throw you.

So that's the 470 Exam—about 230 questions to be done in about an hour. Of course, the actual test will take longer, as the proctor spends time reading directions, allowing breaks between sections, etc. A full-length sample of the 470 Exam is provided in Chapter 7, "Sample Civil Service Job Announcements at the State and Local Level," together with the answers and explanations.

OTHER POSTAL EXAMS

Since Exam 470 only tests aptitudes required for specific positions, positions requiring other skills and abilities use other tests. For example, applicants for clerical jobs take one of the following: Test 710, which measures clerical and verbal abilities; Test 712, which measures typing ability; Test 711, which measures the ability to take and transcribe dictation; and Test 714, which measures data entry ability. Similarly, maintenance technicians, electricians, mechanics, and others take Tests M/N 931, 932, or 933.

How the Exams Are Administered

After you've filled out an application, you must wait for an exam to be scheduled—which may be as long as three years if the previous test was just given. Then, one to three weeks prior to the test date, you'll receive a test kit with your schedule, telling you the time and date of the exam and its location. The kit will also include a sample answer sheet and general information. The test is administered by postal management sectional centers, general mail facilities, and bulk mail centers, each one administering the test for a range of local zip codes.

The answer sheet is scored by machine, with all exam results processed by the National Test Administration Center in Virginia. It usually takes about 6 weeks for your exam to be scored, although it can take as long as 10 weeks. You'll receive your results by mail. A passing score of 70 percent or above makes you eligible for two years. If there are other tests or qualifying factors to be determined—such as drug tests, physical performance tests, or psychological interviews—you won't be asked to complete them until your name moves closer to the top.

How the Postal Service Uses Exam Results

In order to be placed on a register of eligible candidates, you only need to pass the exam. Unless an announcement says otherwise, a passing grade for all exams is 70. If you pass the exam, you'll be notified of your score and your rank on the list. But—and this is a very big but—as with all civil service exams, a passing score does *not* guarantee you a job. In fact, neither does a very high score. It all depends on how many other people took the exam at the same time, how you stand in relation to them, and what specific jobs become open over the next couple of years while that particular list of eligibles is valid. For example, you may have aced the exam and received a 98 percent. However, if dozens of other people also aced it and scored, say, 99 percent, your actual rank could be 67, meaning 67 other people would have to be considered for jobs before you.

If you applied for several different positions, your one test score will be put on as many registers as jobs you applied for. There is a separate register for each job classification. So, if you applied for the positions of city carrier, flat sorting machine clerk, and mail handler, your one score of 98 might be ranked 14 on the carrier list, 67 on the flat sorting machine clerk list, and 3 on the list for mail handler. It all depends on who else applied for those jobs and took the test the same time as you.

If you don't pass the exam, you won't get a score; you'll simply be notified that you failed. Honorably dischared Veterans receive "Preference Points" that are added to their scores before the candidates are ranked. They receive 5 extra points, 10 if they were wounded in combat or are disabled. If their disability is severe enough and is connected to their military service, they are automatically put at the top of the list.

NOTE: Veterans must pass the exam first to receive their points. Points can not be added to a failing score to push it up past the passing mark.

Applicants who passed the test but who weren't hired in the two years can take the test over. Applicants who failed the test can also take it over. In both cases, you must wait till another test is called and then re-register.

Once you're actually on the list, what happens? Each time a vacancy appears, the person in charge of filling the position must call someone from the current top three candidates. The first person called may not always be hired. Sometimes an applicant doesn't pass the pre-screening. Sometimes he or she has found other employment in the meantime and no longer wishes to work at the post office or postpones his or her eligibility (maybe that new job won't work out). Candidates who aren't called stay on the list to wait for the next vacancy.

And so it goes down through the list, opening after opening. You may be called very soon after getting your test results, or you may have to wait months or even the whole two-year eligibility period, or you may not be called at all. It all depends on the local job situation.

What is the average score? The "average" score doesn't have much meaning. Here are some better ways to look at exam results that show how tough both the test and the competition are:

About 50 percent of the applicants usually fail, although the precise percentage varies from test to test. That gives you an idea of how hard the exam is. Yet, even with this high failure rate, applicants who are actually hired usually score 90 percent or more. This gives you an idea of how many people take the test, so many that the U.S.P.S. can consistently hire only the top 10 percent of applicants.

Don't let that shake your enthusiasm for applying for a job or your confidence in your test-taking ability. Because, with your guide in hand, you'll find out . . .

How to Give Yourself the Edge Taking the U.S.P.S. Exam

It's true, the post office exam looks far different from other standardized tests you may have taken. But different does not mean impossible. Familiarity with any test helps improve your score, as does taking the test several times. Your reading this guide, taking the full-length sample practice Exam 470 in the last part, and working through other test-preparation books can help you tremendously.

Here are some other tips to keep in mind to help give yourself a competitive edge:

- **Prepare yourself, but don't paralyze yourself.** Don't fall into either of the twin traps: so much confidence you feel you don't need to prepare, or so little confidence you feel you can't possibly prepare. Set yourself a study plan and follow it.
- **Apply for more than one position.** You'll be ranked highest on the list with fewest eligibles. You can always ask for a transfer once you're hired.

- **Learn the rules** for when you should guess on the test or not, as given in the last part. Each section has a different penalty for guessing. Know which is which to take advantage of it.
- **Listen carefully and read carefully.** The post office may change its exam at any time, and sample questions used here may not be the actual questions found on your particular test. Listen carefully to everything the proctor says, and read carefully when you take the test.
- **Remember** that on the oral instructions section you will be skipping around on the answer sheet. This is to be expected.

P A R T

THREE

Getting State and Municipal Civil Service Jobs

CONTENTS

FINDING JOBS WITH YOUR STATE OR MUNICIPAL GOVERNMENT

Nearly all states and municipalities use trained business, technical, and professional employees in a variety of fields. Young men and women are encouraged to step directly from the classroom into state and municipal service at the bottom rung of any one of the many career ladders. However, these entry-level jobs aren't just for the very young. Except for those few categories with physical qualifications that include age limits (for example, police officers and firefighters), older employees have an equal shot at filling these openings. This allows them to find more security and better benefits for their families than their current position provides—or to change fields entirely. Compare this to the private sector, where midlife career changes are seldom met with success.

Many state constitutions require that appointments and promotions in the state civil service and all its civil divisions be made according to merit and fitness, which is determined, whenever possible, through competitive exams. Entry-level positions are all filled competitively by appointment from appropriate civil service eligible lists. When a vacancy above the entrance level is to be filled, the appointment must be made, if possible, by promotion from within. This increases opportunities for entry-level employees to advance to higher-level positions, while emphasizing the importance of recruiting well-trained, intelligent people for these entrance positions.

You'll probably find that civil service on the state, county, and local levels seems much less intimidating than attempting to land a Federal-level job. The application process is often simpler, and the paperwork demands may be easier depending on the hiring agency and the particular position. Yet all of the opportunities are still there: State and local governments provide a large and expanding source of jobs in a wide variety of occupational fields. More than 11.8 million people work for state and local agencies; nearly three-fourths of this number work in local government, such as counties, municipalities, towns, and school districts.

The Types of Jobs Available at the State and Local Level

Educational services account for the majority of jobs in state and local government. About 5.9 million employees work in public schools, colleges, or other educational services—teachers, college professors, administrators, librarians, guidance counselors, nurses, dietitians, clerks, and maintenance workers. Three-fourths of these work in elementary and secondary schools, which are administered largely by local governments. State employment in education is concentrated chiefly at the college, university, and technical school levels.

The next two largest fields of state and local government employment are health services and highway work. Almost 1.4 million people, including physicians, nurses, medical laboratory technicians, and hospital attendants, are employed in health services. More than 600,000 people, including civil engineers, surveyors, operators of construction machinery and equipment, truck drivers, concrete finishers, carpenters, and construction laborers, work in highway activities such as construction and maintenance.

General government control and financial activities account for about 840,000 workers. These include chief executives and their staffs, legislative representatives, and persons employed in the administration of justice, tax enforcement and other financial work, and general administration. These functions require the services of individuals such as lawyers, judges, and other court officials, city managers, property assessors, budget analysts, stenographers, and clerks.

Police and fire protection is another large field of employment. More than 600,000 persons are engaged in police work, including administrative, clerical, and custodial personnel, as well as uniformed and plainclothes police. Local governments employ all of the 300,000 firefighters, many of whom work only part time.

Other state and local government employees work in a wide variety of activities: local utilities (such as water or electricity), transportation, natural resources, public welfare, parks and recreation, sanitation, correction, local libraries, sewage disposal, and housing and urban renewal. These activities require workers in diverse occupations such as economist, electrical engineer, electrician, pipe fitter, clerk, forester, and bus driver.

Clerical, administrative, maintenance, and custodial work make up a large portion of employment in most government agencies. Among the workers involved in these activities are clerk-typists, stenographers, secretaries, office managers, fiscal and budget administrators, bookkeepers, accountants, carpenters, painters, plumbers, guards, and janitors.

Duties of Some Common State and Local Civil Service Job Categories

The duties and responsibilities of these jobs are essentially the same as in the private sector, only performed for public agencies, services, buildings, etc. Here are some further descriptions of some of the main job categories:

- **Clerical Positions.** Clerical support staff are employed throughout virtually every state and municipal department and are at the center of communications throughout these organizations. They perform a wide variety of clerical and administrative duties necessary for running and maintaining the responsibilities of state and local government.
- **Computer-Related Positions.** Computers are important in almost every branch of the civil service; for many functions of state and municipal government, they are now essential. The duties of computer personnel vary with the size of the installation, the type of equipment used, and the policies of the employer. As computer usage grows in government organizations, so will the need for computer professions and related occupations.
- **Financial, Accounting, Actuarial, and Purchasing Positions.** Officials in government must have up-to-date financial information to make important decisions. Accountants and auditors prepare, analyze, and verify financial reports to furnish this information. In addition, government accountants and auditors maintain and examine the records of government agencies and audit private businesses and individuals whose dealings are subject to government regulations.
- **Law Enforcement Positions.** Highly trained police officers are found in both large and small cities. Of the more than 17,000 cities in the U.S., 55 have populations exceeding a quarter of a million, and these employ about one-third of all police personnel. Of the law enforcement units at state level, two of the best known are the state police and the highway patrol. State police engage in a full range of law enforcement activities, including criminal investigation. Highway patrol units are concerned almost entirely with traffic control and enforcement and have limited general police authority.
- **Firefighting Positions.** Every year, fires take thousands of lives and destroy property worth billions of dollars. Firefighters help protect the public against this danger. Their direct firefighting duties, carried out throughout teamwork, include rescuing victims, administering emergency medical aid, ventilating smoke-filled areas, operating equipment, and salvaging the contents of buildings. Some firefighters operate fire engines, ambulances, emergency rescue vehicles, and fireboats. In addition, most fire departments are responsible for fire prevention and inspect both public and private buildings for this purpose.

- **Investigative Positions.** The range of activities performed by modern state and municipal authorities means that they have a great need for information—hence the need for investigators. Investigators have a wide variety of functions: to examine claims for benefits or compensation to ensure that they are valid and conform with regulations, to gather evidence of fraud and other wrongdoing to be used in various legal actions, and to discover violations of rules and regulations.
- **Social Welfare Positions.** Those involved in the social welfare field are community trouble-shooters. Through direct counseling, referral to other services, or policymaking and advocacy, they help individuals, families, and groups cope with their problems. Those in the area of planning and policy help people understand how social systems operate and propose ways of bringing about needed change in institutions, such as health services, housing, or education. Among the major helping professions, social work is distinguished by a tradition of concern for the poor and the disadvantaged.
- **Legal Positions.** The legal activities of many of the state departments require the services of attorneys of various grades. A great deal of important state legal work is handled by lawyers in the office of the Attorney-General. There are many legal positions, some under specialized titles, which are filled from open-competitive civil service lists. The state offers opportunity for legally trained employees to rise to highly responsible, well-paid positions.
- **Health-Related Positions.** With the continual growth of social services, state and local governments continue to need physicians, medical researchers, nurses, and similar workers in more and more fields. The growth of psychiatric concepts, the development of occupational therapy, the public demand that veterans who need medical care should have it, and the increasing demands of an aging population on society in general and the health-care industry in particular all require a force of health-care practitioners working for the government at the state and local levels as well as at the Federal level.
- **Engineering Positions.** Engineers design machines, processes, systems, and structures. They apply scientific and mathematical theories and principles to solve practical technical problems. In state and local government, most work in 1 of the more than 25 specialties recognized by professional societies. Electrical, mechanical, civil, industrial, chemical, and aerospace engineering are the largest; although many engineers work in design and development, others work in testing, production, operations, and maintenance.
- **Mechanical Positions.** Mechanics are responsible for operating, rebuilding, repairing, or maintaining motor vehicles, heavy machinery, machine shop equipment, electrical equipment, and all types of communications equipment. Most mechanics acquire their skills on the job by following the instructions of experienced workers, reading repair manuals, and solving problems on their own. Increasingly, formal mechanical training acquired in high school, vocational or technical school, community or junior college, or in the Armed Forces is an asset to persons entering mechanic and repairer careers.
- **Custodial and Service Positions.** Custodial and service occupations are available in almost every branch of state and local government. Their duties may include cleaning public buildings and grounds, exterminating pests, operating heavy-duty washing machines in state laundry facilities, removing waste, or removing snow. Many of these positions require no formal education, qualification, or experience; however, certain positions may require training and certification.

Salaries for State, County, and City Jobs

People with Federal jobs receive the same base salary and benefits, no matter where they work in the U.S. A GS-11 in Seattle receives the same as a GS-11 in Miami, except for differences in pay locality. Is there any of this uniformity across the states?

No. Each state operates independently. As an indication of the possible variety from state to state, even for the same position, look at the following chart comparing starting salaries for nine job titles across six states. The information was taken from actual job announcements for state, county, and city jobs. City and county are indicated where applicable.

STATE, COUNTY, AND CITY JOB STARTING SALARY CHART

Position	California	Colorado	Florida	Indiana	New York	Texas
Accountant	$26,868	$30,324	$24,709 (Broward County)	$24,248	$28,738	$26,312 (Lubbock)
Clerk-Typist	$25,800	$16,740	$16,472	$13,208	$20,955 (City of Rochester)	$13,176
Computer Programmer	$30,672	$32,532 (El Paso, CO)	$27,611	$24,934	$28,738	$23,232
Corrections Officer	$25,212	$29,532	$23,024	$18,850	$27,838	$17,244
County Sheriff	$29,052 (Lake City)	$35,148 (Douglas County)	$23,551 (Alachua County)	$29,172 (Marion County)	$5.15/Hour (Cadet Trainee, Monroe County)	$31,236 (Collin County)
Court Clerk	$24,360*	$25,476 (Thornton)	$23,220*	$20,180*	$42,240*	$18,283 (City of Denton)
Firefighter	$37,900 (L.A.)	$31,140 (Colorado Springs)	$23,137 (Brevard County)	$28,310	$34,057 (City of Buffalo)	$26,024 (Houston)
Police Officer	$38,985 (L.A.)	$35,148 (Boulder City)	$24,968	$26,515 (City of Beech Grove)	$34,970 (New York City)	$24,060 (City of Abilene, Cadet in Training)
State Trooper	$31,212 (California Highway Patrol)	Not Available	$24,956 (Highway Patrol)	Not Available	$33,921	$21,852

* Mean Annual Salary, not starting salary which would be lower. From *1997 State Occupational Wage Estimates,* Bureau of Labor Statistics, United States Department of Labor.

The Qualifications That Will Help You Land a Civil Service Job

While civil service may seem more accessible on the state and local levels, and while it may even seem easier to apply for the job, it doesn't necessarily mean it is easier to *get* the job. In some ways, it may even be harder because of the local factor. It all depends on who knows whom—and what they're saying about *you.*

Many of the vacancy listings, you may have noticed, require "good character," so it's here that your sterling reputation will have an advantage. Add to that your impressive work record and sincere desire to do your best while making yourself a secure future. No hard-working screening panel wants to get an application from someone whose attitude is, "Yeah, I'm going to get one of those cushy, do-nothing jobs down at the Parks Department. My cousin is in the Judge's office, so I'm going straight to the top of the list!" Not likely.

Applying for a civil service job on the local level has to be approached with the same care and preparation as on the Federal level. Look for specific job vacancies. Consider different kinds of positions in different departments and on different levels of government. Check back frequently to see what's changed in the listings.

When a vacancy is posted and you fill out an application, be thorough and be careful. Assume nothing. Just because the personnel office may be a short car ride away doesn't mean they'll call you if an answer is confusing or a record is missing.

Applications for the state and local level don't approach the length of the Federal SF-171, but many of the vacancies will require you to submit a resume along with your application. Not every state or municipality will call it that, but it's basically the same thing—a detailed explanation of your background and the knowledge, skills, and abilities you acquired along the way that qualify you for the current position. Give your resume a great deal of time and effort. Phrase your qualities in "result-oriented" language and quantify those results whenever possible. Many positions, especially on the professional level, don't have a competitive test, so your resume is your only real shot at the job. Aim true.

But before you get to that part, you first need a job vacancy. Where do you find them?

Finding Out About Job Openings

Local agencies or municipalities issue a bulletin or job announcement on a regular basis detailing all the vacant positions for that period. You may find these bulletins or announcements in several locations including government offices, local libraries, and newspapers.

The following sections discuss some other ways to find openings for state and local civil service jobs.

DIRECT CONTACT

Contact the human resources or personnel departments of the local government agencies that interest you. Look in the phone book under the "blue pages" and you'll see listings for the Public Works Department, Recycling Department, Recreation Department, and Housing Authority on the city level; for the Human Services Department, Private Industry Council, Senior Citizens Centers, and the Cultural and Historic Affairs Department on the county level; for the Environmental Protection Department, the Lottery Division, the Commerce and Economic Growth Commission, and the Consumer Affairs Division. While not every one of these may be in *your* city, county, or state, the phone book will direct you to dozens of agencies.

YOUR STATE DEPARTMENT OF LABOR OR EMPLOYMENT SERVICES

If this department doesn't post listings itself, someone there can direct you to the right source. Again, the number should be in the phone book. Local libraries, too, can be invaluable in helping you track down local information.

ONLINE EMPLOYMENT SERVICES

These are explained in more detail in the "Webliography" on page 213, but for quick reference, these are the sites that offer state and local information:

- Employment Index (www.employmentindex.com/govjob.html)—local and state government agencies' job listings
- Government and Law Enforcement Jobs (jobsearch.tqn.com/msubgov.htm)—state and local agencies
- Jobs in State Government (usgovinfo.about.com/blstjobs.htm)—index of state sites
- Official State Web sites. All 50 states and the District of Columbia have sites on the Web. Each state offers information of its own choosing.

Many states list employment openings in state government detailing what the job entails, qualification requirements, location, salary and benefits, career path, and application procedures. In addition, some state sites will connect you to county or city sites within the state. Here are the online addresses of every state Web site:

OFFICIAL STATE WEB SITES

State	Web site	State	Web site
Alabama	alaweb.asc.edu/	Missouri	www.state.mo.us/
Alaska	www.state.ak.us/	Montana	www.mt.gov/
Arizona	www.state.az.us/	Nebraska	www.state.ne.us/
Arkansas	www.state.ar.us/	Nevada	www.state.nv.us/
California	www.state.ca.us/	New Hampshire	www.state.nh.us/
Colorado	www.state.co.us/	New Jersey	www.state.nj.us/
Connecticut	www.state.ct.us/	New Mexico	www.state.nm.us/
Delaware	www.state.de.us/	New York	www.state.ny.us/
District of	www.dchomepage.net/	North Carolina	www.state.nc.us/
Columbia		North Dakota	www.state.nd.us/
Florida	www.state.fl.us/	Ohio	www.state.oh.us/
Georgia	www.state.ga.us/	Oklahoma	www.state.ok.us/
Hawaii	www.state.hi.us/	Oregon	www.state.or.us/
Idaho	www.state.id.us/	Pennsylvania	www.state.pa.us/
Illinois	www.state.il.us/	Rhode Island	www.state.ri.us/
Indiana	www.state.in.us/	South Carolina	www.state.sc.us/
Iowa	www.state.ia.us/	South Dakota	www.state.sd.us/
Kansas	www.state.ks.us/	Tennessee	www.state.tn.us/
Kentucky	www.state.ky.us/	Texas	www.state.tx.us/
Louisiana	www.state.la.us/	Utah	www.state.ut.us/
Maine	www.state.me.us/	Vermont	www.state.vt.us/
Maryland	sailor.lib.md.us/mec/	Virginia	www.state.va.us/
Massachusetts	www.state.ma.us/	Washington	www.wa.gov/
Michigan	www.migov.state.mi.us/	West Virginia	www.state.wv.us/
Minnesota	www.state.mn.us/	Wisconsin	www.state.wi.us/
Mississippi	www.state.ms.us/	Wyoming	www.state.wy.us/

Will your own city or town also be online? The answer is probably yes. Your local library will have the Web site address.

How to Give Yourself the Edge Getting a State or Local Job

Take advantage of the local aspect of state and municipal civil service by networking with people who can let you know about job conditions in certain departments and about upcoming openings. While these openings must be posted, you wouldn't want that to be the one month you don't pick up a printed bulletin or check the Web site. Besides, knowing in advance that a vacancy is going to be announced gives you more time to prepare your resume.

When calling about positions, ask about the application procedures—then follow them. Most vacancies will list how to apply right in the announcement, but if you have any questions, call. Don't assume that just because you've applied for a Federal job, the county will follow exactly the same steps, or that one state will follow exactly the same steps as another. The overall process is likely to be the same, but it's the different details that could trip you up.

However, as in the Federal application, be as explicit as possible describing your career achievements. Imagine not only that you're trying to change jobs—which you are—but also that you're applying for a job with a huge pay increase. Justify why you deserve it. *You* know why, but don't assume that the person reviewing your application will.

Finally, be patient. Since state and local governments are much smaller in size, you may expect them to move faster since they're not bogged down with so much bureaucracy. It's better not to expect to hear any quick news. If the news is bad, try again. You're probably still on the list of eligibles and can be considered for the next vacancy. While you're waiting for a response, keep an eye out for other job vacancies that interest you.

SAMPLE CIVIL SERVICE JOB ANNOUNCEMENTS AT THE STATE AND LOCAL LEVEL

Nearly all states and municipalities use trained business, technical, and professional employees in a variety of fields. College men and women who have prepared for such positions are encouraged to step directly from the classroom into the state and municipal service at the bottom rung of any one of the many career ladders in its numerous departments, institutions, and agencies.

Many state constitutions require that appointments and promotions in the state civil service and all of its divisions be made according to examination scores. Their constitutions also state that these exams should be competitive. The entrance positions described in this list are filled by the top-scoring individuals on the state civil service exam. Civil service law usually requires that when a vacancy above the entrance level is to be filled, the appointment must be made, if possible, by promotion from among persons holding positions in a lower grade in the department, office, or institution where the vacancy exists. This law increases opportunities for advancement of those employees who come into the service at the lowest rung of the state or municipal career ladder, and emphasizes the importance of the recruitment of well-trained, intelligent personnel in these entrance positions.

Do not assume that all of the examples listed in the following pages are all-inclusive. While these specifications may present a true picture of the position today, state and municipal services do not remain static. Fluctuations in the labor market, reorganization within departments, and other factors affect not only the duties of the position, but also the *existence* of the position.

State Bank Examiner Trainee, Bank Examiner
JOB DESCRIPTION

Bank Examiner Trainees begin a two-year training program which will include field assignments supervised by the banking department's examining staff; department-sponsored training, which is conducted in-house or through specialized schools; and training sessions at selected banks. During the in-bank training, trainees have the opportunity to observe and participate in the major operations of commercial banks, savings banks, and foreign branches or agencies. Upon successful completion of the first year of training, trainees advance automatically to the Bank Examiner Trainee II level. Although training will follow the same basic format during the second year, the nature of the work while on field assignments will grow in scope as the trainee progresses. Performance as a trainee and in the prescribed training and development programs will be observed and evaluated. An appointee not meeting required standards can be terminated at any time after the initial eight weeks and before the completion of the two-year traineeship. Upon successful completion of the two-year traineeship, individuals are automatically advanced to Bank Examiner without further examination.

Bank Examiners assist in conducting in-depth examinations of banking and other financial service institutions regulated by the State Banking Department. They either perform on-site examinations and reviews of institutions' financial condition, operating procedures, and management controls or, when assigned to one of the department's specialized office divisions, review and analyze field examination reports and periodic financial reports submitted by various types of institutions. The field examinations and office analyses are conducted to ensure that the operations and policies of state-chartered financial institutions conform with state banking laws and the banking Superintendent's rules and regulations.

REQUIREMENTS

On or before the date of the written test, candidates must have a bachelor's or graduate degree (from an accredited college or university) in one of the following major areas of study: accounting, auditing, banking, business administration, economics, or finance. Course work must have included, or been supplemented by, six credit hours of accounting. You must include with your application a list of all accounting courses successfully completed and the number of credit hours received for each. Failure to include this information can result in your disqualification.

TEST INFORMATION

There will be a written test, which you must pass in order to be considered for appointment. This written test is designed to test for knowledge, skills, and/or abilities in such areas as:

1. *Understanding and interpreting written material:* These questions test how well you comprehend written material. You will be provided with brief reading selections and asked questions relating to the selections. All of the information required to answer the questions will be presented in the selections; you are not required to have any special knowledge relating to the content area covered in the selections.

2. *Elementary accounting:* These questions test for familiarity with accounting principles and practices at an elementary level. The questions will attempt to test for recognition of accounting terminology, concepts, and relationships; for ability to record accounting transactions; and for acquaintance with financial statements and books of account.

3. *Preparing written material:* These questions will be designed to test how well you can express yourself in writing. Particular emphasis is placed upon two major aspects of written communication: how to clearly and accurately express given information and how to present written material in the most logical and comprehensive manner.

4. *Understanding and interpreting tabular material:* These questions are designed to test your ability to understand, analyze, and use the internal logic of data presented in tabular form. You may be asked to complete tables, to draw conclusions from them, to analyze data trends or interrelationships, and to revise or combine data sets. The concepts of rate, ratio, and proportion will be tested. Mathematical operations will be simple, and computational speed and accuracy will not be major factors in the test.

State or Municipal Correction Officer
JOB DESCRIPTION

This is a law enforcement position that requires close contact with inmates. A Correction Officer may be assigned to supervise inmates of either sex. A Correction Officer, under supervision, maintains security within correctional facilities and is responsible for the custody, control, care, job training, and work performance of inmates of detention and correctional facilities, and performs related work. Correction Officers are required to work rotating tours and shifts, including nights and Saturdays, Sundays, and holidays.

EXAMPLES OF TYPICAL TASKS

Maintains constant watch over and supervises activities of detainees, sentenced inmates, civil prisoners, etc. Enforces maximum security and maintains constant control over departmental property, keys, gates, etc. Performs tours in cell blocks, dormitories or other housing areas, prison wards or detention areas, dining areas, recreation areas, exercise areas, inmate work sites or other locations. May be assigned to continuous surveillance of prisoners or detainees while they are in transit.

Maintains security of prisoners or detainees hospitalized outside of prison wards or when outside the fixed security areas maintained by the department. May help locate escaped inmates. Enforces additional emergency security measures in special situations. Enforces maximum security when assigned to tasks of receiving prisoners or detainees, periodically counting them or checking for contraband. Enforces security during movement of vehicles, articles, and visitors into and out of correctional facilities.

Is responsible for adherence to all directives, rules, and regulations of the Department of Correction, all applicable laws, court orders, and administrative requirements. Reports all inmate violations and infractions of standing or special orders, inmate grievances and proper requests, and unusual incidents. Performs duties as assigned in connection with activities for or by prisoners which are intended to improve their adjustment to society.

REQUIREMENTS

Education

High school graduation or evidence of having passed an examination for the high school equivalency diploma. Foreign education will be evaluated to determine comparability to education received in domestic accredited educational institutions to determine the extent to which it will be credited toward meeting the requirements or for additional credit in this examination.

Age

Candidates must not have reached their twenty-ninth birthday by the first date of the filing period. However, they must have reached their twentieth birthday by the date of appointment.

Exceptions to age requirements: All persons who were engaged in military duty, as defined in Section 243 of the Military Law, may deduct from their actual age the length of time spent in such military duty provided the total deduction for military duty does not exceed six years, of which not more than four years may be for voluntary service.

Character

Proof of good character is an absolute prerequisite to appointment. The following are among the factors that would ordinarily be cause for disqualification:

1. Conviction of an offense the nature of which indicates lack of good moral character or disposition toward violence or disorder or which is punishable by one or more years imprisonment;
2. Repeated convictions of an offense where such convictions indicate a disrespect for the law;
3. Discharge from employment where such discharge indicates poor behavior or inability to adjust to discipline;
4. Addiction to narcotics or to a controlled substance or excessive use of alcoholic beverages;
5. Dishonorable discharge from the Armed Forces. In accordance with provisions of law, persons convicted of a felony are not eligible for appointment to these positions.

Eligibles must also meet, at the time of appointment, the standards for obtaining firearms permits.

Investigation

At the time of investigation and at the time of appointment, candidates must present originals or certified copies of all required documents, including but not limited to proof of date and place of birth by transcript of record of the Bureau of Vital Statistics or other satisfactory evidence, naturalization papers if necessary, proof of any military service, and proof of meeting educational requirements. Any willful misstatement or failure to present any required documents will be cause for disqualification. Investigation must be completed prior to appointment.

Probationary Period

The probationary period is one year. As part of the probationary period, probationers will be required to successfully complete a prescribed training course. Unsatisfactory probationers will be terminated.

TEST INFORMATION

Education and experience weigh 100 percent; a minimum score of 75 percent is required. There is a written test; a minimum score of 70 percent is required. There are also qualifying physical and medical exams.

EDUCATION AND EXPERIENCE

Education and experience will be calculated on the basis of candidates' responses. This rating will be verified on the basis of information contained in the Experience Paper. Therefore, the Experience Paper must be filled out completely and in detail, including exact dates, number of hours per week worked, and salary earned. Candidates are advised to list *all* education and experience for which credit may be given as described below, since they will not be permitted to add any education or experience once they have filed their applications. Education or experience will not be found acceptable unless satisfactory and verifiable. Education and experience listed on the Experience Paper will receive credit only if described clearly and in detail.

The maximum score is 100. Applicants who meet the minimum educational requirement will receive a score of 75. Additional credit will be given to candidates who have additional education and/or experience as explained in the following paragraphs.

Experience Credit

Up to eight years of paid work experience, including military service but not including self-employment, may be given experience credit. Additional credit may also be given for up to four of the eight years of experience if such experience falls within the specialized experience described below. However, each year of specialized experience may be credited under only one category of specialized experience.

Full-time experience means 30 hours or more per week on a regular basis. Part-time experience is less than 30 hours per week but must be at least 15 hours per week to receive credit.

General Experience

At least six months with each employer. General Experience credit will be granted as follows: one point for 6–17 months; two points for 18–29 months; three points for 30–41 months; four points for 42–53 months; five points for 54–65 months; six points for 66–77 months; seven points for 78–89 months; eight points for 90 months and above.

Specialized Experience

At least 12 months with each employer. Specialized Experience credit will be granted as listed below.

For experience as a correction officer, military policeman assigned to a disciplinary facility, or equivalent correctional experience: three points for 12–21 months; six points for 22–33 months; nine points for 34–45 months; 12 points for 46 months and above.

For experience as a police officer, military policeman, parole officer, probation officer, court officer, or equivalent law enforcement experience; two points for 12–21 months; four points for 22–33 months; six points for 34–45 months; eight points for 46 months and above.

For experience as a supervisor or for each year of active duty in military service culminating in honorable discharge or separation, provided at least one year was served: one point for 12–21 months; two points for 22–33 months; three points for 34–45 months; four points for 46 months and above.

Part-Time Experience

Part-time experience is considered 15 to 29 hours per week. Candidates must have a total of at least 12 months of part-time experience to receive any credit. To earn this credit, candidates must have worked at least six months for each employer. Credit will be granted as follows: one point for 12–34 months; two points for 35–57 months; three points for 58–82 months; four points for 83 months and above.

Education Credit

One point will be given for 15 to 36 semester-hours of education at an accredited college. An additional one point will be given for 37 to 72 semester-hours of education at an accredited college. An additional one point will be given for 73 or more semester-hours of education at an accredited college. An additional one point will be given for completion of at least three courses in criminal justice, law enforcement, or correctional administration, or completion of a certificate program in any of these areas at an accredited college. An additional one point will be given for possession of an associate, baccalaureate, or any other degree from an accredited college.

Rating of Education and Experience

In addition to the Experience Paper, candidates must fill out and submit an Answer Sheet in accordance with the Instruction Sheet. The Answer Sheet submitted by the candidate will be the basis for calculating a rating and for ranking on the eligible list, subject to changes after investigation of information contained in the Experience Paper. Candidates will not be allowed to make any changes on their Experience Papers or Answer Sheets once they have filed for this examination. Candidates who fail to submit an Answer Sheet or who fail to fill in their identifying information and responses to the questions listed in the Instruction Sheet will be marked Not Qualified in the Education and Experience Test.

TEST INFORMATION

Qualifying Written Test

The qualifying written test will be of the multiple-choice type and will be designed to measure the ability to learn to perform the duties of the position as described above. It may include questions on understanding written instructions, human relations and communication, filling out forms and maintaining records, basic arithmetic, report writing including English usage, and related areas.

Qualifying Physical and Medical Examination

Eligibles will be rejected for any medical and/or psychiatric condition that impairs their ability to perform the duties of the class of positions for which they are being examined. Medical reexamination of probationary and permanent employees in these titles may be required.

ADVANCEMENT

Employees in the title of Correction Officer are accorded promotion opportunities to the title of Captain.

State or Municipal Social Worker
JOB DESCRIPTION

Under supervision, is responsible for the provision of psychosocial services to children, adults, families, and/or groups in a public agency or setting, such as a municipal hospital, prison health service, or social services center; performs related tasks.

EXAMPLES OF TYPICAL TASKS

Conducts or participates in the intake process to obtain information relevant to formulating a psychosocial evaluation and social work treatment plan; interviews patients/clients, relatives, agency staff, or members of the community regarding patients'/clients' ability to function in the community; implements treatment plan by providing individual and group counseling and/or concrete services; plans for discharge and/or aftercare; makes referrals to agencies or community resources, or provides direct services; confers and consults with professional and technical personnel in implementing a multidisciplinary approach to patient/client care; attends meetings, staff conferences, social work staff meetings and rounds; orients and educates members of other professional disciplines in social work concepts and functions; participates in work of selected staff committees; serves as liaison with community agencies; may supervise fieldwork placement of graduate and undergraduate social work students; may supervise volunteers and other auxiliary personnel; initiates and/or participates in special studies and research projects; maintains appropriate case records and statistical reports and prepares other reports as required; may practice within one or more social work specialities, i.e., casework, group work, or community organization; determines the desirability of the placement of children; provides adoption services; assists unmarried pregnant women by arranging for maternity shelter care and by planning for suitable care of the child; interviews children and parents to discuss behavior problems and to determine appropriate services indicated; prepares children and parents to accept services; analyzes neighborhood or area problems and needs; evaluates alternate care arrangements for the elderly; provides social work services in a prison setting.

REQUIREMENTS
Education

A master's degree in social work from an accredited school of social work. Foreign education will be evaluated by the Department of Personnel to determine comparability to education received in domestic accredited educational institutions.

Certificate Requirements

All candidates will be required to have a valid certificate of Certified Social Worker (CSW) issued by the State Department of Education within one year of the date of appointment. This certificate must be presented to the appointing officer at the time of appointment or, if it is obtained after appointment, at the time it is received. Employees who fail to obtain their certificate within one year after their appointment will automatically have their probationary period extended for no more than six months.

TEST INFORMATION

Education and experience is weighted 100 percent, with a score of 70 percent required. There will be no competitive test other than an evaluation of education and experience.

Your education and experience rating will be based on your statements on the Experience Paper, which must be filled out completely and in detail, including dates and number of hours worked per week. List all education and experience for which credit may be given as described below, since you will not be able to add information after filing has closed. Education or experience will not be found acceptable unless it is verifiable. Education and experience listed on the Experience Paper will receive credit only to the extent that they are described clearly and in detail.

You will receive a score of 70 for meeting the minimum requirements.

After the minimum requirements are met, you may receive credit for a maximum of an additional 9 years of experience, accrued within the last 10 years, on the basis of the categories described below. Each year of experience may be credited under only one category.

1. One point will be granted for each year of full-time paid social work experience, prior to receiving the master's degree in social work, in a recognized child welfare, adult, or family services agency, or in a hospital, mental health, or prison setting.
2. Three points will be granted for each year of full-time paid social work experience, subsequent to receiving the master's degree in social work, in a recognized child welfare, adult, or family services agency, or in a hospital, mental health, or prison setting.

Additionally, three points will be credited for possession, at the time of filing the application, of a valid certificate of Certified Social Worker (CSW) issued by the State Department of Education.

The maximum rating that can be granted on the education and experience test is 100.

ADVANCEMENT

Employees in the title of Social Worker are accorded promotion opportunities, when eligible, to the title of Supervisor I (Social Work).

State or Municipal Clerical/Secretarial Positions

JOB DESCRIPTIONS

Clerk-Typist I and II, and Intermittent Clerk-Typist II are positions that involve typing and clerical duties, such as providing information, composing short letters and memos, sorting, filing, and checking materials. These duties vary in complexity from limited (Clerk-Typist I) to moderate (Clerk-Typist II).

Clerk Stenographer I and II involve taking dictation and transcribing the notes. Other duties from limited to moderate complexity include typing, providing information, composing letters and memos, and sorting and filing materials.

Library Assistants perform moderately complex clerical work in a library, such as maintaining files and records, sorting and shelving books, and checking materials for accuracy.

REQUIREMENTS

All applicants must achieve a passing score on a written examination.

TEST INFORMATION

The clerical examination is made up of three major parts: a written test, a typing test, and a stenography test. The parts of the test that you take will depend upon the position(s) for which you have applied. Applicants for Clerk-Typist I and II, Clerk Stenographer I and II, and Intermittent Clerk-Typist II must take a typing test. For these job titles, the written test will be weighted 50 percent and the typing test score will be weighted 50 percent. Applicants for Clerk Stenographer I and II must pass a stenography test. The stenography test will not be weighted as part of the final score. You must pass all parts of the test to be considered for employment. Any part of the tests may be canceled and the weight added to the remaining parts.

Written Test

The written test for these positions contains eight sections. The number of questions an applicant answers will depend upon the position(s) for which he or she has applied. The time allotted for the written test is 1 hour and 42 minutes. The type and number of questions for each position are as follows.

NUMBER OF QUESTIONS BY JOB TITLE

Subject Matter	Clerk-Typist II, Clerk Stenographer I and II, Clerk Library Assistant I	Area Typist I Intermittent Clerk-Typist II
Name and number checking (perceptual speed and accuracy)	65	65
Sorting file material (coding)	10	10
Alphabetizing (filing)	15	15
Taking telephone messages (following directions)	15	15
Capitalization/punctuation/grammar (language usage)	15	15
Effective expression	10	10
Spelling	25	25
Arithmetic operations	—	15

Typing Test

The typing performance test will consist of a four-minute practice exercise followed by the actual test, which will have an eight-minute time limit. A score of 30 words per minute, after deduction for errors, must be achieved in order to pass the typing performance test. Applicants *may* provide their own typewriters for the typing test.

Stenography Test

The stenography test will consist of a three-minute practice exercise followed by the actual test, which will have a three-minute time limit. Dictation will be given at the rate of 80 words per minute. Applicants will have 30 minutes to transcribe their notes into answers on an answer sheet. Applicants for Clerk Stenographer I must not have more than 10 percent errors on the stenography test. Applicants for Clerk Stenographer II must not have more than 5 percent errors on the test. Any stenography system including the use of a shorthand machine is acceptable. Applicants who wish to use shorthand machines must provide their own.

State Assistant Fire Marshal, Fire Marshal in the Department of Public Welfare

JOB DESCRIPTION

Assistant Fire Marshals and Fire Marshals are responsible for the implementation, direction, and coordination of the fire safety program at state mental hospitals and state schools for the mentally retarded. Employees inspect institutional buildings and grounds for fire hazards. They test and maintain fire-fighting and fire prevention equipment to ensure proper operating conditions. Employees are responsible for organizing and training fire brigades, which serve as first-level firefighting teams at the institutions. Assistant Fire Marshals and Fire Marshals conduct fire drills and train institutional personnel in emergency evacuation procedures. In the event of a fire, employees are responsible for the proper utilization of personnel and equipment to extinguish or control the fire and to evacuate occupants until outside firefighting companies arrive. Employees are responsible for writing reports of fires and reports of fire prevention inspections. Employees are also responsible for maintaining cooperative working relationships with local fire departments.

The duties of Assistant Fire Marshals and Fire Marshals are similar in nature, but different in the degree of responsibility. A Fire Marshal is responsible for the supervision of the Assistant Fire Marshal and has total responsibility for the fire safety program at a state institution. The Assistant Fire Marshal performs work as assigned, but generally will work independently and under minimum supervision. Employees may be required to work rotating shifts depending on the institution at which they are employed.

REQUIREMENTS

Applicants must be state residents, of good moral character, and physically capable of performing the duties of the position. Residency means a current address in the state and the intention to remain a resident.

For Assistant Fire Marshal:

1. Two years of experience in firefighting and fire prevention work and such training as may have been gained through graduation from a standard high school or vocational school; or
2. Any equivalent combination of experience and training.

For Fire Marshal:

1. Four years of experience in firefighting and fire prevention work and such training as may have been gained through graduation from a standard high school or vocational school; or
2. Any equivalent combination of experience and training.

Acceptable training is training in fire prevention or firefighting that can be substituted for the required experience at the rate of 300 clock hours or 18 semester hours for one year's experience to a maximum substitution of one year for the Assistant Fire Marshal and two years for the Fire Marshal position. Training can be administered by colleges, states, or other jurisdictions, fire departments, or the military services. To receive credit, these courses must be relevant to civilian firefighting or fire prevention.

Acceptable experience is full-time paid experience as a fire inspector or firefighter with a fire department. Volunteer fire department experience evaluation is dependent on the estimated number of hours per month the applicant served as a firefighter or participated in fire prevention programs. This experience will be converted to full-time equivalency on the basis of a 40-hour week. *However, time spent on a standby basis or in routine maintenance or in organizing social activities will not be credited.* Military and industrial fire prevention or firefighting experience is acceptable as full-time experience if fire prevention and firefighting were major duties. If candidates fully meet the experience requirements, high school graduation will be assumed.

TEST INFORMATION

There is no written test. The examination will consist of a rating of each candidate's experience and training. Applicants must attain passing scores to have their names placed on eligible lists. All applicants will be notified in writing of their examination results.

ELIGIBLE LISTS

Names of successful candidates will be placed on employment and promotion lists in order of final earned ratings. Promotion lists are limited to current employees with regular or probationary civil service status. Candidates' eligibility for employment will continue for 24 months. Promotion eligibility will continue for 36 months.

State or Municipal Computer Specialist (Data Base Administration)
JOB DESCRIPTION

This class of positions encompasses technical or supervisory responsibilities for the design, implementation, enhancement, and maintenance of Data Base Management Systems performed at varying levels of difficulty and with varying degrees of latitude for independent initiative and judgment. There are three assignment levels within this class of positions. All personnel perform related work.

1. *Assignment Level I:* Under supervision, with considerable latitude for the exercise of independent judgment, is responsible for the maintenance, design, and enhancement of Data Base Management Systems; for assisting other computer personnel with technical advice, as required, including identification, coding, and implementation of complex technical programming projects; performs tasks such as are indicated below under Examples of Typical Tasks.
2. *Assignment Level II:* Under supervision, with considerable latitude for the exercise of independent judgment, performs logical and physical data administration functions working with applications and systems programmers and other technical personnel of the data processing installation; performs tasks such as are indicated below under Examples of Typical Tasks. Supports applications and systems programmers and other technical personnel of the data processing installation in determining data specifications for new information systems or for enhancement of existing systems. Sets standards, ensures that there is no data redundancy, and may lead design reviews to ensure adherence to standards and that the systems design is both complete and feasible. Performs tasks such as are indicated below under Examples of Typical Tasks.
3. *Assignment Level III:* Under general supervision with wide latitude for the exercise of independent initiative and judgment, performs the following: supervises a unit of Data Base Administration Specialists and is fully responsible for execution of projects of the highest complexity in the design, implementation, enhancement, and maintenance of the Data Base Management Systems of the data processing installation. Performs tasks such as are indicated below under Examples of Typical Tasks.

EXAMPLES OF TYPICAL TASKS

Assists analysts with technical design considerations. Develops approaches for modifying existing systems. Maintains state-of-the-art knowledge in computer systems technology. Is responsible for the maintenance and enhancement of general purpose applications software. Ensures the completeness and accuracy of coded programs, creates program test data and program test plans, and prepares system acceptance test plans and systems test data. Provides on-the-job programming training of subordinate technical personnel to ensure efficient and accurate utilization of state-of-the-art techniques. Ensures that the data center is knowledgeable in the hardware and software requirements, job flow, required inputs, and expected outputs; prepares operational specifications.

Controls and coordinates logical, internal, and external data element definition and data relationships for all applications. Defines physical structures and organizations of data bases/data sets to best meet the logical requirements of the applications, reviewing and modifying as new requirements are specified. Monitors the performance of the data base software and tunes as necessary to optimize performance. For new applications, estimates performance via simulation or benchmark test. Performs approved updates to dictionary system and makes dictionary information available to analysts and programmers. Generates all DBMS control blocks and data structures required by application programs. Defines and implements procedures for backup/recovery/restart for all data. Monitors DBMS output from recovery and backup executions. Determines appropriate reorganization frequency for the data base. Determines device storage space requirements for the data base and data compression strategies. Ensures data security using the features of the DBMS or, if necessary, developing requirement specifications for security routines. Provides training for application programmers, systems programmers, and operations personnel in the use of DBMS and special purpose utility software. Provides application programming DBMS-related diagnostic error detection support. Coordinates implementation of applications changes across multiple divisions of the data processing installation. Develops approaches for addressing security violation detection and tracking and auditing the integrity of the data in the data base. Reviews and approves application systems prior to implementation for adherence to DBA standards in design, systems and programming specifications, systems tests, and final documentation. Develops data definition, documentation, programming, testing, and systems acceptance standards. Provides program specification for internal Data Base Administration programs. Directs the activities of the Data Base Administration librarians. Assists in the selection of appropriate DB access methods.

REQUIREMENTS

1. A bachelor's degree from an accredited college and four years of satisfactory full-time paid applications or systems programming experience involving the use of either COBOL, BAL, PL/1, or FORTRAN, at least one year of which shall have been in a data base management environment; or
2. An associate's degree from an accredited college or completion of two years of study (60 credits) at an accredited college and six years of satisfactory full-time paid applications or systems programming experience involving the use of either COBOL, BAL, PL/1, or FORTRAN, at least one year of which shall have been in a data base management environment; or
3. High school graduation or evidence of having passed an examination for a high school equivalency diploma and eight years of satisfactory full-time paid applications or systems programming experience involving the use of either COBOL, BAL, PL/1, or FORTRAN, at least one year of which shall have been in a data base management environment; or
4. Education and/or experience that is equivalent to (1), (2), or (3). However, all candidates must have the four years of experience described under subdivision 1.

Foreign education will be evaluated by the Department of Personnel to determine comparability to education received in domestic accredited educational institutions to determine the extent to which it will be credited toward meeting the requirements for this examination.

All qualified candidates must pass a background investigation by the Department of Investigation in order to be eligible for this position.

TEST INFORMATION

Written, weight 100, 70 percent required. The test may include questions on techniques of supervision and administration in a computer environment; design, implementation, enhancement, and maintenance of Data Base Management Systems, including logical and physical data administration functions; and other related areas.

ADVANCEMENT

Employees in the title of Computer Specialist (Data Base Administration) are accorded promotion opportunities, when eligible, to the title of Computer Systems Manager.

State or Municipal Public Health Assistant
JOB DESCRIPTION

Under direct supervision, the public health assistant assists medical staff in a public health clinic by performing nonprofessional duties; performs related work.

EXAMPLES OF TYPICAL TASKS

Performs vision, hearing, and simple urinanalysis tests; weighs and measures patients; takes pulse, respiration rates, and temperatures; collects specimens; prepares patients for examination and helps professional staff perform examination; operates related equipment; may administer simple first aid; interviews clients to obtain identifying and routine medical information; explains clinic procedures; answers routine questions and makes appropriate referrals; makes and receives related telephone calls; comforts children; reports relevant observations and information to the professional staff; accompanies nurses on home visits; prepares, maintains, and files medical folders, charts, and forms; reviews for completeness and enters data onto appropriate documents; labels specimens; arranges appointments; sends and receives medical records and notices; collects and records statistical data; maintains logs and schedules; requests, arranges, and maintains equipment and supplies; does light housekeeping and cleaning of instruments and equipment.

REQUIREMENTS

1. High school graduation or its equivalent; or
2. Successful completion of the eleventh grade of high school and one year of full-time paid experience performing health-related or clerical duties; or
3. Experience and/or education which is equivalent to (1) or (2).

However, all candidates must have successfully completed the eleventh grade of high school.

TEST INFORMATION

Written, weight 100, 70 percent required. The written test will be of the multiple-choice type and may include questions on reading and understanding instructional material, medical charts, and statistical forms; completing forms; filing and organizing simple data; spelling, simple arithmetic, and measurements; working cooperatively with staff and interacting with patients; and related information.

State Electrical and Mechanical Engineers
JOB DESCRIPTION

Employees in these positions perform professional engineering work, within their specialties, in the design, construction, and inspection of a variety of electrical and mechanical systems and equipment for state buildings and facilities, such as office buildings, colleges, hospitals, water and sewage treatment plants, steam generating plants, parks and recreation areas, highway interchanges, and rest areas. The work performed must conform to accepted engineering standards, agency rules and regulations, and safety laws and codes.

Engineers I perform entry-level work, normally including engineering assignments involving component parts of a system when the controlling parameters for such systems have been developed. The work does not normally involve coordinating their specialties with other architectural or engineering disciplines.

Engineers II perform more advanced work with responsibility for complete engineering projects. They work with considerable independence in developing the technical details of the projects. Their work requires coordinating their specialties with other architectural and engineering disciplines and contact with other public agencies, consultants, or contractors to obtain compliance with state standards and needs.

Consultants perform highly advanced engineering work. They are involved in developing solutions to design and construction problems that require advanced and innovative application of engineering principles. They are normally recognized agency experts with responsibility for advising management on the advantages, disadvantages, and effects of utilizing technology and/or changing existing engineering and materials standards. Work is normally self-generated and in response to unusual construction, design, or administrative problems and is performed with considerable independence in approach and scheduling.

Electrical Engineers and Consultants work on such projects, or parts of projects, as complete electrical distribution systems, and substations; conversion of a facility to a total electrical utility base; tunnel and highway interchange lighting and signaling; electrical servicing of highways; parking lot illumination; security and intrusion alarm systems; fire detection and suppression systems; temperature and motor controls; intercommunications systems; and elevators.

Mechanical Engineers and Consultants work on such projects as mechanical systems for internal water supply and other plumbing systems; heating, including steam generation, air conditioning, ventilation, and refrigeration, for buildings and water and sewage treatment plants; components of recreational facilities, such as pumps and filtration for swimming pools and plumbing for camping sites; locks and gates for dams or similar projects; fire suppression and detection; and air pollution control systems.

Employees in these jobs may occasionally travel. For positions where travel is required, offers of employment will be made only to applicants who are willing to travel. If transportation by government vehicle or public transportation is not available or feasible, employees may be required to arrange their own transportation. Travel expenses of employees will be reimbursed at specified rates.

In addition, employees in these jobs are occasionally required to work an unusual schedule or work overtime to meet emergency situations or project deadlines. In such cases, employees are paid overtime or given compensatory time off, as appropriate, in accordance with state Personnel Rules and/or the union contract.

These positions are in the Department of General Services, the primary employing agency; the Departments of Public Welfare, Education, Transportation, and Community Affairs; the State Public Utility Commission; and the State Fish Commission. There are 13 filled Electrical Engineer positions and 12 filled Mechanical Engineer positions.

REQUIREMENTS

Necessary Special Requirement

Certain positions in these job titles will require licensure as a professional engineer by the state or a reciprocal jurisdiction. These are positions where there can be no exemption from such licensure, as defined under Section 5, Exemption from Licensure, of the Professional Engineers Registration Law (as amended).

For Electrical Engineer I:

1. One year as an Electrical Engineer Trainee in state employment; or
2. One year of experience in designing, constructing, or reviewing components of electrical engineering projects that required the application of problem-solving techniques, including loading and capacity calculations and the preparation of drawings; and a bachelor's degree in electrical engineering or closely related field.

For Electrical Engineer II:

1. One year as an Electrical Engineer I in state employment; or
2. Two years of experience in designing, constructing, or reviewing components of electrical engineering projects which required the application of problem-solving techniques including electrical loading and capacity calculations and the preparation of drawings and specifications for the solutions; and a bachelor's degree in electrical engineering or closely related field.

For Electrical Engineering Consultant:

1. One year as an Electrical Engineer II in state employment; or
2. One year of experience in designing, reviewing, or constructing engineering systems for commercial, educational, or governmental facilities which required the application of problem-solving techniques, including electrical loading or power capacity calculations and the preparation of drawings and specifications for the solutions; and a bachelor's degree in electrical engineering or closely related field.

For Mechanical Engineer I:

1. One year as a Mechanical Engineer Trainee in state employment; or
2. One year of experience in designing, constructing, or reviewing components of mechanical engineering projects that required the application of problem-solving techniques including loading and capacity calculations and the preparation of drawings; and a bachelor's degree in mechanical engineering or closely related field.

For Mechanical Engineer II:

1. One year as a Mechanical Engineer I in state employment; or
2. Two years of experience in designing, constructing, or reviewing components of mechanical engineering projects which required the application of problem-solving techniques and the preparation of drawings; and a bachelor's degree in mechanical engineering or closely related field.

For Mechanical Engineering Consultant:

1. One year as a Mechanical Engineer II in state employment; or
2. One year of experience in designing, reviewing, or constructing engineering systems for commercial, educational, or governmental facilities that required the application of problem-solving techniques, including loading or capacity calculations and the preparation of drawings and specifications for the solutions; and a bachelor's degree in mechanical engineering or closely related field.

Note: Any equivalent combination of experience and training can be substituted for the above experience and training.

EVALUATION POLICY

Clarification of the Necessary Special Requirement (NSR)

This NSR means some selected positions in these job titles will require licensure as a professional engineer (PE). When a vacancy is to be filled in a position which requires licensure, only candidates who possess a PE license, as defined above, will be considered for employment to the position. After you are on the eligible list for these jobs, you should immediately advise the Civil Service Commission of any changes concerning your PE license.

Acceptable Experience and Training

The phrase "any equivalent combination of experience and training" means that generally:

1. Applicants who do not have an engineering degree in the appropriate discipline can substitute any combination of appropriate engineering experience and education that totals four years and possession of an Engineer-in-Training (EIT) certificate or PE license for the required degree.
2. Applicants can substitute graduate training in the appropriate engineering discipline or a closely related field for the required experience at the rate of 30 semester hours (or equivalent) of coursework for each year of experience. Students in the final term of qualifying training may apply.
3. A bachelor's degree in a closely related electrical engineering field includes a bachelor of engineering or engineering technology degree in such fields as electrical power, electrical science engineering, electrical design, and electrical science and systems.
4. A bachelor's degree in a closely related mechanical engineering field includes a bachelor of engineering or engineering technology degree in such fields as mechanical analysis and design, mechanical design, mechanical engineering and analysis.

Applicants for the Electrical/Mechanical Engineering Consultant job titles must have experience involving a total electrical/mechanical system. Qualifying experience or training must have included engineering assignments that required the application of engineering problem-solving techniques involving loading and capacity calculations and the preparation of drawings appropriate to the jobs applied for. Acceptable experience will normally commence after receipt of a bachelor's degree in the appropriate discipline. In the absence of such degree, the appropriate engineering experience will not normally commence until after award of an EIT certificate.

Applicants must be of good moral character and be capable of performing the physical activities of the job. State residency is not required for any of these job titles.

TEST INFORMATION

The tests will consist of a rating of your experience and training. Applicants will receive a score based on the experience and training reported on the Application for Employment and Application Supplement for Electrical Engineers or Application Supplement for Mechanical Engineers. It is therefore important to provide complete and accurate information. Failure to do so may delay the processing of the application or result in a lower than deserved score. Call any of the Commission offices if there are any problems or questions.

Applicants who do not pass the tests or who would like to try for a better score may be retested after six months during the life of this announcement. A new application and application supplement are required for a retest.

If these tests do not produce enough candidates for a particular geographic area, a testing program will be announced locally. That announcement will tell when and how to apply.

State or Municipal Exterminator

JOB DESCRIPTION

Under general supervision, performs work in the prevention, control, and elimination of insects, vermin, and other pests from buildings and surrounding areas; performs related work.

EXAMPLES OF TYPICAL TASKS

Inspects areas of infestation; selects and uses the most effective insecticides, rodenticides, baits, traps, etc., for exterminating pests as required; prepares poisonous insecticides, rodenticides, etc., used in exterminating; may prepare reports as required, including records of equipment usage, work schedules, and exterminating operations performed.

REQUIREMENTS

1. One year of satisfactory, full-time paid experience in the preparation, testing, or application of pesticides; or
2. Successful completion of a pesticide application course acceptable to the Department of Environmental Conservation for meeting the requirements for a Commercial Pesticide Applicator Certificate in Structural and Rodent Control.

Candidates who claim to meet the minimum requirements as described in (2) above (successful completion of a pesticide application course) *must* list the name of the course and the full name of the institution where the course was taken. All candidates will be required to possess a valid Commercial Pesticide Applicator Certificate in Structural and Rodent Control issued by the Department of Environmental Conservation within 18 months of the date of appointment.

TEST INFORMATION

There will be no competitive test other than an evaluation of your training and/or experience.

Training and Experience

Training and Experience test, weight 100. A score of at least 70 percent is needed in order to pass. The training and experience rating will be based on candidates' statements on the Experience Paper which must be filled out completely and in detail, including dates and number of hours worked per week. List and describe all vocational courses and experience for which credit may be given as described below. Training or experience will not be found acceptable unless it is verifiable. Training and experience listed on the Experience Paper will receive credit only to the extent that they are described clearly and in detail. A score of 70 percent will be given for meeting the minimum requirements.

After the minimum requirements are met, credit may be given for a maximum of an additional five years of experience on the following basis:

1. Up to two points, depending on quality, will be given for each year of full-time, paid experience in the preparation and testing of pesticides.
2. Up to four points, depending on quality, will be given for each year of full-time, paid experience in the application of pesticides.
3. Four points will be given for the successful completion of a pesticide application course acceptable to the Department of Environmental Conservation for meeting the requirements for a Commercial Pesticide Applicator Certificate in Structural and Rodent Control.
4. Six points will be given for the possession of a valid Commercial Pesticide Applicator Certificate in Structural and Rodent Control issued by the Department of Environmental Conservation.

Physical Test

Candidates will be required to satisfactorily complete the following physical test:

1. *Stair climb:* Eligibles will be required to walk/run up 81 steps (approximately 10 short flights of stairs) and return to the starting point within three minutes.
2. *Agility:* Eligibles will be required to rise from a supine position, scale a vault box 3 feet high, sprint 3 yards to a maze of obstacles, dodge through a tunnel approximately 4 yards in length, and sprint back approximately 10 yards to the finish line within 35 seconds.
3. *Wall climb:* Eligibles will be required to climb three steps to a foothold 44 inches high. The eligible must then step or climb over a 26-inch wall to a platform. The eligible must then descend to the ground by stepping or climbing back over the wall and climbing to the ground within two minutes.

Medical evidence to allow participation in the physical test may be required and the Department of Personnel reserves the right to exclude from the physical test eligibles who, upon examination of such evidence, are apparently medically unfit. Eligibles will take the physical test at their own risk of injury, although every effort will be made to safeguard them.

ADVANCEMENT

Employees in the title of Exterminator are accorded promotion opportunities, when eligible, to the title of Foreman (Exterminators).

State Laundry Washman and Supervisor
JOB DESCRIPTION

Laundry Washmen perform semi-skilled manual work in the operation of heavy-duty washing machines in a state laundry facility. They operate washing machines, extractors, conditioning tumblers, and dryers; use proper amounts of laundry chemicals; load machines; and keep the equipment and surrounding area clean.

Laundry Supervisors supervise the operation of a state laundry facility. They plan, direct, and coordinate laundry operations, requisition materials and supplies, arrange for repairs to equipment or machinery, and train others in work methods, safety hazards, and rules and regulations.

These jobs are in state hospitals and centers operated by the Department of Public Welfare throughout the state. The Department currently has 36 filled Laundry Washman jobs and 24 filled Laundry Supervisor jobs. A few job openings are expected during the coming year. In the past two years, there have been three appointments to Laundry Washman and seven to Laundry Supervisor. Contact the personnel office at the place where you want to work for more information on possible job openings.

REQUIREMENTS
For Laundry Washman:

1. One year as a Laundry Worker; or
2. One year of experience as a laundry worker or washman in a commercial or industrial laundry and completion of the eighth grade.

For Laundry Supervisor:

1. One year as a Laundry Washman; or
2. Three years of experience in the input, process, and output phases of a commercial or industrial laundry and high school graduation.

Equivalent combinations of experience and training are acceptable for both job titles. If you have enough experience to qualify, you don't need to have completed the schooling specified above. Please make sure you meet all requirements. If you are not sure if you qualify, contact one of the Commission's offices listed at the end of this announcement.

For both positions, applicants must be state residents and of good moral character. They must be willing to work under hot, humid, and noisy conditions, be exposed to unpleasant odors and soiled laundry, and be physically capable of lifting up to 35 pounds, bending, stooping, and standing for long periods. They may be required to pass a physical examination, including a test for color blindness, given by the hiring agency prior to appointment.

TEST INFORMATION

No written test is required. The test is a rating of experience and training. Applicants will receive a score based on their Application and Application Supplement. It is important to provide complete and accurate information. Failure to do so may delay the processing of the application or result in a lower-than-deserved score. Call any of the Commission's offices if there are any problems or questions.

Retests will not be allowed.

If these tests do not produce enough names for a localized area, another test may be announced for that area *only*.

Test Results

Employment and Promotion lists will be established. Applicants will be notified in writing of their test results.

State or Municipal Consumer Services Specialist Trainee

JOB DESCRIPTION

Consumer Services Specialist Trainees perform a variety of activities and tasks in connection with the investigations and resolution of consumer complaints against the investor-owned electric, steam, gas, telecommunications, and water utilities. These complaints include inadequate or substandard service, interruptions in service, disconnection of service, meter problems, billing problems, rate problems, deposit arrangements, deferred payment agreements, transferred balances, utility company policy, or other disputes requiring investigations and formal reply by the Department. They also discuss energy conservation matters with consumers and provide information on utility regulation.

Consumer Services Specialists Trainees also identify trends or problems in complaint handling which are investigated by staff in the Division of Consumer Services Policy and Compliance Section. Upon satisfactory completion of a one-year traineeship, they advance to the position of Consumer Services Specialist I without further examination.

REQUIREMENTS

On or before the date of the written test, candidates must meet the following requirements:

1. A minimum of two years of experience in any one or any combination of the following:
   a. Construction, inspection, repair, or testing of electric or gas meters
   b. Testing gas for heat content and purity
   c. Telephone plant construction, maintenance, or operation
   d. Telephone commercial or traffic operations
   e. Drafting or analyzing utility billing statements
   f. Satisfactory equivalent combination of such experience; or
2. Graduation from a two-year technical institute or college with an associate's degree in electronics, electrical technology, instrument technology, engineering technology, computer technology, or applied science; or
3. Completion of two years of a four-year engineering or engineering technology course; or
4. A satisfactory equivalent combination of the above training experience.

TEST INFORMATION

There will be a *written test* and an *oral test*. Candidates must pass both in order to be considered for appointment. Only candidates who pass the written test will be notified to appear for the oral test. The Department of Civil Service reserves the right to call to the oral test only that number of successful written test candidates necessary to fill existing and anticipated positions. Only passing scores on the written test will be used in computing final scores.

Scope of Written Test

The written test will be designed to test for knowledge, skills, and/or abilities in such areas as:

1. Understanding and interpreting tabular material
2. Understanding and interpreting written material
3. Reading of meters, scales, and gauges
4. Evaluating conclusions in the light of known facts
5. Basic interviewing

Scope of Oral Test

The oral test will be designed to evaluate, against the background of the position, the ability to:

1. Identify and deal effectively with consumer problems
2. Communicate orally
3. Establish satisfactory relationships with others in a complaint-oriented situation

State or Municipal Bus Maintainer

JOB DESCRIPTION

Maintain, inspect, test, alter, and repair the electrical, mechanical, hydraulic, pneumatic, and air-conditioning equipment of buses, trucks, and other automotive vehicles.

EXAMPLES OF TYPICAL TASKS

Inspect, test, alter, and repair diesel and gasoline engines, clutches, transmissions, axles, generators, compressors, air-conditioning systems, brake assemblies, and electrical accessories. Diagnose troubles and irregularities and make the necessary repairs and adjustments. Align wheels and repair steering equipment. Reline and adjust brakes and clutches. Operate power machine tools and portable power tools and use hand tools as required to rebuild and repair automotive components. If assigned, perform inspection work on new equipment and material at manufacturing plants. Record data and keep records.

REQUIREMENTS

Candidates must meet one of the following requirements:

1. Four years of full-time paid experience at the mechanic (journeyman) level repairing passenger automobiles, trucks, buses, or aircraft, including engines, transmissions, brakes, electrical systems, and automotive air conditioning; or
2. Three years of full-time paid experience at the mechanic (journeyman) level as described above, plus graduation from a recognized trade high school, vocational high school, or community college with a major sequence of courses of study in auto mechanics or a closely related field.

On the Experience Paper, applicants must indicate which of the two alternative requirements described above they are presenting for qualification.

The following types of experience are *not* acceptable: auto body and fender mechanic, auto or truck assembly line mechanic, dealership "make-ready" mechanic, gas station attendant, specialty replacement shop mechanic, salvage and junkyard mechanic.

License

At the time of appointment, eligibles must possess a valid state driver's license. Eligibles must also possess, at the time of the appointment interview, either a commercial driver's license or a valid learner's permit for a commercial driver's license. Eligibles will be appointed subject to the receipt of a commercial driver's license at the end of a special training course. Serious moving violations, license suspensions, or accident record may be cause for disqualification.

TEST INFORMATION

This examination will consist of four parts: a competitive education and experience test, a qualifying written test, a qualifying medical test, and a qualifying physical test. Information on each of the four parts is given below. Candidates must pass all parts to be eligible for employment.

Competitive Education and Experience Test

Weight 100, 70 percent required. There will be no competitive test other than an evaluation of education and experience. After the minimum requirements have been met, additional credit will be given, as stated in the rating key below, for a maximum of 10 additional years of full-time paid experience at the mechanic (journeyman) level, as described in the minimum requirements, or as a supervisor of such mechanics. Education and experience rating will be based on candidate's statements on the Experience Paper, which must be filled out completely and in detail, including names and addresses of employers, dates, salary, and number of hours per week worked for all claimed relevant experience; and including full details of all claimed relevant education. Candidates must list all education and experience for which credit may be given as described below. Once a candidate has filed an application, the candidate will not be permitted to add additional education and experience for purposes of having such education and experience evaluated beyond the minimum requirements.

Education and experience will not be found acceptable unless they are verifiable. Education and experience listed on the Experience Paper will receive credit only to the extent that they are described clearly and in detail.

Rating Key

A rating of 70 percent will be granted for meeting the minimum requirements as stated above. After the minimum requirements have been met, experience for a maximum of 10 additional years will be credited as follows:

1. Two points per year for each additional year of full-time paid experience at the mechanic (journeyman) level as described in minimum requirements above.
2. Three points per year for each additional year of full-time paid experience as a supervisor of those performing the duties described in minimum requirements above.

In addition, candidates who have full-time paid experience at the mechanic (journeyman) level repairing diesel engines on buses, trucks, or other automotive equipment, will receive an additional two points per year for each year of such experience. For mechanic or supervisory experience, credit will be given to the nearest full quarter of a year.

The maximum rating in this Education and Experience test is 100 percent.

Qualifying Written Test

Minimum of 70 percent required. Prior to appointment, eligibles will be required to pass a multiple-choice qualifying test. This test may include questions on safe, proper, and efficient work practices related to maintenance operations in a bus repair shop; proper selection and safe use of hand tools, power tools, and machinery, as required for the performance of work related to bus maintenance and repair; technical knowledge and ability to perform maintenance, repair, and trouble-shooting of engines, transmissions, chassis, running gear, air conditioning, and electrical and mechanical accessories as used in buses, trucks, and other vehicles; reading and interpreting specifications and drawings and performing related mathematical calculations; record keeping; and other related areas.

Candidates who fail the qualifying written test will not be permitted to file again for this examination until at least six months after the date on which they take and fail such qualifying written test.

Qualifying Medical Test

Eligibles will be required to pass a qualifying medical test. Rejection will be based on determination by the examining physician that a condition will interfere with the eligible's ability to engage in the activities performed in this class of positions.

Qualifying Physical Test

Medical evidence to allow participation in the qualifying physical test may be required, and the Department of Personnel reserves the right to exclude from the physical test eligibles who, upon examination of such evidence, are apparently medically unfit. Eligibles will take the physical test at their own risk of injury, although every effort will be made to safeguard them.

The qualifying physical test will consist of two subtests. In one subtest, eligibles will be required to squat without falling and without using any support to keep from falling and to rise to an erect position without falling and without using any support to keep from falling. In the second subtest, eligibles will be required to lift a 50-pound barbell off the floor, raise it to a stop position at shoulder level by bending the arms, press it over the head to a vertical, fully-extended arm position, return it to a stop position at shoulder level by bending the arms, and put the barbell back on the floor. All lifting of the 50-pound barbell must be done under full control and solely by the eligible's sheer muscular effort.

State or Municipal Life Actuaries
JOB DESCRIPTION

Senior Actuaries (Life) assist higher level actuaries in checking actuarial reserve formulae and calculations of net premiums and reserves for life insurance, retirement benefits, annuities, disability, and double indemnity life insurance, and life insurance departments of savings banks under the jurisdiction of the Insurance Department. They also prepare statistical tables in the development of trends of reserves, and check methods and calculations of approximations employed for special reserve liabilities.

Associate Actuaries (Life) in the Department of Audit and Control are responsible for planning and developing difficult projects and studies. These could include such areas as development of funding procedures to match the expanding benefit structure, continuing analyses of the actuarial gains and/or losses of the systems' operations, and formulating applications of new actuarial concepts to the existing systems. In the Insurance Department, they recommend solutions to difficult actuarial problems connected with valuation of reserves; assist in the preparation of valuation reports covering methods, procedures, and accuracy of reserve valuations submitted by domestic life insurance companies; analyze mortality experience; and examine adequacy of premium rates for life insurance and annuities. They also assist in investigation and studies of problems of reserves, annual statements, policy forms, rates, and other matters.

Principal Actuaries (Life) perform actuarial studies in various phases of life insurance and retirement systems. These studies include the testing of the effectiveness of current department regulations and consideration of the need for modification of such regulations and/or the addition of new regulations. They determine proper reserve bases for life insurance annuities, disability benefits, accidental death benefits, and contingent liabilities of life insurance companies and fraternal societies. They review proposals by domestic life insurance companies to revise their valuation procedures to provide for the application of electronic data processing equipment for upgrading of such equipment at their home offices. They also review policy forms for actuarial compliance with the Insurance Law and regulations concerning credit life insurance, minimum cash values, and guidelines concerning wholesale insurance, and determine the reasonableness of accident and health rates.

Supervising Actuaries (Life) supervise the Actuarial Bureau staff in the annual review of reserve valuation of domestic life companies and the fraternal societies and supervise the adherence to regulations pertaining to life insurance, particularly credit life. They review studies of experience and recommend new regulations and modification of current regulations, supervise the actuarial review of policy forms, and assist in establishing actuarial guidelines. Concerning nonprofit hospital and medical corporations, they review and approve premium rates and experience rating formulas. They also recommend approval of employee benefits programs, assist in providing actuarial considerations for policy decisions to be made by the superintendent, and assist in the actuarial review of proposed legislation.

REQUIREMENTS

Candidates must meet the following requirements:

For Senior Actuary:

1. Successful completion of 3 of the 10 parts of the examination of the Society of Actuaries; and
2. One year of full-time paid experience in professional actuarial work.

For Associate Actuary:

1. Successful completion of 4 of the 10 parts of the examination of the Society of Actuaries; and
2. Two years of full-time paid experience in professional actuarial work.

For Principal Actuary:

1. Successful completion of 6 of the 10 parts of the examination of the Society of Actuaries; and
2. Three years of full-time paid experience in professional actuarial work of which one year shall have been in one or more of the following: directing actuarial computations for regular and special policy forms as to premium rates, reserves, and nonforfeiture values of life insurance policies or annuities; independently investigating and drawing professionally sound conclusions regarding such actuarial problems as approximate reserve methods, valuation procedure, or determination of special reserve items; and drafting, or directing the drafting of, policy forms, riders, and/or endorsements for adoption.

For Supervising Actuary:

1. Successful completion of 8 of the 10 parts of the examination of the Society of Actuaries; and
2. Four years of full-time paid experience in professional actuarial work of which two years shall have been in one or more of the following: directing and drawing professionally sound conclusions from studies concerning mortality experience and expense analyses; responsibility for determining the specific liability items to be reported in the annual statements of life insurance companies, retirement systems, fraternal societies, etc.; responsibility for correspondence with official governmental regulatory agencies or insurance companies regarding actuarial aspects of life insurance contracts or methods, policy changes, dividends, net costs, procedures, reinstatements, etc.; responsibility for the calculation of reserve liabilities including the determination of insurance in force, valuation standards, methods of valuation; and preparation of written reports including conclusions and recommendations on methods, standards, and results of actuarial investigations.

TEST INFORMATION

There is no written test. The training and experience of those applicants who meet the minimum qualifications will be evaluated against the general background of the position(s). It is essential, therefore, that you give complete and accurate information on your application.

FOUR

Examination Preparation

CONTENTS

HOW TO PREPARE YOURSELF FOR CIVIL SERVICE EXAMINATIONS

When you receive a notice in the mail telling you when and where to take your civil service exam, you should feel a certain amount of satisfaction, even optimism. The fact that you're scheduled for a test indicates your application passed the initial screening and met the minimum requirements for the job. That alone is a huge hurdle, and now you're over it.

However, in a certain way, this accomplishment can bring with it even *more* fear. What if you do poorly on the test? What if you do well, but someone else does better? What if this is your one big chance at civil service work—and you blow it? Before, the process seemed impersonal. If you weren't called for a test, you could give yourself any number of explanations—from an application that was never delivered or that fell behind a filing cabinet, to a screening clerk who overlooked something and mistakenly thought your application was incomplete. But, if anything goes wrong at this point, you might think, the fault can only be laid at one doorstep.

Take a deep breath. Now release.

While no one can *guarantee* you a job-winning score on the exam—and beware anyone who does—there are steps you *can* take to improve your performance. This book is one of them. Over the past seven chapters, you've been learning about the process of finding civil service employment and putting together the kind of application that will get you noticed. Now you'll find out in more detail about the civil service tests themselves. The format of the tests will be explained, and you'll get actual samples—each with an answer key and explanations to the answers.

Whoever said *"Familiarity breeds contempt"* wasn't talking about test-taking. In the world of tests, familiarity breeds *better scores*. Just knowing what to expect improves your performance. Taking the test several times also improves your performance. That's why so many college-bound high-schoolers take college entrance exams over and over again. Very often these aren't poor students who do so miserably on the exams that they must retake them. These are students who get competitive scores the first time, but know that the second time they are likely to score even higher. And they want those few extra points of competitive edge.

On the civil service exam, a few points more or less can mean the difference between getting the job and not getting the job. It may seem unfair, but it's true. And it's certainly fairer than having Uncle Joe hire his nephew. However, this book is *your* "first chance" to take the test and familiarize yourself with it—*your* chance to improve your performance and gain the competitive edge.

Understanding the Exam Announcement

The announcement already told you the kind of competitive exam you'll be taking—whether it's an assembled or an unassembled test. Reminder: An *assembled* test means that the applicants assemble at the same time and in the same place to take the exam; it might be a written test, a performance test, or a combination of the two. The written test is usually in a multiple-choice format. An *unassembled* test means, essentially, that there is no test. This is a common procedure for the more professional positions that require experience and/or an advanced degree. In an unassembled test, you're given a competitive score, based on the application form detailing your work history, whatever education or training you've had (and sometimes must provide proof of), and the Life Experience Paper, if requested, by a screening panel. This competitive score functions as your test score and it's used to rank you against other applicants for the job. Some positions require a written test, physical test, a grade based on your education and training, and a Life Experience Paper.

Obviously, for all exams, the better your score the better your chance of being appointed. Tests are usually rated on a scale of 100, with 70 as the usual passing grade. If not, the announcement will explain the scoring.

The announcement also explains what areas will be covered on the test. For example, the announcement for clerk typist said that the written test would cover name and number checking, sorting file material, alphabetizing, taking telephone messages, following directions, capitalization/punctuation, grammar, effective expression, spelling, and arithmetic operations. The announcement for bus maintainer said that the qualifying physical test would consist of two subtests. In one subtest, eligibles will be required to squat without falling and without using any support to keep from falling, then rise to an erect position without falling and without using any support to keep from falling. In the second subtest, eligibles will be required to lift a 50-pound barbell off the floor, raise it to a stop position at shoulder level by bending the arms, press it over the head to a vertical, fully-extended arm position, return it to a stop position at shoulder level by bending the arms, and put the barbell back on the floor. All lifting of the 50-pound barbell must be done under full control and solely by the eligible's sheer muscular effort.

In addition to specifying what the test covers, sometimes the announcement includes a few sample questions.

Some Questions (and Answers!) About the Exam

By now, *you* probably have a few questions. Here are answers to the most common ones:

"CAN I STUDY FOR THE CIVIL SERVICE TEST?"

No, you can't study in the traditional sense, like in school, where you memorized facts. But, you *can* prepare in three simple ways:

- **Take sample tests.** This is an ideal way to prepare yourself. The more samples you complete, the more comfortable you'll feel with the actual test. Take the sample tests under "normal" test conditions— that is, find a quiet table or desk and time yourself, using only as much time as the directions allow.
- **Increase the amount you read every day, especially nonfiction.** Your reading ability is crucial since your ability to understand the test questions determines whether or not you'll answer them correctly. Be an active reader. *Think* about what you've read. Underline and look up any words you don't understand.
- **Practice the physical test.** The announcement will provide details: so many push-ups to be done, so many stairs to be climbed within limited time, so many pounds to be carried, etc.

"SHOULD I GUESS?"

Whether you should guess or not depends on the particular test, or the particular section of the test. In most cases, the answer is *yes;* it's to your benefit to guess. Here's why:

Most sections in civil service exams only score every *correct* answer. You're not penalized for wrong answers, you just don't receive any credit for them. So a guess can't hurt you, and you have a one-in-four or one-in-five chance of getting lucky and getting a higher score. If you leave an answer blank, you're losing a risk-free opportunity to add points. Of course, if you can make an educated guess, so much the better. The best way to make an educated guess is to eliminate those answers you definitely know to be wrong. Narrow down the field of possible answers, and you increase your chances of getting the right answer. Even if you can only eliminate one choice, your odds are one in three; eliminate two choices, and your odds become one in two or fifty/fifty.

CAUTION: While *most* sections of exams don't penalize for wrong answers, some might. For example, part of the Federal Clerical Exam and parts of some postal exams penalize wrong answers. That means that the number of wrong answers is subtracted from the number of right answers. However, sometimes only a portion (one-fourth, for instance) of the wrong answers is subtracted from the number of correct answers. Whenever there is a penalty for wrong answers, don't rush to fill in answers, especially at the end when time is running out. When you're being penalized for wrong answers and you can't make any kind of educated guess, a blank answer may be better.

"HOW WILL I KNOW IF A TEST PENALIZES WRONG ANSWERS?"

The printed instructions at the beginning of the exam should tell you if there's a penalty for wrong answers or for guessing. If you're not sure, ask the proctor. You're entitled to have this information.

"IF TESTS ARE RATED ON A PERFECT SCORE OF 100, DOES THAT MEAN I HAVE TO ANSWER 100 QUESTIONS? HOW CAN I DO THAT WITH A TIME LIMIT?"

In some cases, you might even have to answer *more* than 100 questions. Most exams don't have exactly 100 questions. Regardless of how many questions you have to answer, your score will often be reported on a scale of 0 to 100. All this means is that when you have fewer than 100 questions, your answers will be worth more points. When you have more than 100 questions, correct answers will be worth fewer points.

"WHAT'S THE SINGLE MOST IMPORTANT TIP FOR GETTING A GOOD SCORE?"

Read carefully. This is the single greatest factor that determines whether you choose the right answer or the wrong one. If the directions for an entire section say to choose the word that means the *opposite* of the underlined word, and you choose the word that means the *same* as the underlined word, you'll mark wrong answers for a whole series of questions. If the directions tell you to "Mark (D) if all the names being compared are *alike*," and you mark (D) when all the names are *different*, you'll drastically—and needlessly—lower your score. There's no doubt that you know the meaning of *opposite* and *same*, *alike* and *different*. But under the pressure and stress of taking the exam, you may automatically do the opposite—like pointing left when you mean right.

Read the directions carefully. Pay close attention to qualifying words like *most, least, only, best, probably, definitely, not, all, every,* and *except.* They're often the key to "pointing right" when you mean right.

Then read everything else carefully too. Even arithmetic problems have directions for each section, and word problems—well, you get it.

How to Give Yourself the Edge Taking Civil Service Examinations

By the time you finish this book and take all of the practice exams, you should feel confident in your ability to do well on "the real thing." If you want extra practice, retake the exams in this book, using a blank piece of paper for your answers. Or buy one of the books that focus exclusively on a single type of exam.

Some key points to remember:

- **Be an active reader every day.** Whether you've already received notice of your exam date or haven't even applied yet and have just skipped to this chapter—begin today to be an active reader. Read more nonfiction. Question what you read. Look up words you dohn't know.
- **Practice those parts of the test that you can.** Guides like this will help you with the written tests. If you have a physical test coming up, find out what you'll have to do and practice those activities. If you're not sure which job you'll be applying for, skim the announcements for similar positions and practice those activities.

And on the day of the test:

- **Make an educated guess when there's no penalty for wrong answers.** If you don't know from the test booklet whether you'll be penalized or not, ask the proctor.
- **Skim, underline, then read.** Remember that three-point approach to handling reading-based questions.
- **Read carefully.** Understanding the directions and the questions is essential to getting a better score.
- **Relax.** Other people have taken this test and passed, people who are no better than you and who were just as anxious at the time. Breathe deep and tell yourself that you can do this—because you really can.

And good luck!

PREPARING FOR MULTIPLE-CHOICE TESTS

All multiple-choice tests consist of a question booklet or booklets and a separate answer sheet. The question booklets begin with general instructions for taking the test. It's here that you'll learn the rules and regulations governing your exam, number of questions, timing, signals, etc. If there are specific directions for different types of questions, you will find these in the question booklet before each new type of question.

You may usually write in the question booklet. So, you can put a question mark next to the number of a question you want to return to, calculate the answers to math questions, cross out eliminated answer choices, underline key words, or even just plain doodle in the margins. The one thing you must *not* do with a question booklet is use it as an answer sheet. If you aren't allowed to write in the test booklet, you can use scratch paper for figuring and for writing notes to yourself about guesses and when time will run out on each part of the exam. The scratch paper will be collected but it will *NOT* be scored.

Your answers *must* be on the separate answer sheet in order to be counted and scored. It's the only record that's kept. Mark every answer in the correct place on the answer sheet. Mark your answer choice by blackening its circle darkly and completely. A correct answer response looks like this: ● .

Here are some examples of incorrectly marked responses: ⊘⊗⊗ .

The scoring machine might not notice these marks. If your answer isn't registered by the scoring machine, you can't get any credit for it. You must mark only one answer for each question. If there's more than one answer marked for any question, even if one of the answers is correct, the machine will give no credit for that question. It is possible to change your mind and change your answer. However, when you change an answer, you must be careful to fully and cleanly erase the first answer. And mark your new choice with extra care. You don't want the scoring machine to misread your choice. Never cross out an answer in favor of a new choice. You must erase. Ⓐ⊗Ⓒ● will not work. The machine will read both old and new answers and will give you no credit.

Another very important aspect of working with the separate answer sheet is to mark every question in the right place. The scoring machine doesn't read question number and answer choice. The machine only scans the page for a pattern of blackened spaces. If you've marked an answer in the wrong place, it will be scored as wrong (unless, of course, the same letter was coincidentally the correct answer for the space in which you made your mark). If you notice that you've slipped out of line, erase all your answers from the point of the error and redo all of those questions. While you'll usually have adequate time, it's not unlimited; you can't waste it erasing and reanswering large blocks of questions. Furthermore, an error of this type may fluster you and lead to errors of judgment in later questions. What's worse, if you misplace a question and don't catch your error, every answer from then on could be wrong. Positions and promotions have been lost for this reason. Even if you inspect your answer sheet later, as you're allowed to do, and you discover a skipped line and the following block of answers wrong, the grade won't be changed. There's no definite way to prove that you did indeed miss a line rather than simply leave one blank and answer the rest wrong.

For these reasons, it's best not to skip any questions. Some people will look for easy questions to answer first. If you can do this without losing your place, fine. But if you have any doubts, don't do it. Answer the questions one by one. Unless you're being penalized for wrong answers, don't omit a question.

The questions on multiple-choice exams consist of the question itself and four or five answer choices. The answer choices are lettered A through D or E. On the answer sheet next to each number are lettered circles. Each question has one BEST answer. You must read the question carefully, think, choose the best answer, and blacken the circle that contains the letter of that answer. This method of answering is much easier than filling in a blank or circling a portion of a sentence or paragraph. Provided that you mark your answers neatly, there is no room for scoring error in marking a multiple-choice answer sheet. You can be sure of accuracy and objectivity.

Directions are always written and must be read. Furthermore, a large proportion of questions are either reading comprehension/interpretation questions or are questions that are based upon material that the test-taker must read. Since reading is so key to success with multiple-choice questions, we're devoting a large part of this chapter to reading and reading-based questions and will tackle those sample questions first. Once you've mastered the techniques of dealing with reading-based questions, you will be well-equipped to tackle all aspects of your civil service exam.

Reading-Based Questions

Some exams include classic reading-comprehension questions that present a passage and then ask questions on the details of the passage and, perhaps, on its meaning. Other exams require candidates to indicate proper behavior based on their reading of printed procedures and regulations. Still another type of reading-based question requires candidates to reason and choose next steps on the basis of information presented in a reading passage. There are, of course, nearly as many variations of the reading-based question as there are test-makers. In fact, reading skill enters into form-completion questions, arithmetic problems based on fact situations, and judgment questions as well.

Before you begin to devote attention to strategies for dealing with reading-based questions, give some thought to your present reading habits and skills. Of course, you already know how to read. But how well do you read? Do you concentrate? Do you get the point on your first reading? Do you notice details?

Between now and the test day, work to improve your reading concentration and comprehension. Your daily newspaper provides excellent material for this. Make a point of reading all the way through any article that you begin. Do not be satisfied with the first paragraph or two. Read with a pencil in hand. Underscore details and ideas that seem to be crucial to the meaning of the article. Notice points of view, arguments, and supporting information. When you have finished the article, summarize it for yourself. Do you know the purpose of the article? The main idea presented? The attitude of the writer? The points over which there is controversy? Did you find certain information lacking? As you answer these questions, skim back over your underlinings. Did you focus on important words and ideas? Did you read with comprehension? As you repeat this process day after day, you'll find that your reading will become more efficient. You will read with greater understanding and will get more from your newspaper.

One aspect of your daily reading that deserves special attention is vocabulary building. The effective reader has a rich, extensive vocabulary. As you read, make a list of unfamiliar words. Also include in your list words that you understand within the context of the article, but that you cannot really define. When you put aside your newspaper, go to the dictionary and look up *every* new and unfamiliar word. Write the word and its definition in a special notebook. Writing the words and their definitions helps seal them in your memory far better than just reading them, and the notebook serves as a handy reference for your own use.

Success with reading-based questions depends on more than comprehension. You must also know how to draw the answers from the reading selection and be able to distinguish the *best* answer from a number of answers that all seem to be good ones, or from a number of answers that all seem to be wrong.

Strange as it may seem, it's a good idea to approach reading comprehension questions by reading the questions first. *Not the answer choices,* just the questions themselves. The questions will alert you to look for certain details, ideas, and points of view *while* you read. Use your pencil. Underscore key words in the questions. These will help direct your attention as you read.

Next, skim the selection very rapidly to get an idea of its subject matter and its organization. If key words or ideas pop out at you, underline them, but do not consciously search out details in the preliminary skimming.

Now read the selection carefully, with comprehension as your main goal. Underscore the important words as you have been doing in your newspaper reading.

Finally, return to the questions. Read each one carefully. Be sure you know what it asks. Misreading of questions is a major cause of error on reading-comprehension tests. Read *all* the answer choices. Eliminate the obviously incorrect answers. You may be left with only one possible answer. If you find yourself with more than one possible answer, reread the question. Pay attention to catch words that might destroy the validity of a seemingly acceptable answer. These include expressions like *under all circumstances, at all times, never, always, under no condition, absolutely, entirely,* and *except when.* Then skim the passage once more, focusing on the underlined segments. By now you should be able to conclude which answer is *best.*

Reading-based questions may take a number of different forms. In general, some of the most common forms are as follows:

1. **Question of fact or detail.** You may have to mentally rephrase or rearrange, but you should find the answer stated in the body of the selection.
2. **Best title or main idea.** The answer may be obvious, but the incorrect choices to the "main idea" question are often half-truths that are easily confused with the main idea. They may misstate the idea, omit part of the idea, or even offer a supporting idea quoted directly from the text. The correct answer is the one that covers the largest part of the selection.
3. **Interpretation.** This type of question asks you what the selection means, not just what it says. On police exams, questions based upon definitions of crimes, for example, fall into this category. On firefighter exams, questions based upon categories of building styles might fall into the realm of interpretation.
4. **Inference.** This is the most difficult type of reading comprehension question. It asks you to go beyond what the selection says to predict what might happen next. You might have to choose the best course of action to take, based upon given procedures and a fact situation, or you may have to judge the actions of others—what are they likely to do next? Your answer must be based upon the information in the selection and your own common sense, but not upon any other information you may have about the subject. A variation of the inference question might be stated as, "The author would expect that . . ." To answer this question, you must understand the author's point of view, then make an inference from that viewpoint based upon the information in the selection.
5. **Vocabulary.** Some civil service reading sections, directly or indirectly, ask the meanings of certain words as used in the selection.

Let's now work together on some typical reading-comprehension selections and questions.

READING SELECTION FOR QUESTIONS 1 TO 4

For this first selection, just read but do not answer the questions yet.

The recipient gains an impression of a typewritten letter before beginning to read the message. Factors that give a good first impression include margins and spacing that are visually pleasing, formal parts of the letter that are correctly placed according to the style of the letter, copy that is free of obvious erasures and overstrikes, and transcript that is even and clear. The problem for the typist is how to produce that first, positive impression.

There are several general rules that a typist can follow when he or she wishes to prepare a properly spaced letter on a sheet of letterhead. The width of a letter should ordinarily not be less than four inches, nor more than six inches. The side margins should also have a proportionate relation to the bottom margin, as well as the space between the letterhead and the body of the letter. Usually the most appealing arrangement is when the side margins are even, and the bottom margin is slightly wider than the side margins. In some offices, however, a standard line length is used for all business letters, and the secretary then varies the spacing between the date line and the inside address according to the length of the letter.

1. The best title for the preceding paragraph is
   (A) Writing Office Letters
   (B) Making Good First Impressions
   (C) Judging Well-Typed Letters
   (D) Good Placing and Spacing for Office Letters

   1. Ⓐ Ⓑ Ⓒ Ⓓ

2. According to the preceding paragraphs, which of the following might be considered the way that people quickly judge the quality of work that has been typed?
   (A) by measuring the margins to see if they are correct
   (B) by looking at the spacing and cleanliness of the typescript
   (C) by scanning the body of the letter for meaning
   (D) by reading the date line and address for errors

   2. Ⓐ Ⓑ Ⓒ Ⓓ

3. According to the preceding paragraphs, what would be definitely undesirable as the average line length of a typed letter?
   (A) 4 inches
   (B) 5 inches
   (C) 6 inches
   (D) 7 inches

   3. Ⓐ Ⓑ Ⓒ Ⓓ

4. According to the preceding paragraphs, when the line length is kept standard, the secretary
   (A) does not have to vary the spacing at all because this also is standard.
   (B) adjusts the spacing between the date line and inside address for different lengths of letters.
   (C) uses the longest line as a guideline for spacing between the date line and inside address.
   (D) varies the number of spaces between the lines.

   4. Ⓐ Ⓑ Ⓒ Ⓓ

Okay. The next time you'll begin by first skimming just the questions and underscoring key words. Go back and do that now. Your underscored questions should look more or less like this:

1. The best title for the preceding paragraphs is . . .
2. According to the preceding paragraphs, which of the following might be considered the way that people quickly judge the quality of work that has been typed?
3. According to the preceding paragraphs, what would be definitely undesirable as the average line length of a typed letter?
4. According to the preceding paragraphs, when the line length is kept standard, the secretary . . .

After you skim the questions, you'll then skim the selection. This quick reading should give you an idea of the structure of the selection and of its overall meaning. Go back and skim the selection now.

Next go back and read the selection carefully. Underscore words that seem important or that you think hold keys to the question answers. Your underscored selection should look something like this:

The recipient gains an impression of a typewritten letter before beginning to read the message. Factors that give a good first impression include margins and spacing that are visually pleasing, formal parts of the letter that are correctly placed according to the style of letter, copy that is free of obvious erasures and overstrikes, and transcript that is even and clear. The problem for the typist is how to produce that first, positive impression.

There are several general rules that a typist can follow when he or she wishes to prepare a properly spaced letter on a sheet of letterhead. The width of a letter should ordinarily not be less than four inches, nor more than six inches. The side margins should also have a proportionate relation to the bottom margin, as well as the space between the letterhead and the body of the letter. Usually the most appealing arrangement is when the side margins are even, and the bottom margin is slightly wider than the side margins. In some offices, however, a standard line length is used for all business letters, and the secretary then varies the spacing between the date line and the inside address according to the length of the letter.

Finally, read the questions and answer choices, and try to choose the correct answer for each question. The correct answers are: 1. **(D)**, 2. **(B)**, 3. **(D)**, 4. **(B)**. Did you get them all right? Whether you made any errors or not, read these explanations.

1. **(D)** The best title for any selection is the one that takes in all of the ideas presented without being too broad or too narrow. Choice (D) provides the most inclusive title for this passage. A look at the other choices shows you why. Choice (A) can be eliminated because the passage discusses typing a letter, not writing one. Although the first paragraph states that a letter should make a good first impression, the passage is clearly devoted to the letter, not the first impression, so choice (B) can be eliminated. Choice (C) puts the emphasis on the wrong aspect of the typewritten letter. The passage concerns how to type a properly spaced letter, not how to judge one.

2. **(B)** Both spacing and cleanliness are mentioned in paragraph 1 as ways to judge the quality of a typed letter. The first paragraph states that the margins should be "visually pleasing" in relation to the body of the letter, but that does not imply margins of a particular measure, so choice (A) is incorrect. Meaning is not discussed in the passage, only the look of the finished letter, so choice (C) is incorrect. The passage makes no mention of errors, only the avoidance of erasures and overstrikes, so choice (D) is incorrect.

3. **(D)** This answer comes from the information provided in paragraph 2, that the width of a letter "should not be less than four inches nor more than six inches." According to this rule, seven inches is an undesirable line length.

4. **(B)** The answer to this question is stated in the last sentence of the reading passage. When a standard line length is used, the secretary "varies the spacing between the date line and the inside address according to the length of the letter." The passage offers no support for any other choice.

Let's try another.

READING SELECTION FOR QUESTIONS 5 TO 9

First skip down to the questions below the next paragraph and underscore the words which you consider to be key. Then come back and skim the reading selection to get an idea of the subject matter and how it is organized. Then finally read the selection carefully and underscore the words that you think are especially important. Do not answer the questions yet.

Cotton fabrics treated with XYZ Process have features that make them far superior to any previously known flame-retardant-treated cotton fabrics. XYZ Process treated fabrics endure repeated laundering and dry cleaning; are glow resistant as well as flame resistant; when exposed to flames or intense heat form tough, pliable, and protective chars; are inert physiologically to persons handling or exposed to the fabric; are only slightly heavier than untreated fabrics; and are susceptible to further wet and dry finishing treatments. In addition, the treated fabrics exhibit little or no adverse change in feel, texture, and appearance, and are shrink-, rot-, and mildew-resistant. The treatment reduces strength only slightly. Finished fabrics have "easy care" properties in that they are wrinkle resistant and dry rapidly.

5. It is most accurate to state that the author in the preceding selection presents   5. Ⓐ Ⓑ Ⓒ Ⓓ
   (A) facts but reaches no conclusion concerning the value of the process.
   (B) a conclusion concerning the value of the process and facts to support that conclusion.
   (C) a conclusion concerning the value of the process unsupported by facts.
   (D) neither facts nor conclusions, but merely describes the process.

6. Of the following articles, for which is the XYZ Process most suitable?   6. Ⓐ Ⓑ Ⓒ Ⓓ
   (A) nylon stockings
   (B) woolen shirt
   (C) silk tie
   (D) cotton bedsheet

7. Of the following aspects of the XYZ Process, which is *not* discussed in the preceding selection?   7. Ⓐ Ⓑ Ⓒ Ⓓ
   (A) costs
   (B) washability
   (C) wearability
   (D) the human body

8. The main reason for treating a fabric with XYZ Process is to   8. Ⓐ Ⓑ Ⓒ Ⓓ
   (A) prepare the fabric for other wet and dry finishing treatment.
   (B) render it shrink-, rot-, and mildew-resistant.
   (C) increase its weight and strength.
   (D) reduce the chance that it will catch fire.

9. Which of the following would be considered a minor drawback of the XYZ process   9. Ⓐ Ⓑ Ⓒ Ⓓ
   (A) it forms chars when exposed to flame
   (B) it makes fabrics mildew-resistant
   (C) it adds to the weight of fabrics
   (D) it is compatible with other finishing treatments

Did you skim your questions first? They should look something like this:

5. It is the most accurate to state that the author, in the preceding selection, <u>presents</u>
6. Of the following articles, for which is the <u>XYZ Process most suitable</u>?
7. Of the following <u>aspects</u> of the XYZ Process, which is *not* <u>discussed</u> in the preceding selection?
8. The <u>main reason for treating</u> a fabric with the XYZ Process is to
9. Which of the following would be considered a <u>minor drawback</u> of the XYZ Process?

After you read and underlined, this fact-filled selection might look something like this:

Cotton fabrics treated with XYZ Process have features that make them far superior to any previously known flame-retardant-treated cotton fabrics. XYZ Process treated fabrics endure repeated laundering and dry cleaning; are glow resistant as well as flame resistant; when exposed to flames or intense heat form tough, pliable, and protective chars; are inert physiologically to persons handling or exposed to the fabric; are only slightly heavier than untreated fabrics; and are susceptible to further wet and dry finishing treatments. In addition, the treated fabrics exhibit little or no adverse change in feel, texture, and appearance, and are shrink-, rot-, and mildew-resistant. The treatment reduces strength only slightly. Finished fabrics have "easy care" properties in that they are wrinkle resistant and dry rapidly.

Now go back and read each question and all its answer choices, then try to choose the correct answer for each question.

The correct answers are: 5. **(B)**, 6. **(D)**, 7. **(A)**, 8. **(D)**, 9. **(C)**. How did you do on these? Read the explanations.

5. **(B)** This is a combination main idea and interpretation question. If you cannot answer this question readily, reread the selection. The author clearly thinks that the XYZ Process is terrific and says so in the first sentence. The rest of the selection presents a wealth of facts to support the initial claim.

6. **(D)** At first glance you might think that this is an inference question requiring you to make a judgment based upon the few drawbacks of the process. Closer reading, however, shows you that there is no contest for correct answer here. This is a simple question of fact. The XYZ Process is a treatment for cotton fabrics.

7. **(A)** Your underlinings should help you with this question of fact. Cost is not mentioned; all other aspects of the XYZ Process are. If you are having trouble finding mention of the effect of the XYZ Process on the human body, add to your vocabulary list "inert" and "physiologically."

8. **(D)** This is a main idea question. You must distinguish between the main idea and the supporting and incidental facts.

9. **(C)** Obviously a drawback is a negative feature. The selection mentions only two negative features. The treatment reduces strength slightly, and it makes fabrics slightly heavier than untreated fabrics. Only one of these negative features is offered among the answer choices.

You should be getting better at reading and at answering questions. Try this next selection on your own. Remember the steps: (1) Skim and underline the questions. (2) Skim the selection. (3) Read and underline the selection. (4) Read questions and answer choices and mark your answers. (5) Then check your answers against the answers and explanations that follow the selection.

READING SELECTION FOR QUESTIONS 10 TO 12

Language performs an essentially social function: It helps us get along together, communicate, and achieve a great measure of concerted action. Words are signs that have significance by convention, and those people who do not adopt the conventions simply fail to communicate. They do not "get along," and a social force arises that encourages them to achieve the correct associations. By "correct" we mean as used by other members of the social group.

Some of the vital points about language are brought home to an English visitor to America, and vice versa, because our vocabularies are nearly the same—but not quite.

10. As defined in the preceding selection, usage of a word is "correct" when it is
    (A) defined in standard dictionaries.
    (B) used by the majority of persons throughout the world who speak the same language.
    (C) used by a majority of educated persons who speak the same language.
    (D) used by other persons with whom we are associating.

10. Ⓐ Ⓑ Ⓒ Ⓓ

11. In the preceding selection, the author is concerned primarily with the
    (A) meaning of words.
    (B) pronunciation of words.
    (C) structure of sentences.
    (D) origin and development of language.

11. Ⓐ Ⓑ Ⓒ Ⓓ

12. According to the preceding selection, the main language problem of an English visitor to America stems from the fact that an English person
    (A) uses some words that have different meanings for Americans.
    (B) has different social values than the Americans.
    (C) has had more exposure to non-English speaking persons than Americans have had.
    (D) pronounces words differently than Americans do.

12. Ⓐ Ⓑ Ⓒ Ⓓ

The correct answers are: 10. **(D)**, 11. **(A)**, 12. **(A).**

10. **(D)** The answer to this question is stated in the next-to-last sentence of the selection.
11. **(A)** This main idea question is an easy one to answer. You should have readily eliminated all of the wrong choices.
12. **(A)** This is a question of fact. The phrasing of the question is quite different from the phrasing of the last sentence, but the meaning is the same. You may have found this reading selection more difficult to absorb than some of the others, but you should have had no difficulty answering this question by eliminating the wrong answers.

Now try this reading selection and its questions. Explanations follow the correct answers. Follow the procedure you have learned, and be sure to read the explanations even if you have a perfect score.

READING SELECTION FOR QUESTIONS 13 TO 18

Since almost every office has some contact with data-processed records, a Senior Stenographer should have some understanding of the basic operations of data processing. Data processing systems now handle about one third of all office paper work. On punched cards, magnetic tape, or on other mediums, data are recorded before being fed into the computer for processing. A machine such as the key punch is used to convert the data written on the source document into the coded symbols on punched cards or tapes. After data has been converted, it must be verified to guarantee absolute accuracy of conversion. In this manner data becomes a permanent record that can be read by electronic computers that compare, store, compute, and otherwise process data at high speeds.

One key person in a computer installation is a programmer, the man or woman who puts business and scientific problems into special symbolic languages that can be read by the computer. Jobs done by the computer range all the way from payroll operations to chemical process control, but most computer applications are directed toward management data. About half of the programmers employed by business come to their positions with college degrees; the remaining half are promoted to their positions without regard to education, from within the organization on the basis of demonstrated ability.

13. Of the following, the best title for the preceding selection is   13. Ⓐ Ⓑ Ⓒ Ⓓ
    (A) The Stenographer as Data Processor
    (B) The Relation of Key Punching to Stenography
    (C) Understanding Data Processing
    (D) Permanent Office Records

14. According to the preceding selection, a Senior Stenographer should   14. Ⓐ Ⓑ Ⓒ Ⓓ
    understand the basic operations of data processing because
    (A) almost every office today has contact with data-processed records
        by computer.
    (B) any office worker may be asked to verify the accuracy of data.
    (C) most offices are involved in the production of permanent records.
    (D) data may be converted into computer language by typing on a key punch.

15. According to the preceding selection, the data that the computer understands   15. Ⓐ Ⓑ Ⓒ Ⓓ
    is most often expressed
    (A) as a scientific programming language.
    (B) as records or symbols punched on tape, cards, or other mediums.
    (C) as records on cards.
    (D) as records on tape.

16. According to the preceding selection, computers are used most often to handle   16. Ⓐ Ⓑ Ⓒ Ⓓ
    (A) management data.
    (B) problems of higher education.
    (C) the control of chemical processes.
    (D) payroll operations.

17. Computer programming is taught in many colleges and business schools. The   17. Ⓐ Ⓑ Ⓒ Ⓓ
    preceding selection implies that programmers in industry
    (A) must have professional training.
    (B) need professional training to advance.
    (C) must have at least a college education to do adequate programming tasks.
    (D) do not need college education to do programming work.

18. According to the preceding selection, data to be processed by computer   18. Ⓐ Ⓑ Ⓒ Ⓓ
    should be
    (A) recent.
    (B) complete.
    (C) basic.
    (D) verified.

The correct answers are: 13. **(C)**, 14. **(A)**, 15. **(B)**, 16. **(A)**, 17. **(D)**, 18. **(D)**.

13. **(C)** Choosing the best title for this selection is not easy. Although the Senior Stenographer is mentioned in the first sentence, the selection is really not concerned with stenographers or with their relationship to key punching. Eliminate choices (A) and (B). Permanent office records are mentioned in the selection, but only along with other equally important uses for data processing. Eliminate choice (D). When in doubt, the most general title is usually correct.

14. **(A)** This is a question of fact. Any one of the answer choices could be correct, but the answer is given almost verbatim in the first sentence. Take advantage of answers that are handed to you.

15. **(B)** This is a question of fact, but it is a tricky one. The program language is a symbolic language, not a scientific one. Reread carefully and eliminate choice (A). (B) includes more of the information in the selection than either (C) or (D) and so is the best answer.

16. **(A)** This is a question of fact. The answer is stated in the next to the last sentence.

17. **(D)** Remember that you are answering the questions on the basis of the information given in the selection. In spite of any information you may have to the contrary, the last sentence of the selection states that half the programmers employed in business achieved their positions by moving up from the ranks without regard to education.

18. **(D)** Judicious underlining proves very helpful to you in finding the correct answer to this question buried in the middle of the selection. Since any one of the answers might be correct, the way to deal with this question is to skim the underlined words in the selection, eliminate those that are not mentioned, and choose the appropriate answer.

In the past few years, the federal government has introduced a new style of reading comprehension question into many of its exams. The reading selection itself is very short, and it is followed by only one question. At first glance, the task is deceptively simple. However, the paragraph is often dense with information and difficult to absorb. The question may be phrased in a circular, oblique, or negative fashion. Total concentration is needed for answering this type of reading question. On the plus side, this style of reading question is always scored on a "right answers only"—there's no penalty for wrong answers—basis; so read carefully, think, eliminate obviously wrong answers, and guess if necessary.

READING SELECTION FOR QUESTION 19

The modern conception of the economic role of the public sector (government), as distinct from the private sector, is that every level of government is a link in the economic process. Government's contribution to political and economic welfare must, however, be evaluated not merely in terms of its technical efficiency, but also in the light of its acceptability to a particular society at a particular state of political and economic development. Even in a dictatorship this principle is formally observed, although the authorities usually destroy the substance by presuming to interpret to the public its collective desires.

19. The paragraph best supports the statement that   19. Ⓐ Ⓑ Ⓒ Ⓓ
    (A) it is not true that some levels of government are not links in the economic process
    (B) all dictatorships observe the same economic principles as other governments
    (C) all links in the economic process are levels of government
    (D) the contributions of some levels of government do not need to be evaluated for technical efficiency and acceptability to society
    (E) no links in the economic process are institutions other than levels of government

The correct answer is **(A).** This answer can be inferred from the first sentence of the paragraph, which states that *every level of government is a link in the economic process.* It can be deduced that its contradictory statement, *some levels of government are not links in the economic process,* cannot be true. Response B is not supported by the paragraph because it goes beyond the information given. The third sentence of the paragraph states that a dictatorship observes (at least formally) *one* of the same principles as other governments. It cannot be concluded from this that dictatorships observe more than this one principle in common with other governments.

Responses C and E represent incorrect interpretations of the information given in the first sentence, which states that *every level of government is a link in the economic process.* It cannot be inferred from this statement that *all links in the economic process are levels of government,* only that some are. We know that the category "all levels of government" is contained in the category "links in the economic process," but we do not know if other links in the economic process exist that are not levels of government. In regard to response E, it cannot be inferred that *no links in the economic process are institutions other than levels of government,* because that would be the same as saying that all links in the economic process are levels of government.

Response D is not supported by the passage because the second sentence implies that the contributions of *all* levels of government must be evaluated for technical efficiency and acceptability to society. There is nothing to suggest that the contributions of some levels of society do *not* need to be evaluated.

Note that in this question the correct answer follows basically from one sentence in the paragraph—the first sentence. The rest of the paragraph presents additional information about the public sector and its effects on society, which is relevant to the discussion but not necessary to make the inference. Part of your task in the Reading section is to understand what you read and then to discern what conclusions follow logically from statements in the paragraph. Consequently, in this test, you will find some questions necessitate the use of all or most of the statements presented in the paragraph, while others, such as this one, require only one statement to infer the correct answer.

READING SELECTION FOR QUESTION 20

All property is classified as either personal property or real property, but not both. In general, if something is classified as personal property, it is transient and transportable in nature, while real property is not. Things such as leaseholds, animals, money, and intangible and other moveable goods are examples of personal property. Permanent buildings and land, on the other hand, are fixed in nature and are not transportable.

20. The paragraph best supports the statement that   20. Ⓐ Ⓑ Ⓒ Ⓓ
   (A) if something is classified as personal property, it is not transient and transportable in nature
   (B) some forms of property are considered to be both personal property and real property
   (C) permanent buildings and land are real property
   (D) permanent buildings and land are personal property
   (E) tangible goods are considered to be real property

20. The correct answer is **(C).** The answer can be inferred from information contained in the first, second, and fourth sentences. The first sentence is a disjunction; that is, it presents two mutually exclusive alternatives—*all property is classified as either personal property or real property, but not both.* The second sentence states that *if something is classified as personal property, it is transient and transportable in nature.* The fourth sentence states that *permanent buildings and land . . . are fixed in nature and are not transportable.* It can be concluded that, since permanent buildings and land are

not transient and transportable in nature, they are not personal property. In view of the disjunction in the first sentence, it can be seen that they must be real property.

Response A is incorrect because it contradicts the information presented in the second sentence.

Response B is incorrect because it contradicts the first sentence, which states that *all property is classified as either personal property or real property, but not both.* Response D contradicts the information presented in the second and fourth sentences. The second sentence states that *if something is classified as personal property, it is transient and transportable in nature.* The fourth sentence indicates that permanent buildings and land do not have these qualities. Therefore, it can be concluded that they are not personal property.

Response E seems to be derived from the third sentence, which says that intangible goods are examples of personal property. However, it cannot be concluded from this statement that tangible goods are real property. In fact, the third sentence gives examples of tangible goods that are personal property.

READING SELECTION FOR QUESTION 21

Personnel administration begins with the process of defining the quantities of people needed to do the job. Thereafter, people must be recruited, selected, trained, directed, rewarded, transferred, promoted, and perhaps released or retired. However, it is not true that all organizations are structured so that workers can be dealt with as individuals. In some organizations, employees are represented by unions, and managers bargain directly only with these associations.

21. The paragraph best supports the statement that
    (A) no organizations are structured so that workers cannot be dealt with as individuals
    (B) some working environments other than organizations are structured so that workers can be dealt with as individuals
    (C) all organizations are structured so that employees are represented by unions
    (D) no organizations are structured so that managers bargain with unions
    (E) some organizations are not structured so that workers can be dealt with as individuals

21. Ⓐ Ⓑ Ⓒ Ⓓ

21. The correct answer is **(E)**. This conclusion can be derived from information contained in the third sentence of the paragraph, which states that *it is not true that all organizations are structured so that workers can be dealt with as individuals.* From this statement, it can be inferred that *some organizations are not structured so that workers can be dealt with as individuals.*

Response A is incorrect because it contradicts the information in the third and fourth sentences of the paragraph. With its double negation, response A is in effect saying that all organizations are structured so that workers can be dealt with as individuals. This flatly contradicts the third sentence and also contradicts the fourth sentence, which says that *in some organizations, employees are represented by unions, and managers bargain with these associations.*

Response B is not supported by the paragraph because the paragraph gives no information about working environments other than organizations. Response C is not supported by the paragraph because the paragraph says only that employees are represented by unions in *some* organizations. One cannot generalize from this to say that employees are represented by unions in *all* organizations.

Response D is incorrect because it contradicts the fourth sentence, which says that managers bargain with unions in some organizations.

Note that in this question the correct answer follows basically from one sentence in the paragraph—the third sentence. The rest of the paragraph presents additional information about personnel administration that is relevant to the discussion, but not necessary to make the inference. Part of your task in the Reading section is to *understand* what you read, and then to *discern* what conclusions follow logically from statements in the paragraph. Consequently, in this test, you'll find some questions require the use of all or most of the statements presented in the paragraph, while others, such as this one, require only one statement to infer the correct answer.

READING SELECTION FOR QUESTION 22

Many kinds of computer programming languages have been developed over the years. Initially, programmers had to write instructions in machine language. If a computer programming language is a machine language, then it is a code which can be read directly by a computer. Most high-level computer programming languages, such as Fortran and Cobol, use strings of common English phrases which communicate with the computer only after being converted or translated into a machine code.

22. The paragraph best supports the statement that   22. Ⓐ Ⓑ Ⓒ Ⓓ
   (A) all high-level computer programming languages use strings of common
        English phrases which are converted to a machine code
   (B) if a computer programming language is a machine language, then it is
        not a code which can be read directly by a computer
   (C) if a computer programming language is a code which can be read
        directly by a computer, then it is not a machine language
   (D) if a computer programming language is not a code which can read
        directly by a computer, then it is not a machine language
   (E) if a computer programming language is not a machine language, then
        it is a code which can be read directly by a computer

22. The correct answer is **(D)**. The answer can be derived from the information presented in the third sentence. That sentence states that *if a computer programming language is a machine language, then it is a code which can be read directly by a computer.* From this statement it can be seen that all machine languages are codes which can be read directly by a computer and that if a computer programming language is not such a code, then it is not a machine language.

Response A goes beyond the information presented in the paragraph, which states only that *most* high level computer programming languages use strings of common English phrases.

Response B represents a complete contradiction of the third sentence of the paragraph. Response C contradicts the paragraph. We know from the paragraph that at least some coded languages which can be read directly by a computer are machine languages.

Response E is incorrect because the paragraph does not say whether or not computer languages that are *not* machine languages are codes which can be read directly by a computer.

Many exams contain reading passages that relate to legal definitions or laws or to standard designations or to specified rules of procedure. You're not expected to have any knowledge of these definitions or rules. All the information you need to answer the questions will be given to you in the reading selection. Even if you happen to know that a definition is wrong or that a procedure is not according to current practice, you must still answer on the basis of the information on the page. When reading these passages, pay special attention to details relating to exceptions, special preconditions, combinations of activities, choices of actions, and prescribed time sequences. Sometimes the printed procedure specifies that certain actions occur only when there is a combination of factors such as that water pressure has dropped *and* staircase collapse is imminent or, perhaps, that a person has actually broken a window *and* has a gun. At other times, the procedures give choices of action under certain circumstances. You must read carefully to determine if the passage requires a combination of factors or gives a choice, then make the appropriate judgment. When a time sequence is specified, be certain to follow that sequence in the prescribed order.

The remaining reading selections require the special attention to sequence, combinations, and choices that we have just described.

READING SELECTION FOR QUESTIONS 23 TO 26

Label

BREGSON'S CLEAR GLUE HIGHLY FLAMMABLE	PRECAUTIONS
A clear quick-drying glue.	Use with adequate ventilation.
For temporary bonding, apply glue to one surface and join immediately.	Close container after use.
For permanent bonding, apply glue to both surfaces, press together after it dries.	Keep out of reach of children.
Use for bonding plastic to plastic, plastic to wood, and wood to wood only.	Avoid prolonged breathing of vapors and repeated contact with skin.
Will not bond at temperatures below 60°	

23. Assume that you, as a member of a repair crew, have been asked to repair a wood banister in the hallway of a house. Since the heat has been turned off, the hallway is very cold except for the location where you have to make the repair. Another repair crew worker is working at that same location using a blow torch to solder a pipe in the wall. The temperature at that location is about 67°. According to the instructions on the above label, the use of this glue to make the necessary repair is
    (A) advisable because the glue will bond wood to wood
    (B) advisable because the heat from the soldering will cause the glue to dry quickly
    (C) inadvisable because the work area temperature is too low
    (D) inadvisable because the glue is highly flammable

23. Ⓐ Ⓑ Ⓒ Ⓓ

24. According to the instructions on the label, this glue should *not* be used for which of the following applications
    (A) affixing a pine table leg to a walnut table
    (B) repairing leaks around pipe joints
    (C) bonding a plastic knob to a cedar drawer
    (D) attaching a Lucite knob to a Lucite drawer

24. Ⓐ Ⓑ Ⓒ Ⓓ

25. According to the instructions on the label, using this glue to bond ceramic

tile to a plaster wall by coating both surfaces with glue, letting the glue
dry, and then pressing the tile to the plaster wall is
   (A) advisable because the glue is quick drying and clear
   (B) advisable because the glue should be permanently affixed to the one surface of the tile only
   (C) inadvisable because the glue is not suitable for bonding ceramic tile to plaster walls
   (D) inadvisable because the bonding should be a temporary one

26. The precaution described in the label, to "use with adequate ventilation"

means that
   (A) the area you are working in should be very cold
   (B) there should be sufficient fresh air where you are using the glue
   (C) you should wear gloves to avoid contact with the glue
   (D) you must apply a lot of glue to make a permanent bond

The correct answers are: 23. **(D)**, 24. **(B)**, 25. **(C)**, 26. **(B)**.

23. **(D)** In all caps, the label clearly states: BREGSON'S CLEAR GLUE, HIGHLY FLAMMABLE. Since another repair crew worker is working at the same location using a blow torch, it would be most foolhardy to use the glue at this location at this time.

24. **(B)** The glue is for bonding one surface to another, not for repairing leaks. Further, the use of the glue is specific to wood and plastics.

25. **(C)** The glue is suited for bonding plastic to plastic, plastic to wood, and wood to wood only. It will not bond ceramic tile to plaster.

26. **(B)** This is really a vocabulary question. "Sufficient ventilation" means "adequate fresh air."

READING SELECTION FOR QUESTIONS 27 TO 30

All automotive accidents, no matter how slight, are to be reported to the Safety Division by the employee involved on Accident Report Form S-23 in duplicate. When the accident is of such a nature that it requires the filling out of the State Motor Vehicle Report Form MV-104, this form is also prepared by the employee in duplicate, and sent to the Safety Division for comparison with the Form S-23. The Safety Division forwards both copies of Form MV-104 to the Corporation Counsel, who sends one copy to the State Bureau of Motor Vehicles. When the information on the Form S-23 indicates that the employee may be at fault, an investigation is made by the Safety Division. If this investigation shows that the employee was at fault, the employee's dispatcher is asked to file a complaint on Form D-11. The foreman of mechanics prepares a damage report on Form D-8 and an estimate of the cost of repairs on Form D-9. The dispatcher's complaint, the damage report, the repair estimate and the employee's previous accident record are sent to the Safety Division where they are studied together with the accident report. The Safety Division then recommends whether or not disciplinary action should be taken against the employee.

27. According to the preceding paragraph, the Safety Division should be

notified whenever an automotive accident has occurred by means of
   (A) Form S-23
   (B) Forms S-23 and MV-104
   (C) Forms S-23, MV-104, D-8, D-9, and D-11
   (D) Forms S-23, MV-104, D-8, D-9, D-11, and employee's accident record

28. According to the preceding paragraph, the forwarding of the Form
MV-104 to the State Bureau of Motor Vehicles is done by the

  (A) Corporation Counsel
  (B) dispatcher
  (C) employee involved in the accident
  (D) Safety Division

28. Ⓐ Ⓑ Ⓒ Ⓓ

29. According to the preceding paragraph, the Safety Division investigates
an automotive accident if the

  (A) accident is serious enough to be reported to the State Bureau of
Motor Vehicles
  (B) dispatcher files a complaint
  (C) employee appears to have been at fault
  (D) employee's previous accident record is poor

29. Ⓐ Ⓑ Ⓒ Ⓓ

30. Of the forms mentioned in the preceding paragraph, the dispatcher is
responsible for preparing the

  (A) accident report form
  (B) complaint form
  (C) damage report
  (D) estimate of cost of repairs

30. Ⓐ Ⓑ Ⓒ Ⓓ

The correct answers are: 27. **(A)**, 28. **(A)**, 29. **(C)**, 30. **(B)**.

27. **(A)** The first sentence makes it clear that regardless of whatever other forms might need to be filed, all automobile accidents should be reported to the Safety Division on Form S-23.

28. **(A)** Follow the steps carefully. The employee fills out Form MV-104 in duplicate and sends both copies to the Safety Division. The Safety Division, in turn, sends both copies to the Corporation Counsel who then sends one copy on to the State Bureau of Motor Vehicles.

29. **(C)** The Safety Division investigates if the information on the Form S-23 indicates that the employee may have been at fault.

30. **(B)** If the employee was indeed at fault, the dispatcher files a complaint on Form D-11.

READING SELECTION FOR QUESTION 31

When a person commits a traffic violation, a Police Officer should:

1. Inform the violator of the offense committed.
2. Request the violator to show his or her driver's license, vehicle registration, and insurance identification card. Failure to produce this required material may result in additional tickets. (Taxis, buses, and other rented vehicles do not require insurance identification cards.)
3. Enter only one infraction on each ticket.
4. Use a separate ticket for each additional infraction.

31. Police Officer Herrmann has been assigned to curb traffic violations
at the intersection of Main Street and Central Avenue. Officer Herrmann
observes a taxi cab going through a red light at this intersection and signals
the driver to pull over. The officer informs the cab driver of his violation

31. Ⓐ Ⓑ Ⓒ Ⓓ

and asks for the required material. The driver surrenders his license and registration to the officer. Police Officer Herrmann should
(A) issue the cab driver a ticket for the red light violation and issue him a separate ticket for not surrendering his insurance card
(B) issue the cab driver one ticket including both the red light violation and the absence of the insurance card
(C) issue the cab driver a ticket only for the red light violation
(D) issue the cab driver a ticket only for not having an insurance card

The correct answer is **(C).**

31. **(C)** The taxi driver violated the law by going through a red light. Officer Herrmann correctly informed the driver of this infraction and must issue a ticket. If the violator had been driving a private automobile, Officer Herrmann would have had to issue a separate ticket for his not producing an insurance card (see rules 3 and 4). However, in this case, the exception applies. The exception is that taxis, along with buses and rented vehicles, do not need to have insurance identification cards. You have to read carefully to determine exactly which rule applies in this case.

READING SELECTION FOR QUESTIONS 32 AND 33

Police Officers on patrol may observe a recently vacated building that can create a safety hazard. In such situations, Police Officers should follow these procedures, in the order given:

1. Walk through the vacated building to determine if a safety hazard exists.
2. If a safety hazard exists, notify the supervisor on patrol.
3. Write an entry in the Activity Log.
4. Report the facts concerning the safety hazard in the vacant building to the Telephone Switchboard Operator.
5. Place barriers in front of the vacated building if directed by the Patrol Supervisor.

32. Police Officer Wolff notes that a building on his patrol route has recently been vacated. What action should Officer Wolff take next?   32. Ⓐ Ⓑ Ⓒ Ⓓ
(A) Report the safety hazard in the vacant building to the Telephone Switchboard Operator.
(B) Radio the supervisor on patrol.
(C) Make an entry in his Activity Log.
(D) Determine if there is a safety hazard.

33. Police Officer Furumoto has noticed a safety hazard in a vacant building. He first notified the supervisor on patrol and then made an entry in the Activity Log. He is about to place barriers in front of the building to safeguard the public. Officer Furumoto is acting   33. Ⓐ Ⓑ Ⓒ Ⓓ
(A) correctly. Public safety is the Police Officer's first duty.
(B) incorrectly. The Patrol Supervisor did not direct him to place barriers.
(C) incorrectly. He must first report the safety hazard to the Telephone Switchboard Operator.
(D) incorrectly. He should radio for additional Police Officers to assist him in protecting the public from this hazard.

The correct answers are: 32. **(D)**, 33. **(C)**.

32. **(D)** The introductory sentence says that a recently vacated building can create a safety hazard, not that it necessarily does so. Officer Wolff must enter the building and look around to determine whether or not there is indeed a safety hazard. Only if he decides that there is a hazard, should he proceed with notification and other actions.

33. **(C)** The procedure lists steps to be taken in the order given. While Officer Furumoto is justly concerned with public safety, the hazard in the vacant building hardly constitutes a pressing emergency. Having made the entry in the Log, his next act must be to notify the Telephone Switchboard Operator. Then he must await instructions from the Patrol Supervisor. The Supervisor may feel that the hazard does not warrant barricades.

READING SELECTION FOR QUESTIONS 34 AND 35

Police Officer DiSisto has observed that there is a pattern to criminal activity in her sector. She has noticed that burglaries tend to occur on High Street while auto thefts occur on York Street. Most rapes take place on Chapel Street and most assaults on Whitney. The rapes occur between 10 P.M. and 4 A.M., auto thefts between midnight and 6 A.M., burglaries between 10 A.M. and 4 P.M., and assaults between 6 P.M. and 10 P.M. Auto thefts seem most common on Monday, Tuesday, and Thursday. Assaults occur most often on Friday, Saturday, and Sunday. Most rapes happen over the weekend and most burglaries on Monday, Wednesday, and Saturday.

34. Police Officer DiSisto would most likely be able to reduce the incidence of rape by concentrating her patrol on   34. Ⓐ Ⓑ Ⓒ Ⓓ
    (A) York Street between midnight and 8 A.M.
    (B) Chapel Street between 7 P.M. and 3 A.M.
    (C) High Street between 2 A.M. and 10 P.M.
    (D) Chapel Street between 4 P.M. and midnight

35. Auto theft is a special problem in the precinct, and Police Officer DiSisto's supervisor has requested that she make a special effort to eliminate auto theft on her patrol. Officer DiSisto should request assignment to patrol on   35. Ⓐ Ⓑ Ⓒ Ⓓ
    (A) Sunday through Thursday from 10 P.M. to 6 A.M.
    (B) Friday through Wednesday from 3 A.M. to 4 P.M.
    (C) Monday through Friday from 8 A.M. to 4 P.M.
    (D) Wednesday through Sunday from 2 P.M. to 10 P.M.

The correct answers are: 34. **(B)**, 35. **(A)**.

34. **(B)** You must read for details and then use these details to reason. This type of question highlights the value of reading the questions before you read the paragraph. Question 34 deals with rape; question 35 with auto theft. In your initial reading of the paragraph, you will underscore details concerning rape and auto theft, ignoring information relating to burglary and assault. With your information thus narrowed, note that the rape area is Chapel Street. Eliminate choices (A) and (C). The rapes occur in the six-hour span from 10 P.M. to 4 A.M. Choice (B) covers five hours of this six-hour span while (D) covers only the two hours from 10 P.M. to midnight.

35. **(A)** Approach this question in the same way. Auto theft appears to be a midweek event. Only choices (A) and (C) include the three target days of Monday, Tuesday, and Thursday. Auto thefts occur under cover of darkness making (C) a poor choice.

READING SELECTION FOR QUESTION 36

Harassment occurs when a person annoys or alarms another person, but does not intend or cause physical injury.

Menacing occurs when a person threatens to cause serious physical injury to another person, but does not cause a serious physical injury.

Assault occurs when a person causes physical injury to another person.

36. On a foggy Friday night after a work, a group of men met at Jolly-O Tavern for a few beers. The conversation centered on the merits of the two local hockey teams, and Warren Wu stoutly defended his favorite team against that of Tomas Ramos. Ramos could stand just so much taunting. As he became more angry, Ramos told Wu that he had better "shut up" before he, Tomas Ramos, knocked Wu's block off. Wu continued to praise his team, whereupon Ramos gave him such a punch to the jaw that Wu's lip was split and a tooth was knocked out. Based on the definitions above, Ramos should be charged with

    36. Ⓐ Ⓑ Ⓒ Ⓓ

  (A) harassment, menacing, and assault

  (B) menacing and assault

  (C) assault

  (D) no crime

The correct answer is **(C).**

36. **(C)** The fact of assault seems clear. Ramos caused physical injury to Wu. According to the definitions, assault is the only charge. Harassment requires that no injury be intended, but Ramos stated intent to harm Wu. Menacing requires that no injury be caused. These definitions are mutually exclusive. Only one can apply. Definitions of other crimes may allow for one definition to be included within another. Careful reading is the number one requirement.

Judgment Questions

The need for reading skills is universal. The need for good judgment is a very close second. Even entry-level employees who work under close supervision have moments when they must rely on their own good judgment in dealing with an emergency situation or in choosing priorities when there's no supervisor to consult. Almost all multiple-choice civil service exams include some questions designed to measure judgment either directly or indirectly. For test-taking purposes, we define judgment as a process of combining knowledge and understanding with common sense. Some examples of judgment questions include:

37. Decisions about handcuffing or restraining inmates are often up to the Correction Officers involved. An officer is legally responsible for exercising good judgment and for taking necessary precautions to prevent harm both to

    37. Ⓐ Ⓑ Ⓒ Ⓓ

the inmate involved and to others. In which one of the following situations is handcuffing or other physical restraint most likely to be needed?

(A) An inmate seems to have lost control of his senses and is banging his fists repeatedly against the bars of his cell.

(B) During the past two weeks, an inmate has deliberately tried to start three fights with other inmates.

(C) An inmate claims to be sick and refuses to leave his cell for a scheduled meal.

(D) During the night an inmate begins to shout and sing, disturbing the sleep of other inmates.

The correct answer is **(A)**.

37. **(A)** The inmate who repeatedly bangs his fists against the bars of his cell is in immediate danger of causing himself bodily harm. This inmate *must* be restrained. The other inmates require attention, and their situations must be dealt with, but they do not require physical restraint.

38. While you're working on a routine assignment, a co-worker asks you to help her for a few minutes so she can complete an assignment that has top priority and must be completed immediately. Of the following, the *best* action for you to take should be to   **38.** Ⓐ Ⓑ Ⓒ Ⓓ

(A) tell her to find somebody who doesn't look busy and ask that person for help

(B) tell her you will help her as soon as you complete your own work

(C) help her to complete her assignment and then go back to your work

(D) tell her that your work is as important to you as her work is to her and continue to work on your own assignment

The correct answer is **(C)**.

38. **(C)** There are a number of points to take into consideration: Your own task is described as routine, the co-worker's assignment is described as one which has top priority; and the co-worker has asked for only a few minutes of your time. If you were involved in "rush" work yourself, you might refuse to help until you had finished your own task, but under these circumstances, help get the priority work done. A side benefit to be considered here is to maintain a good relationship with the co-worker so that you, too, may request assistance at some time when your job demands it.

39. A police officer stationed along the route of a parade has been ordered not to allow cars to cross the route while the parade is in progress. An ambulance driver on an emergency run attempts to drive an ambulance across the route while the parade is passing. Under these circumstances, the officer should   **39.** Ⓐ Ⓑ Ⓒ Ⓓ

(A) ask the driver to wait while the officer calls headquarters and obtains a decision

(B) stop the parade long enough to permit the ambulance to cross the street

(C) direct the ambulance driver to the shortest detour available, which will add at least ten minutes to the run

(D) hold up the ambulance in accordance with the order

The correct answer is **(B)**.

39. **(B)** Without any knowledge of police rules, common sense dictates that saving of lives is the number one priority. An ambulance on an emergency run is on a mission to save a life. Lifesaving takes precedence over the desire for an uninterrupted parade despite the officer's prior orders.

40. An office worker frequently complains to the building custodian that her office is poorly illuminated. The best action for the building custodian to follow is to   40. Ⓐ Ⓑ Ⓒ Ⓓ
    (A) ignore the complaints as those of an habitual crank
    (B) inform the worker that illumination is a fixed item built into the building originally and evidently is the result of faulty planning by the architect
    (C) request a licensed electrician to install additional ceiling lights
    (D) investigate for faulty illumination features in the room, such as dirty lamp globes, and incorrect lamp wattages

The correct answer is **(D)**.

40. **(D)** The repeated complaints may be quite legitimate if the lighting problem has not been corrected. Do not dismiss the officer worker as a "crank." The custodian should check out the fixtures personally before calling in an electrician. Costs can be held down by having house staff perform those tasks for which they are qualified.

41. Suppose that one of your neighbors walks into the police precinct where you are an Administrative Aide and asks you to make 100 photocopies of a flyer he intends to distribute in the neighborhood. Of the following, what action should you take in this situation?   41. Ⓐ Ⓑ Ⓒ Ⓓ
    (A) Pretend that you do not know the person and order him to leave the building.
    (B) Call a police officer and report the person for attempting to make illegal use of police equipment.
    (C) Tell the person that you will make the copies when you are off duty.
    (D) Explain that you cannot use police equipment for nonpolice work.

The correct answer is **(D)**.

41. **(D)** Where calm, reasoned explanation is offered as an answer choice, it is nearly always the correct answer. There is no need to be impolite or hostile toward the neighbor. He may not even realize that he is asking you to do something that is not permitted. He will respect you for obeying the rules.

42. A police officer, walking a beat at 3 A.M., notices heavy smoke coming out of a top floor window of a large apartment house. Out of the following, the action the officer should take *first* is to: 42. Ⓐ Ⓑ Ⓒ Ⓓ
    (A) make certain that there really is a fire
    (B) enter the building and warn all the occupants of the apartment house
    (C) attempt to extinguish the fire before it gets out of control
    (D) call the fire department

The correct answer is **(D)**.

42. **(D)** A police officer is a police officer and not a firefighter. Eliminate choices (A) and (C) at once. It is the job of the firefighters to ascertain whether or not there really is a fire and to put it out. Since the building is a large one and fires spread rapidly, the practical move is to call the fire department

immediately rather than trying to run through the building alone trying to rouse all occupants. Firefighters will have greater manpower to do this efficiently and are trained in nighttime rousing procedures.

43. An elevator inspector on routine inspection for the Building Department notices a number of dangerous situations in the basement of the building she is in. Of the following conditions that she notices, which is the most dangerous and should be reported immediately?
    (A) Gas is leaking from a broken pipe.
    (B) The sewer pipe is broken.
    (C) Water is seeping into the basement.
    (D) The basement is unlighted.

43. Ⓐ Ⓑ Ⓒ Ⓓ

The correct answer is **(A)**.

43. **(A)** Leaking gas can be ignited, causing a fire. If a large amount of gas collects in the basement and is ignited, an explosion and fire are likely. This is the greatest hazard. The broken sewer pipe and the water seepage can create health hazards and should be reported and repaired, but these corrections do not represent the same emergency situations as the gas leak. An unlit basement is also a safety hazard, but even less of an emergency.

44. There are times when an employee of one city department should notify and seek assistance from employees of another department. A parking enforcement agent is checking meters on a busy one-way street. Of the following situations which he notices, which should he report immediately?
    (A) A rat runs out of a building and into the storm sewer across the street.
    (B) A wire is dangling over the sidewalk giving off sparks.
    (C) A car is parked directly in front of a hydrant.
    (D) Two men are sitting on the front steps of a building sharing a marijuana joint.

44. Ⓐ Ⓑ Ⓒ Ⓓ

The correct answer is **(B)**.

44. **(B)** The most urgent hazard is that caused by the sparking wire. A quick call to the Police Department will get the area sealed off and a repair crew to attend to the wire. The Health Department could be notified of rodents in the building, but pest infestation is a chronic problem rather than an emergency. The parking enforcement agent can ticket the illegally parked car. The two men sharing one joint pose no danger.

Communication Skills Questions

No one works entirely alone. Every person must at times communicate information to someone else. The communication may be in the form of written memos or reports or may be oral. No matter the form of the communication, it must be clear, readily understood, and it must convey all the necessary information. Most city civil service exams include some measure of ability to organize and communicate information. Where the communication is very likely to be written, this measure may be by the way of questions on grammar and English usage. These questions do not ask rules of grammar; rather they offer a choice of sentences and ask which one contains an error, or which is the best and most correct sentence of the group. Where the communication is more likely to be telephoned in to a central post, the measure of ability to communicate may offer a set of facts and ask how you would best organize those facts into a clear and accurate report. Some examples:

*Select the sentence that is **best** with regard to grammar and proper usage.*

45. (A) There are several ways to organize a good report.

    (B) Several ways exist in organizing a good report.

    (C) To organize a good report, several ways exist.

    (D) In the organization of a good report, there must be several ways.

45. Ⓐ Ⓑ Ⓒ Ⓓ

The correct answer is **(A)**.

    45. **(A)** While all four choices get the message across, the first is most straightforward.

46. (A) The personnel office has charge of employment, dismissals, and employee's welfare.

    (B) Employment, together with dismissals and employees' welfare, are handled by the personnel office.

    (C) The personnel office takes charge of employment, dismissals, and etc.

    (D) The personnel office is responsible for the employment, dismissal, and welfare of employees.

46. Ⓐ Ⓑ Ⓒ Ⓓ

The correct answer is **(D)**.

46. **(D)** This statement is clear and correct. Choice (A) is incorrect in that the personnel department is in charge of the welfare of more than one employee; the word would have to be "employees'." In choice (B), the subject of the sentence is "employment," which is singular. The verb would have to be "is." "Together with dismissals and employees' welfare" is a parenthetical expression giving additional information, but is not part of the subject. The Latin abbreviation, "etc." means "and so forth." The word "and" before "etc." is superfluous and is incorrect.

*Select the sentence that is **incorrect.***

47. (A) In the case of members who are absent, a special letter will be sent.

    (B) The visitors were all ready to see it.

    (C) I like Leaf's poem "To a Mountain Daisy."

    (D) John told William that he was sure he had seen it.

47. Ⓐ Ⓑ Ⓒ Ⓓ

The correct answer is **(D)**.

47. **(D)** This sentence is incorrect because it is unclear. Who is the second *he*? Was John sure that William had seen it or that he had seen it himself? If you were puzzled by choice (C), it is indeed correct. A period *always* goes inside the quotation marks, even if it seems logical to place it outside in a case like this. There are no exceptions to the rule governing placement of period or comma inside quotation marks.

48. (A) Being tired, I stretched out on a grassy knoll.

    (B) While we were rowing on the lake, a sudden squall almost capsized the boat.

    (C) Entering the room, a strange mark on the floor attracted my attention.

    (D) Mounting the curb, the empty car crossed the sidewalk and came to rest against a building.

48. Ⓐ Ⓑ Ⓒ Ⓓ

The correct answer is (**C**).

48. (**C**) The way this sentence currently reads, the strange mark entered the room and attracted my attention. Obviously, this is ridiculous. For clarity and correctness, the sentence should be rewritten: "As I entered the room, a strange mark on the floor attracted my attention." The subject of the sentence is "I." In all three other sentences, the subject is clear.

Below are the details of an incident. Following the details of the incident are four statements. Which one of the statements expresses the information most clearly and accurately?

49. Police Officer Franks arrives at the scene of a frame, two-family house in Brooklyn and observes flames leaping from the door onto the porch. A woman on the sidewalk gives him a description of a man she saw running from the house just before she noticed the fire. The information is:

Place of Occurrence:	1520 Clarendon Road, Brooklyn
Time of Occurrence:	6:32 A.M.
Type of Building:	Two-family frame dwelling
Event:	Fire, suspected arson
Suspect:	Male, white, approx 6-foot wearing blue jeans
Witness:	Mary Smith of 1523 Clarendon Road, Brooklyn

49. Ⓐ Ⓑ Ⓒ Ⓓ

Officer Franks is about to radio an alert for the suspect. Which of the following expresses the information *most clearly* and *accurately*?

(A) At 6:32 A.M. Mary Smith of 1523 Clarendon Road, Brooklyn, saw a white male wearing approximately 6-foot blue jeans running from the building across the street.

(B) A white male wearing blue jeans ran from the house at 1520 Clarendon Road at 6:32 A.M. Mary Smith saw him.

(C) At 6:32 A.M. a 6-foot white male wearing blue jeans ran from a burning two-family frame structure at 1520 Clarendon Road, Brooklyn. He was observed by a neighbor, Mary Smith.

(D) A two-family frame house is on fire at 1520 Clarendon Road in Brooklyn. A white male in blue jeans probably did it. Mary Smith saw him run.

The correct answer is (**C**).

49. (**C**) This statement tells what happened, where, and when. It gives a brief description of the suspect and identifies the witness. Choices (A) and (B) neglect to mention the fire; (D) omits the height of the suspect, an important fact, and does not identify the relationship of the witness for later questioning, if necessary.

50. A woman runs to the token clerk at the platform of the subway station to report that her purse was just snatched. She gives the following information to the token clerk:

Time of Occurrence:	1:22 A.M.
Place of Occurrence:	uptown-bound platform, 59th Street Station, 7th Avenue line
Victim:	Juana Martinez
Crime:	purse snatching
Description of Suspect:	unknown, fled down steps to lower platform

50. Ⓐ Ⓑ Ⓒ Ⓓ

The token clerk is about to call for assistance from the transit police. Which of the following expresses the information *most clearly* and *accurately?*

(A) Juana Martinez had her purse snatched on the subway platform at 59th Street Station. She didn't see him.

(B) A purse was just snatched by a man who ran down the steps. This is the 7th Avenue token booth at 59th Street Station. Her name is Juana Martinez.

(C) It is 1:22 A.M. The person who snatched Juana Martinez's purse is downstairs at 59th Street Station.

(D) This is the 59th Street Station, uptown-bound 7th Avenue token booth. A Juana Martinez reports that her purse was just snatched by a man who fled down the steps to a lower platform.

The correct answer is **(D)**.

50. **(D)** This statement gives the precise location, the event, and a direction in which the suspect might be traced. Since the statement says that the event just occurred, the time is irrelevant. The recipient of the message knows to move quickly. Choice (A) does not give enough details to be of use; (B) makes a disjointed statement; (C) makes a flat statement that is not necessarily true. The purse snatcher may have exited by another route.

Other Test Topics

The purpose of civil service exams is to identify candidates who have the aptitude and ability to learn the job easily and to do it well. The subjects tested on the exam are closely related to the duties of the position. Reading, judgment, and self-expression are common to most jobs. Other subjects are more position-specific: arithmetic for cashiers, clerical workers, and many positions in the manual trades; observation and memory for police officers, firefighters, correction officers, court officers, and the like; coding, alphabetizing, name and number checking for office workers; typing for typists; stenography for stenographers; tool recognition for firefighters, custodians, mechanical workers in many trades, etc. The remainder of this chapter will introduce you to just a few of these.

VOCABULARY

51. FRAUDULENT means most nearly

(A) suspicious
(B) unproven
(C) deceptive
(D) unfair
(E) despicable

51. Ⓐ Ⓑ Ⓒ Ⓓ Ⓔ

The correct answer is **(C)**.

51. **(C)** The word *fraudulent* means "characterized by deceit or trickery, especially deliberate misrepresentation." Therefore, response C, *deceptive,* is the best synonym. Responses A, D, and E could be viewed as slightly related to the meaning of *fraudulent*. Response A, *suspicious,* "sensing that something is wrong without definite proof," could describe a person's reaction to a *fraudulent* situation. Response D, *unfair,* and response E, *despicable,* could both be used to describe a

fraudulent act. However, the basic meanings of these three words are completely different from the meaning of *fraudulent.* Response B, *unproven,* is clearly unrelated to the meaning of *fraudulent.*

52. ALTRUISTIC means most nearly
    (A) unselfish
    (B) extended
    (C) unimaginative
    (D) organized
    (E) appealing

    52. Ⓐ Ⓑ Ⓒ Ⓓ Ⓔ

    The correct answer is **(A).**

52. **(A)** To be *altruistic* means "to be concerned for or devoted to the welfare of others." Therefore, response A, *unselfish,* is an excellent synonym. Response B could be viewed as slightly related, since *altruistic* people often extend themselves to help others. However, the basic meaning of *extended,* "stretched out," is completely different from the meaning of *altruistic.* Responses C and D are clearly unrelated to the meaning of *altruistic.* A vague connection exists between *altruistic* and response E, *appealing. Altruistic* people often make appeals on behalf of those less fortunate than themselves. Simultaneously, the generosity of *altruistic* people often makes them very *appealing* to other people. Although this vague connection exists between *altruistic* and *appealing,* they do not share a similar meaning.

ARITHMETIC

53. What is the net amount of a bill of $428 after a discount of 6% has been allowed?
    (A) $401.10
    (B) $402.32
    (C) $401.23
    (D) $402.23

    53. Ⓐ Ⓑ Ⓒ Ⓓ

    The correct answer is **(B).**

53. **(B)** 6% of $428 = $428 × .06 = $25.68
    $428 − 6% = $428 − $25.68 = $402.32

54. If a piece of wood measuring 4 feet 2 inches is divided into three equal parts, each part is
    (A) 1 foot 4 $^2/_3$ inches
    (B) 1 foot 2 $^1/_3$ inches
    (C) 1 foot 4 inches
    (D) 1 foot $^7/_{18}$ inch

    54. Ⓐ Ⓑ Ⓒ Ⓓ

    The correct answer is **(A).**

54. **(A)** 4 feet 2 inches = 50 inches (4 × 12 + 2)

    50 inches ÷ 3 = 16 $^2/_3$ inches = 1 foot 4 $^2/_3$ inches each

55. A federal agency had a personal computer repaired at a cost of $49.20. This amount included a charge of $22 per hour for labor and a charge for a new switch which cost $18 before a 10 percent government discount was applied. How long did the repair job take?

(A) 1 hour, 6 minutes

(B) 1 hour, 11 minutes

(C) 1 hours, 22 minutes

(D) 1 hour, 30 minutes

55. Ⓐ Ⓑ Ⓒ Ⓓ

The correct answer is **(D).**

55. **(D)** $49.20 - (18 - (18 \times .10)) \div 22 = X$

$X = {}^{33}/_{22} = 1.5$ hours or 1 hour, 30 minutes

The cost of the switch after the government discount of 10 percent is applied is $18 - (18 - .10)$ or $16.20. This amount, when subtracted from the total charge of $49.20, leaves $33, which represents the charge for labor. A charge of $33 at the rate of $22 per hour represents 1.5 hours, or 1 hour and 30 minutes, of work.

TABULAR COMPLETION

FINANCE COMPANIES—ASSETS AND LIABILITIES: 1970 to 1980
(*in millions of dollars*)*

ITEM	1970	1975	1980
Total Receivables	Ⓘ	85,994	183,341
Consumer Receivables	31,773	40,814	77,460
Retail passenger car paper and others	11,577	13,399	31,950
Retail consumer goods and loans	20,196	27,415	ⒾⓋ
Business Receivables	22,999	39,286	86,067
Wholesale paper and others	14,084	22,012	48,059
Lease paper and others	8,915	17,274	38,008
Other Receivables	2,341	5,894	19,814
Total Liabilities	60,577	Ⓘⓘⓘ	175,025
Loans and Notes Payable to Banks	7,551	8,617	15,458
Short-term	Ⓘⓘ	7,900	7,885
Long-term	969	717	7,573
Commercial Paper	22,073	25,905	52,328
Other Debt	30,953	54,194	Ⓥ

*Hypothetical data.

56. What is the value of I in millions dollars?
- (A) 54,772
- (B) 57,113
- (C) 63,546
- (D) 68,856
- (E) none of these

57. What is the value of II in millions of dollars?
- (A) 6,582
- (B) 14,522
- (C) 53,026
- (D) 58,236
- (E) none of these

58. What is the value of III in millions of dollars?
- (A) 62,811
- (B) 88,716
- (C) 94,610
- (D) 97,333
- (E) none of these

59. What is the value of IV in millions of dollars?
- (A) 45,610
- (B) 47,610
- (C) 47,611
- (D) 54,117
- (E) none of these

60. What is the value of V in millions of dollars?
- (A) 67,786
- (B) 85,147
- (C) 107,239
- (D) 107,259
- (E) none of these

The correct answers are: 56. **(B)**, 57. **(A)**, 58. **(B)**, 59. **(E)**, 60. **(C)**.

56. **(B)** Add the values for Consumer Receivables, Business Receivables, and Other Receivables.

$31,773 + 22,999 + 2,341 = 57,113$

57. **(A)** Subtract the value for *Long-term* from the value for *Loans and Notes Payable to Banks*.

$7,551 - 969 = 6,582$

58. **(B)** Add the value of 1975 *Loans and Notes Payable to Banks*, *Commercial Paper*, and *Other Debt*.

$8,617 + 25,905 + 54,194 = 88,716$

59. **(E)** Subtract the value of 1980 *Retail passenger car paper and others* from 1980 *Consumer Receivables*.

77,460 – 31,950 = 45,510

60. **(C)** Subtract the sum of the values of *Loans and Notes Payable to Banks* and *Commercial Paper* from 1980 *Total Liabilities*.

175,025 – (15,458 + 52,328) = 107,239

OBSERVATION AND MEMORY

Directions: *You will have three minutes to study the following picture, to note details about people, time and place, and activities. Then you will have to answer five questions about the picture without looking back at the picture.*

*Picture for questions 61 to 65—***At The Bank**

*Answer questions 61 to 65 on the basis of the picture, "**At The Bank.**" Cover the picture with your hand or a piece of paper. Do not look at the picture again.*

61. The teller is
    (A) wearing a striped tie
    (B) wearing glasses
    (C) making change
    (D) left-handed

61. Ⓐ Ⓑ Ⓒ Ⓓ

62. The man wearing a hat is also
    (A) handing money to the teller
    (B) wearing a bow tie
    (C) talking to another man in the line
    (D) smoking a pipe

62. Ⓐ Ⓑ Ⓒ Ⓓ

63. The teller's name is
(A) R. Smith
(B) T. Jones
(C) T. Smith
(D) R. Jones

63. Ⓐ Ⓑ Ⓒ Ⓓ

64. The woman in the striped dress is
(A) carrying a handbag
(B) wearing a pendant
(C) holding gloves
(D) third in line

64. Ⓐ Ⓑ Ⓒ Ⓓ

65. The time of day is
(A) early morning
(B) lunchtime
(C) mid-afternoon
(D) later afternoon

65. Ⓐ Ⓑ Ⓒ Ⓓ

The correct answers are: 61. **(B)**, 62. **(D)**, 63. **(D)**, 64. **(B)**, 65. **(B)**.

MECHANICAL APTITUDE, ELECTRONICS INFORMATION, TOOL RECOGNITION, AUTOMOTIVE KNOWLEDGE

66. The saw shown to the right is used mainly to cut
(A) plywood
(B) odd-shaped holes in wood
(C) along the grain of the wood
(D) across the grain of the wood

66. Ⓐ Ⓑ Ⓒ Ⓓ

The correct answer is **(B).**

66. **(B)** The compass saw is used to cut odd-shaped holes in wood.

67. Four gears are shown in the figure to the right. If gear 1 turns as shown, then the gears turning in the same direction are
(A) 2 and 3
(B) 2 and 4
(C) 3 and 4
(D) 2, 3, and 4

67. Ⓐ Ⓑ Ⓒ Ⓓ

The correct answer is **(C).**

67. **(C)** Gear 1 turns clockwise: gear 2 turns counterclockwise; gears 3 and 4 turn clockwise.

68. After brakes have been severely overheated, what should be checked for?   **68.** Ⓐ Ⓑ Ⓒ Ⓓ
  (A) water condensation in brake fluid
  (B) glazed brake shoes
  (C) wheels out of alignment
  (D) crystallized wheel bearings

The correct answer is **(B)**.

68. **(B)** Overheating the brake shoe will cause the brake material to glaze and become slippery. Slippery brakes are dangerous because they take longer to stop a car.

69. The tool shown to the right is used for   **69.** Ⓐ Ⓑ Ⓒ Ⓓ
  (A) pressure lubricating
  (B) welding steel plate
  (C) drilling small holes in tight places
  (D) holding small parts for heat treating

The correct answer is **(B)**.

69. **(B)** The tool is a welding torch used in making metal joint. Welding is generally done with material made of steel.

70. When working on live 600-volt equipment where rubber gloves might be   **70.** Ⓐ Ⓑ Ⓒ Ⓓ
damaged, an electrician should
  (A) work without gloves
  (B) carry a spare pair of rubber gloves
  (C) reinforce the fingers of the rubber gloves with rubber tape
  (D) wear leather gloves over the rubber gloves

The correct answer is **(D)**.

70. **(D)** Leather gloves offer the best protection over the rubber gloves. The leather can withstand severe conditions before it will tear. The rubber acts as insulation.

ALPHABETIZING, FILING, CLERICAL NAME AND NUMBER CHECKING, CODING

Directions: Each question consists of a capitalized word that is to be filed correctly before one of the alphabetized words listed. Indicate the word before which the key word should be filed by marking the letter of the word on your answer sheet.

Note: Read these directions carefully. The correct answer is the letter of the word before which the key word should be filed.

71. BIOGRAPHY   **71.** Ⓐ Ⓑ Ⓒ Ⓓ
  (A) bible
  (B) bibliography
  (C) bilge
  (D) biology

The correct answer is **(D)**.

71. **(D)** Biography should be filed before *biology*.

Directions: In Column I you will find four names to be filed. The names are lettered w, x, y, and z. In Column II are four possible orders for alphabetizing those names. You are to choose which arrangement constitutes the correct filing order according to the rules for alphabetical filing and mark the letter that precedes the correct order.

72.	Column I	Column II	72. Ⓐ Ⓑ Ⓒ Ⓓ
	(w) Rivera, Ilena	(A) w, x, z, y	
	(x) Riviera, Ilene	(B) z, w, y, x	
	(y) Rivere, I.	(C) w, y, z, x	
	(z) Riviera Ice-Cream Co.	(D) x, z, w, y	

The correct answer is **(C)**.

72. **(C)** The correct order in which to file these names is:

  (w) Rivera, Ilena
  (y) Rivere, I.
  (z) Riviera Ice-Cream Co.
  (x) Riviera, Ilene

Directions: Each question consists of letters or numbers in Columns I and II. For each question, compare each line of Column I with its corresponding line in Column II and decide how many lines in Column II are exactly the same as their counterparts in Column I. Mark your answers as follows:

Mark (A) if only ONE line in Column II is exactly the same as its corresponding line in Column I
Mark (B) if TWO lines in column II are exactly the same as their corresponding lines in Column I
Mark (C) if THREE lines in Column II are exactly the same as their corresponding lines in Column I
Mark (D) if all FOUR lines in Column II are exactly the same as their corresponding lines in Column I

73.	Column I	Column II	73. Ⓐ Ⓑ Ⓒ Ⓓ
	awg3	awg3	
	tyE3	ty3E	
	abhn	abnh	
	24po	24op	

The correct answer is **(A)**.

73. **(A)** Only on the top line are the letter combinations in columns I and II identical. If you got this wrong, look again.

Directions: Each question consists of a set of names and addresses. In each question the name and address in Column II should be exactly like the name and address in Column I. But there are some mistakes.

Mark (A) if there is a mistake only in the NAME
Mark (B) if there is a mistake only in the ADDRESS
Mark (C) if there are mistakes in both NAME and ADDRESS
Mark (D) if there are NO MISTAKES

74.	**Column I**	**Column II**	74. Ⓐ Ⓑ Ⓒ Ⓓ
	Mr. Brett H. Meyers	Mr. Brett H. Meyers	
	72 Nannyhagen Road	72 Nannyhagen Road	
	Haverford, PA 19042	Haverford, PA 19402	

The correct answer is **(B).**

74. **(B)** The name is identical in both columns, as are street address, city, and state. However, there is a number reversal in the zip code. The total addresses are therefore not identical and the answer must be (B).

The most common variety of coding question found on city civil service tests consists of a coding table (you don't need to memorize it) and a series of questions that requires you to demonstrate your understanding of the use of the code and your ability to follow directions in answering the questions. From one exam to another, the chief variations in coding questions tend to be in the number of digits and letters in each question line and in the directions. Indeed, in New York City, on the same day, two exams were given for two different clerical positions. Both exams contained coding questions, but the directions for answering the questions were different on the two exams. One asked that questions be answered on the basis of correctly coded lines; the other on the basis of how many lines contained coding errors. On one exam the questions and directions looked like this:

Directions: *Each letter should be matched with its number in accordance with the following table:*

Letter	P	S	B	O	Q	K	A	M	E	Y
Number	0	1	2	3	4	5	6	7	8	9

For each question, compare each line of letters and numbers carefully to see if each letter is matched correctly to its corresponding number. Mark your answer according to the number of lines in which all of the letters and numbers are matched correctly.

Mark (A) if NONE of the lines is matched correctly
Mark (B) if only ONE of the lines is matched correctly
Mark (C) if TWO of the lines are matched correctly
Mark (D) if all THREE lines are matched correctly

75.			75. Ⓐ Ⓑ Ⓒ Ⓓ
	SEOB	1732	
	YMQA	9756	
	BEPM	2806	

The correct answer is **(A).**

75. **(A)** In the first line, *E* is incorrectly matched with *7*. In the second line, *Q* is incorrectly matched with *5*. In the third line, *M* is incorrectly matched with *6*. Since all of the letters and numbers are matched correctly in none of the lines, the answer is (A).

On the other exam, the directions looked like this:

Directions: The numbers on each line of each question should correspond with the code letters on the same line in accordance with the table below:

Code Letter	M	Q	O	H	B	C	I	N	Y	V
Number	0	1	2	3	4	5	6	7	8	9

In some of the lines below, an error exists in the coding. Compare the numbers and letters in each question very carefully. Mark your answers according to the number of lines in which you find an error or errors.

Mark (A) if only ONE line contains an error or errors
Mark (B) if TWO lines contain errors
Mark (C) if all THREE lines contain errors
Mark (D) if NONE of the lines contains an error

76.   BCMHIOB   4503624   76. Ⓐ Ⓑ Ⓒ Ⓓ
          VYBQNCO   8941752
          MHBCNIV   0345869

The correct answer is **(B).**

76. **(B)** Line 1 contains no errors. It is correctly coded. On the second line, *V* is incorrectly coded as *8*, and *Y* is incorrectly coded as *9*. On the third line, *N* is incorrectly coded as *8*. There are three errors, but the three errors occur on only two lines, so the correct answer is (B).

Summary

The keys to success with multiple-choice questions are care with the use of answer sheets, budgeting of time, and accurate reading of directions and questions.

Study and practice for the specific exam that you must take can, of course, give you a further advantage over the competition. In addition to the practice exams in this book, ARCO has prepared a series of civil service test-prep books that give you instructions and advice for preparing for your specific exam. Most books also contain actual previous exams or exams that we have created to closely resemble the real thing. Taking the real or model exams gives you a chance to learn to pace yourself to finish an exam and to leave time to check it over.

SAMPLE U.S. POSTAL SERVICE EXAMINATION—EXAMS 470 AND 460

The Postal Service requires that all applicants for the following eight positions take the exam titled Battery 470/460:

Postal Clerk

City Carrier

Distribution Clerk, Machine

Flat Sorting Machine Operator

Mail Handler

Mail Processor

Mark-up Clerk, Automated

Rural Carrier

Exams 470 and 460 are identical, except that 460 is titled for rural carrier.

The 470/460 Exam measures general vocabulary and reading level, in addition to special aptitudes needed for a particular position, such as the ability to check and compare addresses, memorize addresses, follow oral directions, and recognize patterns. It's a multiple-choice format.

Practice Test

ANSWER SHEET—FULL-LENGTH PRACTICE TEST

Part A: Address Checking

1. Ⓐ Ⓓ	20. Ⓐ Ⓓ	39. Ⓐ Ⓓ	58. Ⓐ Ⓓ	77. Ⓐ Ⓓ
2. Ⓐ Ⓓ	21. Ⓐ Ⓓ	40. Ⓐ Ⓓ	59. Ⓐ Ⓓ	78. Ⓐ Ⓓ
3. Ⓐ Ⓓ	22. Ⓐ Ⓓ	41. Ⓐ Ⓓ	60. Ⓐ Ⓓ	79. Ⓐ Ⓓ
4. Ⓐ Ⓓ	23. Ⓐ Ⓓ	42. Ⓐ Ⓓ	61. Ⓐ Ⓓ	80. Ⓐ Ⓓ
5. Ⓐ Ⓓ	24. Ⓐ Ⓓ	43. Ⓐ Ⓓ	62. Ⓐ Ⓓ	81. Ⓐ Ⓓ
6. Ⓐ Ⓓ	25. Ⓐ Ⓓ	44. Ⓐ Ⓓ	63. Ⓐ Ⓓ	82. Ⓐ Ⓓ
7. Ⓐ Ⓓ	26. Ⓐ Ⓓ	45. Ⓐ Ⓓ	64. Ⓐ Ⓓ	83. Ⓐ Ⓓ
8. Ⓐ Ⓓ	27. Ⓐ Ⓓ	46. Ⓐ Ⓓ	65. Ⓐ Ⓓ	84. Ⓐ Ⓓ
9. Ⓐ Ⓓ	28. Ⓐ Ⓓ	47. Ⓐ Ⓓ	66. Ⓐ Ⓓ	85. Ⓐ Ⓓ
10. Ⓐ Ⓓ	29. Ⓐ Ⓓ	48. Ⓐ Ⓓ	67. Ⓐ Ⓓ	86. Ⓐ Ⓓ
11. Ⓐ Ⓓ	30. Ⓐ Ⓓ	49. Ⓐ Ⓓ	68. Ⓐ Ⓓ	87. Ⓐ Ⓓ
12. Ⓐ Ⓓ	31. Ⓐ Ⓓ	50. Ⓐ Ⓓ	69. Ⓐ Ⓓ	88. Ⓐ Ⓓ
13. Ⓐ Ⓓ	32. Ⓐ Ⓓ	51. Ⓐ Ⓓ	70. Ⓐ Ⓓ	89. Ⓐ Ⓓ
14. Ⓐ Ⓓ	33. Ⓐ Ⓓ	52. Ⓐ Ⓓ	71. Ⓐ Ⓓ	90. Ⓐ Ⓓ
15. Ⓐ Ⓓ	34. Ⓐ Ⓓ	53. Ⓐ Ⓓ	72. Ⓐ Ⓓ	91. Ⓐ Ⓓ
16. Ⓐ Ⓓ	35. Ⓐ Ⓓ	54. Ⓐ Ⓓ	73. Ⓐ Ⓓ	92. Ⓐ Ⓓ
17. Ⓐ Ⓓ	36. Ⓐ Ⓓ	55. Ⓐ Ⓓ	74. Ⓐ Ⓓ	93. Ⓐ Ⓓ
18. Ⓐ Ⓓ	37. Ⓐ Ⓓ	56. Ⓐ Ⓓ	75. Ⓐ Ⓓ	94. Ⓐ Ⓓ
19. Ⓐ Ⓓ	38. Ⓐ Ⓓ	57. Ⓐ Ⓓ	76. Ⓐ Ⓓ	95. Ⓐ Ⓓ

TEAR HERE

Part B: Memory for Addresses

1 Ⓐ Ⓑ Ⓒ Ⓓ Ⓔ	23 Ⓐ Ⓑ Ⓒ Ⓓ Ⓔ	45 Ⓐ Ⓑ Ⓒ Ⓓ Ⓔ	67 Ⓐ Ⓑ Ⓒ Ⓓ Ⓔ
2 Ⓐ Ⓑ Ⓒ Ⓓ Ⓔ	24 Ⓐ Ⓑ Ⓒ Ⓓ Ⓔ	46 Ⓐ Ⓑ Ⓒ Ⓓ Ⓔ	68 Ⓐ Ⓑ Ⓒ Ⓓ Ⓔ
3 Ⓐ Ⓑ Ⓒ Ⓓ Ⓔ	25 Ⓐ Ⓑ Ⓒ Ⓓ Ⓔ	47 Ⓐ Ⓑ Ⓒ Ⓓ Ⓔ	69 Ⓐ Ⓑ Ⓒ Ⓓ Ⓔ
4 Ⓐ Ⓑ Ⓒ Ⓓ Ⓔ	26 Ⓐ Ⓑ Ⓒ Ⓓ Ⓔ	48 Ⓐ Ⓑ Ⓒ Ⓓ Ⓔ	70 Ⓐ Ⓑ Ⓒ Ⓓ Ⓔ
5 Ⓐ Ⓑ Ⓒ Ⓓ Ⓔ	27 Ⓐ Ⓑ Ⓒ Ⓓ Ⓔ	49 Ⓐ Ⓑ Ⓒ Ⓓ Ⓔ	71 Ⓐ Ⓑ Ⓒ Ⓓ Ⓔ
6 Ⓐ Ⓑ Ⓒ Ⓓ Ⓔ	28 Ⓐ Ⓑ Ⓒ Ⓓ Ⓔ	50 Ⓐ Ⓑ Ⓒ Ⓓ Ⓔ	72 Ⓐ Ⓑ Ⓒ Ⓓ Ⓔ
7 Ⓐ Ⓑ Ⓒ Ⓓ Ⓔ	29 Ⓐ Ⓑ Ⓒ Ⓓ Ⓔ	51 Ⓐ Ⓑ Ⓒ Ⓓ Ⓔ	73 Ⓐ Ⓑ Ⓒ Ⓓ Ⓔ
8 Ⓐ Ⓑ Ⓒ Ⓓ Ⓔ	30 Ⓐ Ⓑ Ⓒ Ⓓ Ⓔ	52 Ⓐ Ⓑ Ⓒ Ⓓ Ⓔ	74 Ⓐ Ⓑ Ⓒ Ⓓ Ⓔ
9 Ⓐ Ⓑ Ⓒ Ⓓ Ⓔ	31 Ⓐ Ⓑ Ⓒ Ⓓ Ⓔ	53 Ⓐ Ⓑ Ⓒ Ⓓ Ⓔ	75 Ⓐ Ⓑ Ⓒ Ⓓ Ⓔ
10 Ⓐ Ⓑ Ⓒ Ⓓ Ⓔ	32 Ⓐ Ⓑ Ⓒ Ⓓ Ⓔ	54 Ⓐ Ⓑ Ⓒ Ⓓ Ⓔ	76 Ⓐ Ⓑ Ⓒ Ⓓ Ⓔ
11 Ⓐ Ⓑ Ⓒ Ⓓ Ⓔ	33 Ⓐ Ⓑ Ⓒ Ⓓ Ⓔ	55 Ⓐ Ⓑ Ⓒ Ⓓ Ⓔ	77 Ⓐ Ⓑ Ⓒ Ⓓ Ⓔ
12 Ⓐ Ⓑ Ⓒ Ⓓ Ⓔ	34 Ⓐ Ⓑ Ⓒ Ⓓ Ⓔ	56 Ⓐ Ⓑ Ⓒ Ⓓ Ⓔ	78 Ⓐ Ⓑ Ⓒ Ⓓ Ⓔ
13 Ⓐ Ⓑ Ⓒ Ⓓ Ⓔ	35 Ⓐ Ⓑ Ⓒ Ⓓ Ⓔ	57 Ⓐ Ⓑ Ⓒ Ⓓ Ⓔ	79 Ⓐ Ⓑ Ⓒ Ⓓ Ⓔ
14 Ⓐ Ⓑ Ⓒ Ⓓ Ⓔ	36 Ⓐ Ⓑ Ⓒ Ⓓ Ⓔ	58 Ⓐ Ⓑ Ⓒ Ⓓ Ⓔ	80 Ⓐ Ⓑ Ⓒ Ⓓ Ⓔ
15 Ⓐ Ⓑ Ⓒ Ⓓ Ⓔ	37 Ⓐ Ⓑ Ⓒ Ⓓ Ⓔ	59 Ⓐ Ⓑ Ⓒ Ⓓ Ⓔ	81 Ⓐ Ⓑ Ⓒ Ⓓ Ⓔ
16 Ⓐ Ⓑ Ⓒ Ⓓ Ⓔ	38 Ⓐ Ⓑ Ⓒ Ⓓ Ⓔ	60 Ⓐ Ⓑ Ⓒ Ⓓ Ⓔ	82 Ⓐ Ⓑ Ⓒ Ⓓ Ⓔ
17 Ⓐ Ⓑ Ⓒ Ⓓ Ⓔ	39 Ⓐ Ⓑ Ⓒ Ⓓ Ⓔ	61 Ⓐ Ⓑ Ⓒ Ⓓ Ⓔ	83 Ⓐ Ⓑ Ⓒ Ⓓ Ⓔ
18 Ⓐ Ⓑ Ⓒ Ⓓ Ⓔ	40 Ⓐ Ⓑ Ⓒ Ⓓ Ⓔ	62 Ⓐ Ⓑ Ⓒ Ⓓ Ⓔ	84 Ⓐ Ⓑ Ⓒ Ⓓ Ⓔ
19 Ⓐ Ⓑ Ⓒ Ⓓ Ⓔ	41 Ⓐ Ⓑ Ⓒ Ⓓ Ⓔ	63 Ⓐ Ⓑ Ⓒ Ⓓ Ⓔ	85 Ⓐ Ⓑ Ⓒ Ⓓ Ⓔ
20 Ⓐ Ⓑ Ⓒ Ⓓ Ⓔ	42 Ⓐ Ⓑ Ⓒ Ⓓ Ⓔ	64 Ⓐ Ⓑ Ⓒ Ⓓ Ⓔ	86 Ⓐ Ⓑ Ⓒ Ⓓ Ⓔ
21 Ⓐ Ⓑ Ⓒ Ⓓ Ⓔ	43 Ⓐ Ⓑ Ⓒ Ⓓ Ⓔ	65 Ⓐ Ⓑ Ⓒ Ⓓ Ⓔ	87 Ⓐ Ⓑ Ⓒ Ⓓ Ⓔ
22 Ⓐ Ⓑ Ⓒ Ⓓ Ⓔ	44 Ⓐ Ⓑ Ⓒ Ⓓ Ⓔ	66 Ⓐ Ⓑ Ⓒ Ⓓ Ⓔ	88 Ⓐ Ⓑ Ⓒ Ⓓ Ⓔ

Part C: Number Series

1. Ⓐ Ⓑ Ⓒ Ⓓ Ⓔ	7. Ⓐ Ⓑ Ⓒ Ⓓ Ⓔ	13. Ⓐ Ⓑ Ⓒ Ⓓ Ⓔ	19. Ⓐ Ⓑ Ⓒ Ⓓ Ⓔ
2. Ⓐ Ⓑ Ⓒ Ⓓ Ⓔ	8. Ⓐ Ⓑ Ⓒ Ⓓ Ⓔ	14. Ⓐ Ⓑ Ⓒ Ⓓ Ⓔ	20. Ⓐ Ⓑ Ⓒ Ⓓ Ⓔ
3. Ⓐ Ⓑ Ⓒ Ⓓ Ⓔ	9. Ⓐ Ⓑ Ⓒ Ⓓ Ⓔ	15. Ⓐ Ⓑ Ⓒ Ⓓ Ⓔ	21. Ⓐ Ⓑ Ⓒ Ⓓ Ⓔ
4. Ⓐ Ⓑ Ⓒ Ⓓ Ⓔ	10. Ⓐ Ⓑ Ⓒ Ⓓ Ⓔ	16. Ⓐ Ⓑ Ⓒ Ⓓ Ⓔ	22. Ⓐ Ⓑ Ⓒ Ⓓ Ⓔ
5. Ⓐ Ⓑ Ⓒ Ⓓ Ⓔ	11. Ⓐ Ⓑ Ⓒ Ⓓ Ⓔ	17. Ⓐ Ⓑ Ⓒ Ⓓ Ⓔ	23. Ⓐ Ⓑ Ⓒ Ⓓ Ⓔ
6. Ⓐ Ⓑ Ⓒ Ⓓ Ⓔ	12. Ⓐ Ⓑ Ⓒ Ⓓ Ⓔ	18. Ⓐ Ⓑ Ⓒ Ⓓ Ⓔ	24. Ⓐ Ⓑ Ⓒ Ⓓ Ⓔ

Part D: Following Oral Instructions

1 Ⓐ Ⓑ Ⓒ Ⓓ Ⓔ   23 Ⓐ Ⓑ Ⓒ Ⓓ Ⓔ   45 Ⓐ Ⓑ Ⓒ Ⓓ Ⓔ   67 Ⓐ Ⓑ Ⓒ Ⓓ Ⓔ

2 Ⓐ Ⓑ Ⓒ Ⓓ Ⓔ   24 Ⓐ Ⓑ Ⓒ Ⓓ Ⓔ   46 Ⓐ Ⓑ Ⓒ Ⓓ Ⓔ   68 Ⓐ Ⓑ Ⓒ Ⓓ Ⓔ

3 Ⓐ Ⓑ Ⓒ Ⓓ Ⓔ   25 Ⓐ Ⓑ Ⓒ Ⓓ Ⓔ   47 Ⓐ Ⓑ Ⓒ Ⓓ Ⓔ   69 Ⓐ Ⓑ Ⓒ Ⓓ Ⓔ

4 Ⓐ Ⓑ Ⓒ Ⓓ Ⓔ   26 Ⓐ Ⓑ Ⓒ Ⓓ Ⓔ   48 Ⓐ Ⓑ Ⓒ Ⓓ Ⓔ   70 Ⓐ Ⓑ Ⓒ Ⓓ Ⓔ

5 Ⓐ Ⓑ Ⓒ Ⓓ Ⓔ   27 Ⓐ Ⓑ Ⓒ Ⓓ Ⓔ   49 Ⓐ Ⓑ Ⓒ Ⓓ Ⓔ   71 Ⓐ Ⓑ Ⓒ Ⓓ Ⓔ

6 Ⓐ Ⓑ Ⓒ Ⓓ Ⓔ   28 Ⓐ Ⓑ Ⓒ Ⓓ Ⓔ   50 Ⓐ Ⓑ Ⓒ Ⓓ Ⓔ   72 Ⓐ Ⓑ Ⓒ Ⓓ Ⓔ

7 Ⓐ Ⓑ Ⓒ Ⓓ Ⓔ   29 Ⓐ Ⓑ Ⓒ Ⓓ Ⓔ   51 Ⓐ Ⓑ Ⓒ Ⓓ Ⓔ   73 Ⓐ Ⓑ Ⓒ Ⓓ Ⓔ

8 Ⓐ Ⓑ Ⓒ Ⓓ Ⓔ   30 Ⓐ Ⓑ Ⓒ Ⓓ Ⓔ   52 Ⓐ Ⓑ Ⓒ Ⓓ Ⓔ   74 Ⓐ Ⓑ Ⓒ Ⓓ Ⓔ

9 Ⓐ Ⓑ Ⓒ Ⓓ Ⓔ   31 Ⓐ Ⓑ Ⓒ Ⓓ Ⓔ   53 Ⓐ Ⓑ Ⓒ Ⓓ Ⓔ   75 Ⓐ Ⓑ Ⓒ Ⓓ Ⓔ

10 Ⓐ Ⓑ Ⓒ Ⓓ Ⓔ   32 Ⓐ Ⓑ Ⓒ Ⓓ Ⓔ   54 Ⓐ Ⓑ Ⓒ Ⓓ Ⓔ   76 Ⓐ Ⓑ Ⓒ Ⓓ Ⓔ

11 Ⓐ Ⓑ Ⓒ Ⓓ Ⓔ   33 Ⓐ Ⓑ Ⓒ Ⓓ Ⓔ   55 Ⓐ Ⓑ Ⓒ Ⓓ Ⓔ   77 Ⓐ Ⓑ Ⓒ Ⓓ Ⓔ

12 Ⓐ Ⓑ Ⓒ Ⓓ Ⓔ   34 Ⓐ Ⓑ Ⓒ Ⓓ Ⓔ   56 Ⓐ Ⓑ Ⓒ Ⓓ Ⓔ   78 Ⓐ Ⓑ Ⓒ Ⓓ Ⓔ

13 Ⓐ Ⓑ Ⓒ Ⓓ Ⓔ   35 Ⓐ Ⓑ Ⓒ Ⓓ Ⓔ   57 Ⓐ Ⓑ Ⓒ Ⓓ Ⓔ   79 Ⓐ Ⓑ Ⓒ Ⓓ Ⓔ

14 Ⓐ Ⓑ Ⓒ Ⓓ Ⓔ   36 Ⓐ Ⓑ Ⓒ Ⓓ Ⓔ   58 Ⓐ Ⓑ Ⓒ Ⓓ Ⓔ   80 Ⓐ Ⓑ Ⓒ Ⓓ Ⓔ

15 Ⓐ Ⓑ Ⓒ Ⓓ Ⓔ   37 Ⓐ Ⓑ Ⓒ Ⓓ Ⓔ   59 Ⓐ Ⓑ Ⓒ Ⓓ Ⓔ   81 Ⓐ Ⓑ Ⓒ Ⓓ Ⓔ

16 Ⓐ Ⓑ Ⓒ Ⓓ Ⓔ   38 Ⓐ Ⓑ Ⓒ Ⓓ Ⓔ   60 Ⓐ Ⓑ Ⓒ Ⓓ Ⓔ   82 Ⓐ Ⓑ Ⓒ Ⓓ Ⓔ

17 Ⓐ Ⓑ Ⓒ Ⓓ Ⓔ   39 Ⓐ Ⓑ Ⓒ Ⓓ Ⓔ   61 Ⓐ Ⓑ Ⓒ Ⓓ Ⓔ   83 Ⓐ Ⓑ Ⓒ Ⓓ Ⓔ

18 Ⓐ Ⓑ Ⓒ Ⓓ Ⓔ   40 Ⓐ Ⓑ Ⓒ Ⓓ Ⓔ   62 Ⓐ Ⓑ Ⓒ Ⓓ Ⓔ   84 Ⓐ Ⓑ Ⓒ Ⓓ Ⓔ

19 Ⓐ Ⓑ Ⓒ Ⓓ Ⓔ   41 Ⓐ Ⓑ Ⓒ Ⓓ Ⓔ   63 Ⓐ Ⓑ Ⓒ Ⓓ Ⓔ   85 Ⓐ Ⓑ Ⓒ Ⓓ Ⓔ

20 Ⓐ Ⓑ Ⓒ Ⓓ Ⓔ   42 Ⓐ Ⓑ Ⓒ Ⓓ Ⓔ   64 Ⓐ Ⓑ Ⓒ Ⓓ Ⓔ   86 Ⓐ Ⓑ Ⓒ Ⓓ Ⓔ

21 Ⓐ Ⓑ Ⓒ Ⓓ Ⓔ   43 Ⓐ Ⓑ Ⓒ Ⓓ Ⓔ   65 Ⓐ Ⓑ Ⓒ Ⓓ Ⓔ   87 Ⓐ Ⓑ Ⓒ Ⓓ Ⓔ

22 Ⓐ Ⓑ Ⓒ Ⓓ Ⓔ   44 Ⓐ Ⓑ Ⓒ Ⓓ Ⓔ   66 Ⓐ Ⓑ Ⓒ Ⓓ Ⓔ   88 Ⓐ Ⓑ Ⓒ Ⓓ Ⓔ

PART A: ADDRESS CHECKING

Sample Questions

You have three minutes to mark your answers to the sample questions on the sample answer sheet below.

Directions: *For each question, compare the address in the left column with the address in the right column. If the two addresses are ALIKE in every way, write A next to the question number. If the two addresses are DIFFERENT in any way, write D next to the question number.*

1. . . . 3380 State Street	3380 S State Street	
2. . . . 2618 Comly Way	2816 Comly Way	
3. . . . Greenvale MA 11548	Greenvale MA 11548	
4. . . . Harrison CO 80523	Harrisan CO 80523	
5. . . . 7214 SW 83rd St	7214 SW 83rd St	

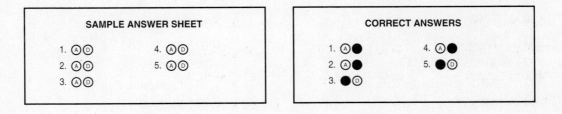

Address Checking

Time: 6 Minutes • 95 Questions

For each question, compare the address in the left column with the address in the right column. If the two addresses are ALIKE in every way, blacken space A on your answer sheet. If the two addresses are DIFFERENT in any way, blacken space D on your answer sheet.

1. . . . 12310 Claire Pl	12310 Claire Pl
2. . . . 24038 Johnson Rd	24038 Johnston Rd
3. . . . 578 Abraham Kazan Blvd	578 Abraham Kazan Blvd
4. . . . 11390 W Dogwood Rd	111390 E Dogwood Rd
5. . . . 11000 West Plaza Cir	11000 West Plaza Cir
6. . . . Canadiqua NY 14424	Canadiqua NY 14424
7. . . . 13450 Montgomery Park	13450 Montegomery Park
8. . . . 16235 Zimbrich Dr	16235 Zimbrench Dr
9. . . . 43961 Remmington Ave	43961 Remmington Ave
10. . . . 11236 Shorewood La	11236 Sherwood La
11. . . . 16002 Dalewood Gardens	1602 Dalewood Gardens
12. . . . 11335 Yarkerdale Dr	11335 Yorkerdale Dr
13. . . . 12305 NE Teutonia Ave	12305 NW Teutonia Ave
14. . . . 1508 Duanesburg Rd	1508 Duanesburg Rd
15. . . . Wachapregue VA 23480	Wachapergue Rd 23480

16. . . . 34001 E Atkinson Cir	34001 E Atkinson Cir
17. . . . 43872 E Tottenham Rd	43873 E Tottenham Rd
18. . . . 13531 Briar Ave NE	13531 Briar Ave NW
19. . . . 22633 N Abingdon Pl	22336 N Abingdon Pl
20. . . . 14615 Leni Lenape Way	14615 Leni Lenape Way
21. . . . 15609 Seaside Ter	15609 Seaside Park
22. . . . 10001 N Magee Ave	10001 N McGee Ave
23. . . . 14617 Quattara Blvd	14716 Quattara Blvd
24. . . . 89 South Timberland Rd	89 South Timberland Rd
25. . . . 18619 Boca Largo Park	18619 Boca Largo Pky
26. . . . 29888 Abbey View Way	29888 Abbey View Way
27. . . . 16567 Handle Rd	16567 Handel Rd
28. . . . 18900 W Passaic Ave	18900 S Passaic Ave
29. . . . 9092 E Trelawne Dr	9092 E Treelawne Dr
30. . . . 8202 NE Morrisville St	8201 NE Morrisville St
31. . . . Emancipation PR 00802	Emancipation PR 00802
32. . . . 11925 Fairfield Cir	11925 Fairfield Dr
33. . . . 41011 Livingston Park A	41011 Livingston Park B
34. . . . 15789 Kearny Rd	157879 Kearny St
35. . . . 31991 Springvale Rd	31991 Springville Rd
36. . . . 14201 W Galbraith Ave	14201 W Galbraith Ave
37. . . . 21235 Laureldale La	21235 Laureldell La
38. . . . 11235 N Coletown Ave	11235 N Coaltown Ave
39. . . . 21003 NE Cronwell Blvd	21003 NE Cromwell Blvd
40. . . . 47989 S Bloomfield Dr	49789 S Bloomfield Dr
41. . . . 22122 Roebling Rd	22122 Rowbeling Rd
42. . . . 4434 N Glenorchard Ln;	4434 N Glenorchard Ln
43. . . . 12087 Neyartnell Pky	12087 Neyartell Pky
44. . . . 31756 Falconbridge Dr	31756 Falconbridge Dr
45. . . . Stambaugh MI 49964	Stanbaugh MI 49964
46. . . . 16735 Haledon Ln	16735 Haledom Ln
47. . . . 133288 La Torneau Ave	133288 La Torneau Ave
48. . . . 10154 Ottercreek Rd	10154 Ottercreek Rd
49. . . . 4867 NE Kellerman Ct	4867 NE Kellerman Ct
50. . . . 15089 Brookhavenn Cir	15089 Brookhaven Dr
51. . . . 12196 SW Westminster Pl	12196 SW Westminster Pl
52. . . . 7800 SE Grantham Way	7800 SE Grantham Way
53. . . . 20697 Indianbluff Dr	20997 Indianbluff Dr
54. . . . 4400 Amberacres Rd	4400 Amberacres Rd
55. . . . 5801 Paulmeadows Dr	5801 Paulmeadows Dr
56. . . . 5101 Pinehurst Ln	5101 Pinehorst Ln

57.	8966 Verona Ct NE	8966 Verona Cir NE
58.	1399 Valhalla Ave NE	1399 Valhalla Ave SE
59.	12397 Reicosky Ln NW	12397 Reikosky Ln NW
60.	3600 Palmetto Ave SE	3600 Palmetto Ave SE
61.	5260 Gettysburg W	5260 Gettysburg W
62.	4563 Terrahaute Dr NW	4563 Terrahaute Dr NW
63.	2190 Glastonbury Dr SE	2190 Glastonberry Dr SE
64.	2207 Hazleton Cir	2207 Hazelton Cir
65.	11300 North Central Ave	11300 North Center Ave
66.	21205 Canadensis Cir	21205 Canadenses Cir
67.	4499 Mt. Carmel Ave	4499 Mt. Carmel St.
68.	4056 Maplewood Ln NW	4056 Mapplewood Ln SW
69.	Tamaqua OH 45624	Tamaqua OH 45624
70.	1257 Zesiger Ave	1257 Zesinger Ave
71.	2697 Remington Ave NW	2697 Remington Ave NW
72.	5409 East Tremont Rd	5409 East Tremont Rd
73.	901 Airymeadows Ln	901 Airymeadows Ln
74.	1795 NE Second Ave	1795 NW Second Ave
75.	PO Box 46972	PO Box 46792
76.	11299 Wolverine Ct SE	11929 Wolverine Ct Se
77.	2000 Bloomnigdale Ave NW	2000 Bloomingdale St NW
78.	3989 Phillipsburg Pl NW	3989 Phillipsberg Pl NW
79.	5700 Inverness Pky SE	5700 Inverness Pky SE
80.	899 Mount Graymore Ave NE	899 Mount Greymore Ave NE
81.	1166 Crockett Ave SE	1166 Crockett Ave SE
82.	89001 Flathollow Trl	89001 Flathollow Trl
83.	Fort Steilacoon WA 98494	Fort Stielacoon WA 98494
84.	2255 Parkridge Cir NW	2255 Partridge Cir NW
85.	5477 Westbury Ave NE	5477 Westbury St NE
86.	35501 Gambrinus Ct SE	3501 Gambrinus Ct SE
87.	11089 Stanhaus St NW	11909 Stanhaus st NW
88.	7700 Cherryhill Dr NW	7700 Cherryhill Cir NW
89.	3303 Allendale Pl SE	3303 Allendale Pl NE
90.	22449 Tatamy Trl	22449 Tatamy Trl
91.	8803 Lawrence Rd S	8803 Lawrence Rd S
92.	12468 Deer Run Ave	12486 Deer Run Ave
93.	Kitatinny AK 99681	Kitatinny AR 99681
94.	700 Equinunk Falls Rd	700 Equinank Falls Rd
95.	297 Montville Valley Ct NW	297 Montville Valley St NW

END OF ADDRESS CHECKING

PART B: MEMORY FOR ADDRESSES

Sample Questions

In this part of the test you will have to memorize the locations (A, B, C, D, or E) of the 25 addresses in the 5 lettered boxes below. Your task is to mark on your answer sheet the letter of the box in which each address belongs.

You will now have five minutes to study the locations of the addresses. Then cover the boxes and answer the questions. You may look back at the boxes if you cannot yet mark the address locations from memory.

The exam provides three practice sessions before the actual test, in addition to these sample questions. Practice I and Practice III supply you with the boxes and permit you to refer to them if necessary. Practice II and the actual Memory for Addresses test do not permit you to look at the boxes.

A	B	C	D	E
2300-3499 Main	3500-3999 Main	4000-4299 Main	1200-2199 Main	2200-2299 Main
Liberty	Willow	Hopper	Magnet	Carrot
4000-4299 Oak	2200-2299 Oak	1200-2199 Oak	3500-3999 Oak	2300-3499 Oak
Iron	Boulder	Window	Press	Forest
1200-2199 Post	2300-3499 Post	3500-3999 Post	2200-2299 Post	4000-4299 Post

1. Willow

2. 2200-2299 Oak

3. 1200-2199 Post

4. 4000-4299 Main

5. Press

6. Carrot

7. 2200-2299 Post

8. 2200-2299 Main

9. 4000-4299 Oak

10. 3500-3999 Main

11. Boulder

12. Forest

13. 1200-2199 Oak

14. 2300-3499 Post

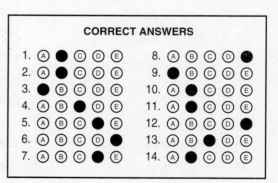

Practice for Memory for Addresses

Directions: The five boxes below are labeled A, B, C, D, and E. In each box are five addresses: Three are street addresses with number ranges and two are unnumbered place names. You have three minutes to memorize the box location of each address. The position of an address within a box is not important. You need only remember the letter of the box in which the address is found. You will use these addresses to answer three sets of practice questions that are NOT scored and one actual test that is scored.

A	B	C	D	E
2300-3499 Main	3500-3999 Main	4000-4299 Main	1200-2199 Main	2200-2299 Main
Liberty	Willow	Hopper	Magnet	Carrot
4000-4299 Oak	2200-2299 Oak	1200-2199 Oak	3500-3999 Oak	2300-3499 Oak
Iron	Boulder	Window	Press	Forest
1200-2199 Post	2300-3499 Post	3500-3999 Post	2200-2299 Post	4000-4299 Post

Practice I

Directions: You have three minutes to mark on your answer sheet the letter of the box in which each of the following addresses is found. Try to do this without looking at the boxes. However, if you get stuck, you may refer to the boxes during this practice exercise. If you must look at the boxes, try to memorize as you do so. This test is for practice only. It will not be scored.

1. 3500-3999 Oak
2. 2300-3499 Post
3. Iron
4. Forest
5. 4000-4299 Main
6. 2300-3299 Oak
7. 3500-3999 Post
8. 2300-3499 Main
9. Magnet
10. Carrot
11. 2200-2299 Post
12. 3500-3999 Main
13. 2200-2299 Main
14. 4000-4299 Oak
15. Liberty
16. Willow
17. 1200-2199 Oak
18. 1200-2199 Main
19. Window
20. Press
21. 2300-3499 Post
22. 4000-4299 Oak

23. 4000-4299 Post
24. 3500-3999 Oak
25. Magnet
26. Boulder
27. Willow
28. 4000-4299 Main
29. 2300-3499 Main
30. 3500-3999 Post
31. 1200-2199 Post
32. Liberty
33. Carrot
34. 2200-2299 Oak
35. 2300-3499 Oak
36. Hopper
37. Iron
38. 2200-2299 Post
39. 3500-3999 Main
40. 2200-2299 Main
41. Forest
42. Windows
43. 3500-3999 Oak
44. 2300-3499 Post

45. 2300-3499 Main
46. 2200-2299 Oak
47. 3500-3999 Post
48. 3500-3999 Oak
49. 2200-2299 Main
50. Magnet
51. Window
52. Willow
53. 4000-4299 Post
54. Press
55. 1200-2199 Oak
56. Boulder
57. 1200-2199 Post
58. 4000-4299 Oak
59. 2300-3499 Oak
60. 4000-4299 Main
61. Carrot
62. Forrest
63. 1200-2199 Main
64. 3500-3999 Main
65. 2300-3499 Post
66. Liberty

67. Hopper
68. 2200-2299 Post
69. Iron
70. 1200-2199 Oak
71. 3500-3999 Post
72. Boulder
73. 2200-2299 Main
74. 1200-2199 Post

75. Press
76. Carrot
77. 4000-4299 Post
78. 4000-4299 Oak
79. 2300-3499 Main
80. 3500-3999 Oak
81. Window
82. Hopper

83. Boulder
84. 1200-2199 Oak
85. 1200-2199 Main
86. 2300-3499 Post
87. Willow
88. Liberty

Practice I Answer Sheet

1 Ⓐ Ⓑ Ⓒ Ⓓ Ⓔ   23 Ⓐ Ⓑ Ⓒ Ⓓ Ⓔ   45 Ⓐ Ⓑ Ⓒ Ⓓ Ⓔ   67 Ⓐ Ⓑ Ⓒ Ⓓ Ⓔ
2 Ⓐ Ⓑ Ⓒ Ⓓ Ⓔ   24 Ⓐ Ⓑ Ⓒ Ⓓ Ⓔ   46 Ⓐ Ⓑ Ⓒ Ⓓ Ⓔ   68 Ⓐ Ⓑ Ⓒ Ⓓ Ⓔ
3 Ⓐ Ⓑ Ⓒ Ⓓ Ⓔ   25 Ⓐ Ⓑ Ⓒ Ⓓ Ⓔ   47 Ⓐ Ⓑ Ⓒ Ⓓ Ⓔ   69 Ⓐ Ⓑ Ⓒ Ⓓ Ⓔ
4 Ⓐ Ⓑ Ⓒ Ⓓ Ⓔ   26 Ⓐ Ⓑ Ⓒ Ⓓ Ⓔ   48 Ⓐ Ⓑ Ⓒ Ⓓ Ⓔ   70 Ⓐ Ⓑ Ⓒ Ⓓ Ⓔ
5 Ⓐ Ⓑ Ⓒ Ⓓ Ⓔ   27 Ⓐ Ⓑ Ⓒ Ⓓ Ⓔ   49 Ⓐ Ⓑ Ⓒ Ⓓ Ⓔ   71 Ⓐ Ⓑ Ⓒ Ⓓ Ⓔ
6 Ⓐ Ⓑ Ⓒ Ⓓ Ⓔ   28 Ⓐ Ⓑ Ⓒ Ⓓ Ⓔ   50 Ⓐ Ⓑ Ⓒ Ⓓ Ⓔ   72 Ⓐ Ⓑ Ⓒ Ⓓ Ⓔ
7 Ⓐ Ⓑ Ⓒ Ⓓ Ⓔ   29 Ⓐ Ⓑ Ⓒ Ⓓ Ⓔ   51 Ⓐ Ⓑ Ⓒ Ⓓ Ⓔ   73 Ⓐ Ⓑ Ⓒ Ⓓ Ⓔ
8 Ⓐ Ⓑ Ⓒ Ⓓ Ⓔ   30 Ⓐ Ⓑ Ⓒ Ⓓ Ⓔ   52 Ⓐ Ⓑ Ⓒ Ⓓ Ⓔ   74 Ⓐ Ⓑ Ⓒ Ⓓ Ⓔ
9 Ⓐ Ⓑ Ⓒ Ⓓ Ⓔ   31 Ⓐ Ⓑ Ⓒ Ⓓ Ⓔ   53 Ⓐ Ⓑ Ⓒ Ⓓ Ⓔ   75 Ⓐ Ⓑ Ⓒ Ⓓ Ⓔ
10 Ⓐ Ⓑ Ⓒ Ⓓ Ⓔ   32 Ⓐ Ⓑ Ⓒ Ⓓ Ⓔ   54 Ⓐ Ⓑ Ⓒ Ⓓ Ⓔ   76 Ⓐ Ⓑ Ⓒ Ⓓ Ⓔ
11 Ⓐ Ⓑ Ⓒ Ⓓ Ⓔ   33 Ⓐ Ⓑ Ⓒ Ⓓ Ⓔ   55 Ⓐ Ⓑ Ⓒ Ⓓ Ⓔ   77 Ⓐ Ⓑ Ⓒ Ⓓ Ⓔ
12 Ⓐ Ⓑ Ⓒ Ⓓ Ⓔ   34 Ⓐ Ⓑ Ⓒ Ⓓ Ⓔ   56 Ⓐ Ⓑ Ⓒ Ⓓ Ⓔ   78 Ⓐ Ⓑ Ⓒ Ⓓ Ⓔ
13 Ⓐ Ⓑ Ⓒ Ⓓ Ⓔ   35 Ⓐ Ⓑ Ⓒ Ⓓ Ⓔ   57 Ⓐ Ⓑ Ⓒ Ⓓ Ⓔ   79 Ⓐ Ⓑ Ⓒ Ⓓ Ⓔ
14 Ⓐ Ⓑ Ⓒ Ⓓ Ⓔ   36 Ⓐ Ⓑ Ⓒ Ⓓ Ⓔ   58 Ⓐ Ⓑ Ⓒ Ⓓ Ⓔ   80 Ⓐ Ⓑ Ⓒ Ⓓ Ⓔ
15 Ⓐ Ⓑ Ⓒ Ⓓ Ⓔ   37 Ⓐ Ⓑ Ⓒ Ⓓ Ⓔ   59 Ⓐ Ⓑ Ⓒ Ⓓ Ⓔ   81 Ⓐ Ⓑ Ⓒ Ⓓ Ⓔ
16 Ⓐ Ⓑ Ⓒ Ⓓ Ⓔ   38 Ⓐ Ⓑ Ⓒ Ⓓ Ⓔ   60 Ⓐ Ⓑ Ⓒ Ⓓ Ⓔ   82 Ⓐ Ⓑ Ⓒ Ⓓ Ⓔ
17 Ⓐ Ⓑ Ⓒ Ⓓ Ⓔ   39 Ⓐ Ⓑ Ⓒ Ⓓ Ⓔ   61 Ⓐ Ⓑ Ⓒ Ⓓ Ⓔ   83 Ⓐ Ⓑ Ⓒ Ⓓ Ⓔ
18 Ⓐ Ⓑ Ⓒ Ⓓ Ⓔ   40 Ⓐ Ⓑ Ⓒ Ⓓ Ⓔ   62 Ⓐ Ⓑ Ⓒ Ⓓ Ⓔ   84 Ⓐ Ⓑ Ⓒ Ⓓ Ⓔ
19 Ⓐ Ⓑ Ⓒ Ⓓ Ⓔ   41 Ⓐ Ⓑ Ⓒ Ⓓ Ⓔ   63 Ⓐ Ⓑ Ⓒ Ⓓ Ⓔ   85 Ⓐ Ⓑ Ⓒ Ⓓ Ⓔ
20 Ⓐ Ⓑ Ⓒ Ⓓ Ⓔ   42 Ⓐ Ⓑ Ⓒ Ⓓ Ⓔ   64 Ⓐ Ⓑ Ⓒ Ⓓ Ⓔ   86 Ⓐ Ⓑ Ⓒ Ⓓ Ⓔ
21 Ⓐ Ⓑ Ⓒ Ⓓ Ⓔ   43 Ⓐ Ⓑ Ⓒ Ⓓ Ⓔ   65 Ⓐ Ⓑ Ⓒ Ⓓ Ⓔ   87 Ⓐ Ⓑ Ⓒ Ⓓ Ⓔ
22 Ⓐ Ⓑ Ⓒ Ⓓ Ⓔ   44 Ⓐ Ⓑ Ⓒ Ⓓ Ⓔ   66 Ⓐ Ⓑ Ⓒ Ⓓ Ⓔ   88 Ⓐ Ⓑ Ⓒ Ⓓ Ⓔ

Practice II

Directions: *The next 88 questions are for practice. Mark your answers on the Practice II answer sheet. Again, your time limit is three minutes. This time, however, you must NOT look at the boxes while answering the questions. You must rely on your memory in marking the box location of each item. This practice test will not be scored.*

1. 2300-3499 Oak
2. 2200-2299 Post
3. 3500-3999 Main
4. 1200-2199 Post
5. Hopper
6. Carrot
7. 4000-4299 Main
8. 1200-2199 Oak
9. 2300-3499 Post
10. Forest
11. Boulder
12. 4000-4299 Oak
13. 2200-2299 Main
14. 1200-2199 Post
15. 3500-3999 Oak
16. Magnet
17. Willow
18. Liberty
19. 3500-3999 Post
20. 1200-2199 Main
21. 2300-3499 Main
22. 2200-2299 Oak
23. Iron
24. Press
25. Window
26. 1200-2199 Main
27. 1200-2199 Oak
28. 2200-2299 Penn
29. Hopper
30. Magnet

31. 4000-4299 Main
32. 2300-3499 Main
33. 400-4299 Oak
34. 2300-3499 Post
35. Boulder
36. Liberty
37. Forest
38. 2200-2299 Oak
39. 4000-4299 Post
40. 3500-3999 Oak
41. Willow
42. Carrot
43. 3500-3999 Post
44. 2200-2299 Main
45. 3500-3999 Main
46. Iron
47. 1200-2199 Main
48. 4000-4299 Oak
49. 2200-2299 Post
50. Press
51. Forest
52. 2200-2299 Main
53. 1200-2199 Oak
54. 2300-3499 Post
55. 3500-3999 Post
56. Hopper
57. Iron
58. 4000-4299 Main
59. 2200-2299 Oak
60. 2300-3499 Oak

61. 4000-4299 Post
62. Carrot
63. Liberty
64. 3500-3999 Oak
65. 2300-3499 Main
66. 3500-3999 Main
67. Willow
68. Boulder
69. 1200-2199 Post
70. Magnet
71. Window
72. 4000-4299 Main
73. 3500-3999 Post
74. 2200-2299 Main
75. 4000-4299 Post
76. 2300-3499 Main
77. 3500-3999 Oak
78. 2200-2299 Oak
79. Willow
80. Hopper
81. 1200-2199 Oak
82. 1200-2199 Post
83. 2200-2299 Main
84. Carrot
85. Iron
86. Liberty
87. 3500-3999 Main
88. 2200-2299 Post

Practice II Answer Sheet

1 Ⓐ Ⓑ Ⓒ Ⓓ Ⓔ	23 Ⓐ Ⓑ Ⓒ Ⓓ Ⓔ	45 Ⓐ Ⓑ Ⓒ Ⓓ Ⓔ	67 Ⓐ Ⓑ Ⓒ Ⓓ Ⓔ
2 Ⓐ Ⓑ Ⓒ Ⓓ Ⓔ	24 Ⓐ Ⓑ Ⓒ Ⓓ Ⓔ	46 Ⓐ Ⓑ Ⓒ Ⓓ Ⓔ	68 Ⓐ Ⓑ Ⓒ Ⓓ Ⓔ
3 Ⓐ Ⓑ Ⓒ Ⓓ Ⓔ	25 Ⓐ Ⓑ Ⓒ Ⓓ Ⓔ	47 Ⓐ Ⓑ Ⓒ Ⓓ Ⓔ	69 Ⓐ Ⓑ Ⓒ Ⓓ Ⓔ
4 Ⓐ Ⓑ Ⓒ Ⓓ Ⓔ	26 Ⓐ Ⓑ Ⓒ Ⓓ Ⓔ	48 Ⓐ Ⓑ Ⓒ Ⓓ Ⓔ	70 Ⓐ Ⓑ Ⓒ Ⓓ Ⓔ
5 Ⓐ Ⓑ Ⓒ Ⓓ Ⓔ	27 Ⓐ Ⓑ Ⓒ Ⓓ Ⓔ	49 Ⓐ Ⓑ Ⓒ Ⓓ Ⓔ	71 Ⓐ Ⓑ Ⓒ Ⓓ Ⓔ
6 Ⓐ Ⓑ Ⓒ Ⓓ Ⓔ	28 Ⓐ Ⓑ Ⓒ Ⓓ Ⓔ	50 Ⓐ Ⓑ Ⓒ Ⓓ Ⓔ	72 Ⓐ Ⓑ Ⓒ Ⓓ Ⓔ
7 Ⓐ Ⓑ Ⓒ Ⓓ Ⓔ	29 Ⓐ Ⓑ Ⓒ Ⓓ Ⓔ	51 Ⓐ Ⓑ Ⓒ Ⓓ Ⓔ	73 Ⓐ Ⓑ Ⓒ Ⓓ Ⓔ
8 Ⓐ Ⓑ Ⓒ Ⓓ Ⓔ	30 Ⓐ Ⓑ Ⓒ Ⓓ Ⓔ	52 Ⓐ Ⓑ Ⓒ Ⓓ Ⓔ	74 Ⓐ Ⓑ Ⓒ Ⓓ Ⓔ
9 Ⓐ Ⓑ Ⓒ Ⓓ Ⓔ	31 Ⓐ Ⓑ Ⓒ Ⓓ Ⓔ	53 Ⓐ Ⓑ Ⓒ Ⓓ Ⓔ	75 Ⓐ Ⓑ Ⓒ Ⓓ Ⓔ
10 Ⓐ Ⓑ Ⓒ Ⓓ Ⓔ	32 Ⓐ Ⓑ Ⓒ Ⓓ Ⓔ	54 Ⓐ Ⓑ Ⓒ Ⓓ Ⓔ	76 Ⓐ Ⓑ Ⓒ Ⓓ Ⓔ
11 Ⓐ Ⓑ Ⓒ Ⓓ Ⓔ	33 Ⓐ Ⓑ Ⓒ Ⓓ Ⓔ	55 Ⓐ Ⓑ Ⓒ Ⓓ Ⓔ	77 Ⓐ Ⓑ Ⓒ Ⓓ Ⓔ
12 Ⓐ Ⓑ Ⓒ Ⓓ Ⓔ	34 Ⓐ Ⓑ Ⓒ Ⓓ Ⓔ	56 Ⓐ Ⓑ Ⓒ Ⓓ Ⓔ	78 Ⓐ Ⓑ Ⓒ Ⓓ Ⓔ
13 Ⓐ Ⓑ Ⓒ Ⓓ Ⓔ	35 Ⓐ Ⓑ Ⓒ Ⓓ Ⓔ	57 Ⓐ Ⓑ Ⓒ Ⓓ Ⓔ	79 Ⓐ Ⓑ Ⓒ Ⓓ Ⓔ
14 Ⓐ Ⓑ Ⓒ Ⓓ Ⓔ	36 Ⓐ Ⓑ Ⓒ Ⓓ Ⓔ	58 Ⓐ Ⓑ Ⓒ Ⓓ Ⓔ	80 Ⓐ Ⓑ Ⓒ Ⓓ Ⓔ
15 Ⓐ Ⓑ Ⓒ Ⓓ Ⓔ	37 Ⓐ Ⓑ Ⓒ Ⓓ Ⓔ	59 Ⓐ Ⓑ Ⓒ Ⓓ Ⓔ	81 Ⓐ Ⓑ Ⓒ Ⓓ Ⓔ
16 Ⓐ Ⓑ Ⓒ Ⓓ Ⓔ	38 Ⓐ Ⓑ Ⓒ Ⓓ Ⓔ	60 Ⓐ Ⓑ Ⓒ Ⓓ Ⓔ	82 Ⓐ Ⓑ Ⓒ Ⓓ Ⓔ
17 Ⓐ Ⓑ Ⓒ Ⓓ Ⓔ	39 Ⓐ Ⓑ Ⓒ Ⓓ Ⓔ	61 Ⓐ Ⓑ Ⓒ Ⓓ Ⓔ	83 Ⓐ Ⓑ Ⓒ Ⓓ Ⓔ
18 Ⓐ Ⓑ Ⓒ Ⓓ Ⓔ	40 Ⓐ Ⓑ Ⓒ Ⓓ Ⓔ	62 Ⓐ Ⓑ Ⓒ Ⓓ Ⓔ	84 Ⓐ Ⓑ Ⓒ Ⓓ Ⓔ
19 Ⓐ Ⓑ Ⓒ Ⓓ Ⓔ	41 Ⓐ Ⓑ Ⓒ Ⓓ Ⓔ	63 Ⓐ Ⓑ Ⓒ Ⓓ Ⓔ	85 Ⓐ Ⓑ Ⓒ Ⓓ Ⓔ
20 Ⓐ Ⓑ Ⓒ Ⓓ Ⓔ	42 Ⓐ Ⓑ Ⓒ Ⓓ Ⓔ	64 Ⓐ Ⓑ Ⓒ Ⓓ Ⓔ	86 Ⓐ Ⓑ Ⓒ Ⓓ Ⓔ
21 Ⓐ Ⓑ Ⓒ Ⓓ Ⓔ	43 Ⓐ Ⓑ Ⓒ Ⓓ Ⓔ	65 Ⓐ Ⓑ Ⓒ Ⓓ Ⓔ	87 Ⓐ Ⓑ Ⓒ Ⓓ Ⓔ
22 Ⓐ Ⓑ Ⓒ Ⓓ Ⓔ	44 Ⓐ Ⓑ Ⓒ Ⓓ Ⓔ	66 Ⓐ Ⓑ Ⓒ Ⓓ Ⓔ	88 Ⓐ Ⓑ Ⓒ Ⓓ Ⓔ

Practice III

Directions: The same addresses from the previous practice sets are repeated in the box below. Each address is in the same box as the original set. You have five minutes to study the locations again. Do your best to memorize the letter of the box in which each address is located. This is your last chance to see the boxes.

A	B	C	D	E
2300-3499 Main Liberty 4000-4299 Oak Iron 1200-2199 Post	3500-3999 Main Willow 2200-2299 Oak Boulder 2300-3499 Post	4000-4299 Main Hopper 1200-2199 Oak Window 3500-3999 Post	1200-2199 Main Magnet 3500-3999 Oak Press 2200-2299 Post	2200-2299 Main Carrot 2300-3499 Oak Forest 4000-4299 Post

Directions: This is your last practice test. Mark the location of each of the 88 addresses on the practice III answer sheet. You will have five minutes to answer these questions. Do NOT look back at the boxes. This practice test will not be scored.

1. Willow
2. Window
3. 1200-2199 Main
4. 3500-3999 Post
5. 4000-4299 Oak
6. 2300-3499 Oak
7. 2200-2299 Post
8. Liberty
9. Carrot
10. Magnet
11. 2300-3499 Main
12. 4000-4299 Main
13. 1200-2199 Oak
14. 2200-2299 Oak
15. Hopper
16. 3500-3999 Main
17. 3500-3999 Oak
18. 2300-3499 Post
19. Press
20. Boulder
21. 4000-4299 Main
22. 1200-2100 Post
23. 2300-3499 Oak
24. Iron
25. Forest
26. 4000-4299 Oak

27. 2300-3499 Main
28. 2200-2299 Post
29. 4000-4299 Post
30. Willow
31. 1200-2199 Oak
32. 3500-3999 Main
33. 2200-2299 Post
34. Forest
35. Magnet
36. 2300-3499 Post
37. 4000-4299 Main
38. 1200-2199 Main
39. Carrot
40. Press
41. 2300-3499 Oak
42. 4000-4299 Oak
43. 3500-3999 Post
44. 4000-4299 Post
45. Liberty
46. Boulder
47. Hopper
48. 2300-3499 Main
49. 2200-2299 Main
50. 3500-3999 Oak
51. Window
52. Willow

53. 2200-2299 Oak
54. 1200-2199 Post
55. 2200-2299 Oak
56. Iron
57. 1200-2199 Main
58. 2300-3499 Oak
59. 4000-4299 Main
60. 4000-4299 Oak
61. 3500-3999 Main
62. 2200-2299 Post
63. 2300-3499 Post
64. 2200-2299 Oak
65. Boulder
66. Willow
67. 1200-2199 Oak
68. 2200-2299 Main
69. 1200-2199 Post
70. 4000-4299 Post
71. Magnet
72. Hopper
73. Carrot
74. 2200-2299 Oak
75. 2300-3499 Oak
76. 2300-3499 Main
77. 4000-4299 Main
78. Forest

79. Press
80. Iron
81. 3500-3999 Post
82. 3500-3999 Oak

83. 1200-2199 Main
84. Liberty
85. Window
86. 1200-2199 Oak

87. 1200-2199 Post
88. 2200-2299 Main

Practice III Answer Sheet

1 Ⓐ Ⓑ Ⓒ Ⓓ Ⓔ
2 Ⓐ Ⓑ Ⓒ Ⓓ Ⓔ
3 Ⓐ Ⓑ Ⓒ Ⓓ Ⓔ
4 Ⓐ Ⓑ Ⓒ Ⓓ Ⓔ
5 Ⓐ Ⓑ Ⓒ Ⓓ Ⓔ
6 Ⓐ Ⓑ Ⓒ Ⓓ Ⓔ
7 Ⓐ Ⓑ Ⓒ Ⓓ Ⓔ
8 Ⓐ Ⓑ Ⓒ Ⓓ Ⓔ
9 Ⓐ Ⓑ Ⓒ Ⓓ Ⓔ
10 Ⓐ Ⓑ Ⓒ Ⓓ Ⓔ
11 Ⓐ Ⓑ Ⓒ Ⓓ Ⓔ
12 Ⓐ Ⓑ Ⓒ Ⓓ Ⓔ
13 Ⓐ Ⓑ Ⓒ Ⓓ Ⓔ
14 Ⓐ Ⓑ Ⓒ Ⓓ Ⓔ
15 Ⓐ Ⓑ Ⓒ Ⓓ Ⓔ
16 Ⓐ Ⓑ Ⓒ Ⓓ Ⓔ
17 Ⓐ Ⓑ Ⓒ Ⓓ Ⓔ
18 Ⓐ Ⓑ Ⓒ Ⓓ Ⓔ
19 Ⓐ Ⓑ Ⓒ Ⓓ Ⓔ
20 Ⓐ Ⓑ Ⓒ Ⓓ Ⓔ
21 Ⓐ Ⓑ Ⓒ Ⓓ Ⓔ
22 Ⓐ Ⓑ Ⓒ Ⓓ Ⓔ

23 Ⓐ Ⓑ Ⓒ Ⓓ Ⓔ
24 Ⓐ Ⓑ Ⓒ Ⓓ Ⓔ
25 Ⓐ Ⓑ Ⓒ Ⓓ Ⓔ
26 Ⓐ Ⓑ Ⓒ Ⓓ Ⓔ
27 Ⓐ Ⓑ Ⓒ Ⓓ Ⓔ
28 Ⓐ Ⓑ Ⓒ Ⓓ Ⓔ
29 Ⓐ Ⓑ Ⓒ Ⓓ Ⓔ
30 Ⓐ Ⓑ Ⓒ Ⓓ Ⓔ
31 Ⓐ Ⓑ Ⓒ Ⓓ Ⓔ
32 Ⓐ Ⓑ Ⓒ Ⓓ Ⓔ
33 Ⓐ Ⓑ Ⓒ Ⓓ Ⓔ
34 Ⓐ Ⓑ Ⓒ Ⓓ Ⓔ
35 Ⓐ Ⓑ Ⓒ Ⓓ Ⓔ
36 Ⓐ Ⓑ Ⓒ Ⓓ Ⓔ
37 Ⓐ Ⓑ Ⓒ Ⓓ Ⓔ
38 Ⓐ Ⓑ Ⓒ Ⓓ Ⓔ
39 Ⓐ Ⓑ Ⓒ Ⓓ Ⓔ
40 Ⓐ Ⓑ Ⓒ Ⓓ Ⓔ
41 Ⓐ Ⓑ Ⓒ Ⓓ Ⓔ
42 Ⓐ Ⓑ Ⓒ Ⓓ Ⓔ
43 Ⓐ Ⓑ Ⓒ Ⓓ Ⓔ
44 Ⓐ Ⓑ Ⓒ Ⓓ Ⓔ

45 Ⓐ Ⓑ Ⓒ Ⓓ Ⓔ
46 Ⓐ Ⓑ Ⓒ Ⓓ Ⓔ
47 Ⓐ Ⓑ Ⓒ Ⓓ Ⓔ
48 Ⓐ Ⓑ Ⓒ Ⓓ Ⓔ
49 Ⓐ Ⓑ Ⓒ Ⓓ Ⓔ
50 Ⓐ Ⓑ Ⓒ Ⓓ Ⓔ
51 Ⓐ Ⓑ Ⓒ Ⓓ Ⓔ
52 Ⓐ Ⓑ Ⓒ Ⓓ Ⓔ
53 Ⓐ Ⓑ Ⓒ Ⓓ Ⓔ
54 Ⓐ Ⓑ Ⓒ Ⓓ Ⓔ
55 Ⓐ Ⓑ Ⓒ Ⓓ Ⓔ
56 Ⓐ Ⓑ Ⓒ Ⓓ Ⓔ
57 Ⓐ Ⓑ Ⓒ Ⓓ Ⓔ
58 Ⓐ Ⓑ Ⓒ Ⓓ Ⓔ
59 Ⓐ Ⓑ Ⓒ Ⓓ Ⓔ
60 Ⓐ Ⓑ Ⓒ Ⓓ Ⓔ
61 Ⓐ Ⓑ Ⓒ Ⓓ Ⓔ
62 Ⓐ Ⓑ Ⓒ Ⓓ Ⓔ
63 Ⓐ Ⓑ Ⓒ Ⓓ Ⓔ
64 Ⓐ Ⓑ Ⓒ Ⓓ Ⓔ
65 Ⓐ Ⓑ Ⓒ Ⓓ Ⓔ
66 Ⓐ Ⓑ Ⓒ Ⓓ Ⓔ

67 Ⓐ Ⓑ Ⓒ Ⓓ Ⓔ
68 Ⓐ Ⓑ Ⓒ Ⓓ Ⓔ
69 Ⓐ Ⓑ Ⓒ Ⓓ Ⓔ
70 Ⓐ Ⓑ Ⓒ Ⓓ Ⓔ
71 Ⓐ Ⓑ Ⓒ Ⓓ Ⓔ
72 Ⓐ Ⓑ Ⓒ Ⓓ Ⓔ
73 Ⓐ Ⓑ Ⓒ Ⓓ Ⓔ
74 Ⓐ Ⓑ Ⓒ Ⓓ Ⓔ
75 Ⓐ Ⓑ Ⓒ Ⓓ Ⓔ
76 Ⓐ Ⓑ Ⓒ Ⓓ Ⓔ
77 Ⓐ Ⓑ Ⓒ Ⓓ Ⓔ
78 Ⓐ Ⓑ Ⓒ Ⓓ Ⓔ
79 Ⓐ Ⓑ Ⓒ Ⓓ Ⓔ
80 Ⓐ Ⓑ Ⓒ Ⓓ Ⓔ
81 Ⓐ Ⓑ Ⓒ Ⓓ Ⓔ
82 Ⓐ Ⓑ Ⓒ Ⓓ Ⓔ
83 Ⓐ Ⓑ Ⓒ Ⓓ Ⓔ
84 Ⓐ Ⓑ Ⓒ Ⓓ Ⓔ
85 Ⓐ Ⓑ Ⓒ Ⓓ Ⓔ
86 Ⓐ Ⓑ Ⓒ Ⓓ Ⓔ
87 Ⓐ Ⓑ Ⓒ Ⓓ Ⓔ
88 Ⓐ Ⓑ Ⓒ Ⓓ Ⓔ

MEMORY FOR ADDRESSES

Time: 5 Minutes • 88 Questions

Directions: *Mark you answer sheet to indicate the location (A, B, C, D, or E) of each of the 88 addresses below. This test will be scored. You are NOT permitted to look at the boxes. Work from memory as quickly and as accurately as you can.*

1. 2300-3499 Main
2. 1200-2199 Oak
3. 4000-4299 Post
4. 2200-2299 Main
5. 1200-2199 Post
6. Iron
7. Boulder
8. Magnet
9. 2300-3499 Oak
10. 4000-4299 Oak
11. 3500-3999 Post
12. 4000-4299 Main
13. Carrot
14. Forest
15. Window
16. 3500-3999 Main
17. 3500-3999 Post
18. 2300-3499 Post
19. 3500-3999 Oak
20. Press
21. Liberty
22. 4000-4299 Oak
23. 3500-3999 Post
24. 1200-2199 Main
25. Window
26. Iron
27. 2200-2299 Main
28. 3500-3999 Oak
29. 2300-3499 Post
30. Willow

31. Forest
32. 1200-2199 Post
33. 1200-2199 Oak
34. 4000-4299 Main
35. Hopper
36. Carrot
37. 2300-3499 Main
38. 2300-3499 Oak
39. 2200-2299 Oak
40. Liberty
41. Magnet
42. 3500-3999 Main
43. 3500-3999 Post
44. 4000-4299 Post
45. 4000-4299 Oak
46. 2200-2299 Main
47. Hopper
48. Willow
49. 2300-3499 Main
50. Window
51. 2300-3499 Main
52. Window
53. Liberty
54. Iron
55. 1200-2199 Oak
56. 2300-3499 Oak
57. 4000-4299 Main
58. 1200-2199 Post
59. Carrot
60. Forrest

61. 2200-2299 Oak
62. 2200-2299 Post
63. 3500-3999 Main
64. 3500-3999 Oak
65. Boulder
66. Magnet
67. 1200-2199 Oak
68. 2200-2299 Main
69. Press
70. 1200-2199 Post
71. 4000-4299 Oak
72. 2200-2299 Post
73. 3500-3999 Main
74. Liberty
75. 4000-4299 Post
76. 2300-3499 Main
77. Window
78. Magnet
79. 1200-2199 Oak
80. 2300-3499 Oak
81. 1200-2199 Main
82. 2300-3499 Post
83. Hopper
84. Press
85. 2200-2299 Oak
86. 4000-4299 Main
87. 3500-3999 Post
88. Forest

END OF MEMORY FOR ADDRESSES

PART C: NUMBER SERIES

Sample Questions

The following sample questions show you the type of question that will be used in Part C. You will have three minutes to answer the sample questions and to study the explanations.

Directions: For each question below, there is at the left a series of numbers that follows some definite order and at the right five sets of two numbers each. You are to look at the numbers in the series at the left and find out what order they follow. Then decide what the next two numbers in the series would be if the same order were continued. Mark your answers on your answer sheet.

1. 42 40 38 35 32 28 24 .... (A) 20 18   (B) 18 14   (C) 19 14   (D) 20 16   (E) 19 15

If you write the steps between the numbers, you will find this pattern emerging: –2, –2, –3, –3, –4, –4, . . . Since it appears that after each two numbers the number being subtracted increases, it is logical to choose answer (C) because 24 – 5 = 19 and 19 – 5 = 14.

2. 2 2 4 2 6 2 8 .... (A) 8 2   (B) 2 8   (C) 2 10   (D) 10 2   (E) 10 12

The series progresses by a factor of +2: 2 4 6 8 10. After each number of the advancing series, we find the number 2. The answer is (C).

3. 88 88 82 82 76 76 70 .... (A) 70 70   (B) 70 65   (C) 64 64   (D) 70 64   (E) 64 48

The pattern in this series is a simple one: Repeat the number, –6; repeat the number, –6; and so on. To complete the series, repeat the number 70 and subtract 6 to yield 64. The answer is (D).

4. 35 46 39 43 43 40 47 .... (A) 47 43   (B) 51 40   (C) 43 51   (D) 70 64   (E) 37 51

This is a more complicated problem. There are really two series that alternate. The first series begins with 35 and ascends by +4: 35 39 43 47 51. The alternating series begins with 4 and descends by –3: 46 43 40 37. The number 43 is not really repeated; the two series really pass each other at that point. In answering a question of this type, you must be careful to maintain the alternation of series. The answer is (E) because 37 continues the descending series and 51 continues the ascending one.

5. 8 10 13 17 22 28 35 .... (A) 43 52   (B) 40 45   (C) 35 42   (D) 42 50   (E) 44 53

The pattern is: +2, +3, +4, +5, +6, +7. Continue the series with 35 + 8 = 43 + 9 = 52 to choose A as the correct answer.

SAMPLE ANSWER SHEET	CORRECT ANSWERS
1. Ⓐ Ⓑ Ⓒ Ⓓ Ⓔ	1. Ⓐ Ⓑ ● Ⓓ Ⓔ
2. Ⓐ Ⓑ Ⓒ Ⓓ Ⓔ	2. Ⓐ Ⓑ ● Ⓓ Ⓔ
3. Ⓐ Ⓑ Ⓒ Ⓓ Ⓔ	3. Ⓐ Ⓑ Ⓒ ● Ⓔ
4. Ⓐ Ⓑ Ⓒ Ⓓ Ⓔ	4. Ⓐ Ⓑ Ⓒ Ⓓ ●
5. Ⓐ Ⓑ Ⓒ Ⓓ Ⓔ	5. ● Ⓑ Ⓒ Ⓓ Ⓔ

Number Series

Time: 20 Minutes • 24 Questions

Directions: For each question below, there is at the left a series of numbers that follows some definite order and at the right five sets of two numbers each. You are to look at the numbers in the series at the left and find out what order they follow. Then decide what the next two numbers in the series would be if the same order were continued. Mark your answers on your answer sheet.

1. 13 12 8 11 18 8 9 .... (A) 8 7   (B) 6 8   (C) 8 6   (D) 8 8   (E) 7 8

2. 13 18 13 17 13 16 13 .... (A) 15 13   (B) 13 14   (C) 13 15   (D) 14 15   (E) 15 14

3. 13 13 10 12 12 10 11 .... (A) 10 10   (B) 10 9   (C) 11 9   (D) 9 11   (E) 11 10

4. 6 5 4 6 5 4 6 .... (A) 4 6   (B) 6 4   (C) 5 4   (D) 5 6   (E) 4 5

5. 10 10 9 8 8 7 6 .... (A) 5 5   (B) 5 4   (C) 6 5   (D) 6 4   (E) 5 3

6. 20 16 18 14 16 12 14 .... (A) 16 12   (B) 10 12   (C) 16 18   (D) 12 12   (E) 12 10

7. 7 12 8 11 9 10 10 .... (A) 11 9   (B) 9 8   (C) 9 11   (D) 10 11   (E) 9 10

8. 13 13 12 15 15 14 17 .... (A) 17 16   (B) 14 17   (C) 16 19   (D) 19 19   (E) 16 16

9. 65 59 53 51 49 43 37 35 ... (A) 29 27   (B) 33 29   (C) 27 24   (D) 33 27   (E) 32 25

10. 73 65 65 58 58 52 52 .... (A) 52 446   (B) 52 47   (C) 47 47   (D) 46 46   (E) 45 45

11. 6 4 8 5 15 13 26 23 .... (A) 69 67   (B) 37 33   (C) 29 44   (D) 75 78   (E) 446 49

12. 19 16 21 18 23 20 25 .... (A) 30 33   (B) 22 27   (C) 28 22   (D) 22 24   (E) 30 27

13. 35 40 5 45 50 5 55 .... (A) 55 5   (B) 60 5   (C) 5 60   (D) 5 55   (E) 60 65

14. 22 20 18 18 16 14 14 .... (A) 14 12   (B) 12 12   (C) 14 10   (D) 14 16   (E) 12 10

15. 11 22 23 13 26 27 17 .... (A) 7 8   (B) 18 36   (C) 18 8   (D) 7 14   (E) 34 35

16. 9 1 10 1 11 1 12 .... (A) 13 14   (B) 13 1   (C) 1 13   (D) 12 1   (E) 12 13

17. 48 10 46 17 44 24 42 .... (A) 31 40   (B) 27 28   (C) 40 38   (D) 28 38   (E) 30 40

18. 8 8 17 26 26 35 44 .... (A) 53 53   (B) 44 53   (C) 44 44   (D) 44 55   (E) 44 54

19. 71 68 62 59 53 50 44 .... (A) 40 32   (B) 38 35   (C) 41 38   (D) 41 35   (E) 41 33

20. 1 7 8 2 7 8 3 .... (A) 4 7   (B) 7 8   (C) 4 5   (D) 7 4   (E) 2 8

21. 1 2 2 1 1 1 2 2 .... (A) 1 1   (B) 1 2   (C) 2 1   (D) 2 2   (E) 1 3

22. 14 25 37 48 60 71 83 .... (A) 92 100   (B) 96 110   (C) 89 98   (D) 95 105   (E) 94 106

23. 35 43 45 53 55 63 65 .... (A) 65 68   (B) 75 83   (C) 73 75   (D) 65 73   (E) 73 83

24. 3 6 12 12 24 48 48 .... (A) 48 96   (B) 96 96   (C) 60 96   (D) 96 192   (E) 60 60

END OF NUMBER SERIES

PART D: FOLLOWING ORAL INSTRUCTIONS

The oral instructions for the sample questions are on page 190.

Sample Questions

Sample Worksheet

Directions: Listen carefully to the instructions read to you and mark each item on this worksheet as directed. Then complete each question by marking the sample answer sheet as directed. For each answer you will darken the answer sheet for a number-letter combination.

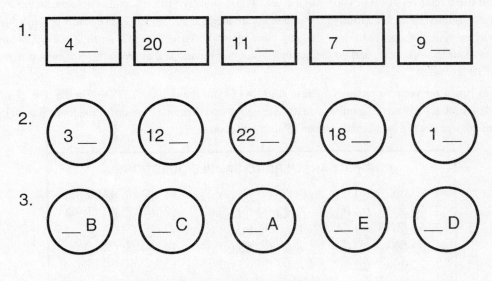

1. | 4 __ | 20 __ | 11 __ | 7 __ | 9 __ |

2. (3 __) (12 __) (22 __) (18 __) (1 __)

3. (__ B) (__ C) (__ A) (__ E) (__ D)

4. X O X X X X O O X O X O X O X X O X

```
                        SAMPLE ANSWER SHEET

     1. Ⓐ Ⓑ Ⓒ Ⓓ Ⓔ       6. Ⓐ Ⓑ Ⓒ Ⓓ Ⓔ      11. Ⓐ Ⓑ Ⓒ Ⓓ Ⓔ
     2. Ⓐ Ⓑ Ⓒ Ⓓ Ⓔ       7. Ⓐ Ⓑ Ⓒ Ⓓ Ⓔ      12. Ⓐ Ⓑ Ⓒ Ⓓ Ⓔ
     3. Ⓐ Ⓑ Ⓒ Ⓓ Ⓔ       8. Ⓐ Ⓑ Ⓒ Ⓓ Ⓔ      13. Ⓐ Ⓑ Ⓒ Ⓓ Ⓔ
     4. Ⓐ Ⓑ Ⓒ Ⓓ Ⓔ       9. Ⓐ Ⓑ Ⓒ Ⓓ Ⓔ      14. Ⓐ Ⓑ Ⓒ Ⓓ Ⓔ
     5. Ⓐ Ⓑ Ⓒ Ⓓ Ⓔ      10. Ⓐ Ⓑ Ⓒ Ⓓ Ⓔ      15. Ⓐ Ⓑ Ⓒ Ⓓ Ⓔ
```

TEAR HERE

SAMPLE ORAL INSTRUCTIONS

Instructions to be read (the words in parentheses should NOT be read aloud):

You are to follow the instructions that I shall read to you. I cannot repeat them.

Look at line 1 on your worksheet. (Pause slightly.) Write a C in the third box. (Pause 2 seconds.) Now on your answer sheet, find the number in that box and darken space C for that number. (Pause 5 seconds.)

Look at line 2 on your worksheet. (Pause slightly.) The number in each circle is the number of employees in a post office. In the circle for the post office holding more than 10 employees, but less than 15, write the letter E next to the number. (Pause 5 seconds.) Now, on your answer sheet, darken the space for the number-letter combination that is in the circle you just wrote in. (Pause 5 seconds.)

Look at the circles on line 3 of your worksheet. (Pause slightly.) In the second circle, write the answer to this question: Which of the following numbers is smallest: 9, 21, 16, 17, 23? (Pause 5 seconds.) In the third circle, write the answer to this question: How many days are there in a week? (Pause 2 seconds.) Now, on your answer sheet, darken the number-letter combinations that are in the circles you wrote in. (Pause 10 seconds.)

Look at line 4 on your worksheet. (Pause slightly.) Count the number of "O's" in the line. (Pause 5 seconds.) Subtract 2 from the number you have counted, and darken the space for the letter B as in baker on your answer sheet next to that number. (Pause 10 seconds.)

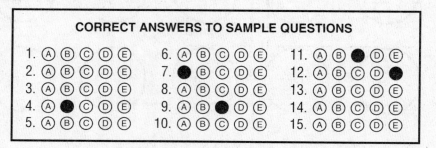

Correctly Filled Worksheet

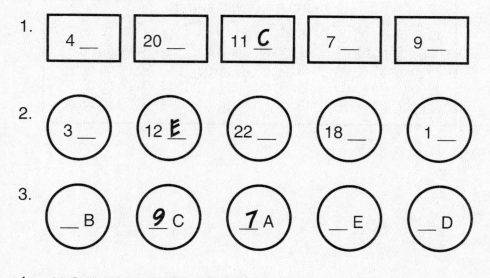

Following Oral Instructions

Time: 25 Minutes (Approximately)
The oral instructions for this part of the test are on page 193.

Worksheet

Directions: Listen carefully to the instructions read to you and mark each item on this worksheet as directed. Then complete each question by marking the answer sheet as directed. For each answer you will darken the answer sheet for a number-letter combination.

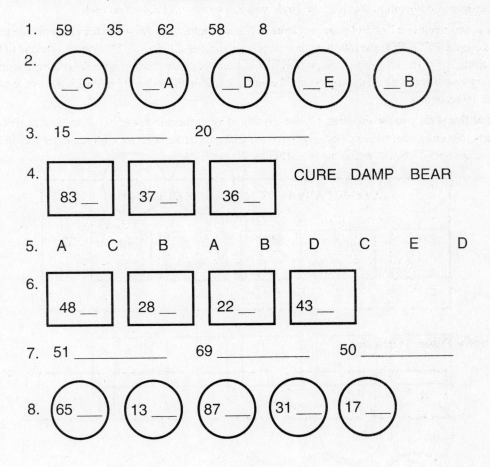

1. 59   35   62   58   8

2. __C   __A   __D   __E   __B

3. 15 _____   20 _____

4. [83 __] [37 __] [36 __]   CURE DAMP BEAR

5. A   C   B   A   B   D   C   E   D

6. [48 __] [28 __] [22 __] [43 __]

7. 51 _____   69 _____   50 _____

8. (65 __) (13 __) (87 __) (31 __) (17 __)

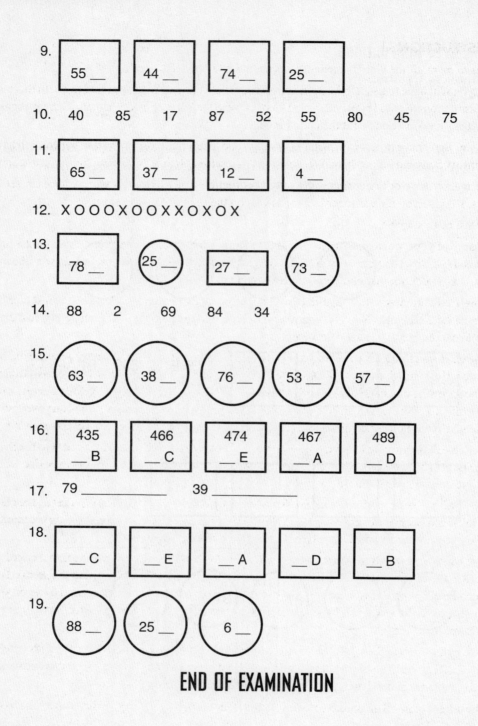

9.

| 55 __ | 44 __ | 74 __ | 25 __ |

10. 40   85   17   87   52   55   80   45   75

11.

| 65 __ | 37 __ | 12 __ | 4 __ |

12. X O O O X O O X X O X O X

13.

| 78 __ | 25 __ | 27 __ | 73 __ |

14. 88   2   69   84   34

15. 63 __   38 __   76 __   53 __   57 __

16.

| 435 __ B | 466 __ C | 474 __ E | 467 __ A | 489 __ D |

17. 79 _____   39 _____

18.

| __ C | __ E | __ A | __ D | __ B |

19. 88 __   25 __   6 __

END OF EXAMINATION

ORAL INSTRUCTIONS

Instructions to be read (the words in parentheses should NOT be read aloud):

On the job, you will have to listen to instructions and then do what you have been told to do. In this test, I will read instructions to you. Try to understand them as I read them; I cannot repeat them. Once we begin, you may not ask any questions until the end of the test.

On the job, you won't have to deal with pictures, numbers and letters like those on the test, but you will have to listen to instructions and follow them. We are using this test to see how well you can follow instructions.

You are to mark your worksheet according to the instruction that I'll read to you. After each set of instructions, I'll give you time to record your answers on the separate answer sheet.

The actual test begins now.

Look on line 1 of your worksheet. (Pause slightly.) Draw a line under the largest number in the line. (Pause 2 seconds.) Now, on your answer sheet, find the number under which you just drew a line and darken box D as in dog for that number. (Pause 5 seconds.)

Look at line 1 on your worksheet again. (Pause slightly.) Draw two lines under the smallest number in the line. (Pause 2 seconds.) Now, on your answer sheet, find the number under which you just drew two lines and darken box E. (Pause 5 seconds.)

Look at the circles in line 2 on your worksheet. (Pause slightly.) In the second circle, write the answer to this question: How much is 6 plus 4? (Pause 8 seconds.) In the third circle, write the answer to this question: Which of the following numbers is largest: 67, 48, 15, 73, 61? (Pause 5 seconds.) In the fourth circle, write the answer to this question: How many months are there in a year? (Pause 2 seconds.) Now, on your answer sheet, darken the letter-number combinations that are in the circles you wrote in. (Pause 10 seconds.)

Now look at line 3 of your worksheet. (Pause slightly.) Write the letter C on the blank next to the right-hand number. (Pause 2 seconds.) Now, on your answer sheet, find the space for the number beside which you wrote and darken box C. (Pause 5 seconds.)

Now look at line 3 of your worksheet again. (Pause slightly.) Write the letter B as in baker on the blank next to the left-hand number. (Pause 2 seconds.) Now, on your answer sheet, find the space for the number beside which you just wrote and darken box B as in baker. (Pause 5 seconds.)

Look at the boxes and words in line 4 on your worksheet. (Pause slightly.) Write the first letter of the second word in the third box. (Pause 2 seconds.) Write the last letter of the first word in the second box. (Pause 2 seconds.) Write the first letter of the third word in the first box. (Pause 2 seconds.) Now, on your answer sheet, darken the space for the letter-number combinations that are in the three boxes you just wrote in. (Pause 10 seconds.)

Look at the letters in line 5 on your worksheet. (Pause slightly.) Draw a line under the fifth letter in the line. (Pause 2 seconds.) Now, on your answer sheet, find the number 56 (pause 2 seconds) and darken the space for the letter under which you drew a line. (Pause 5 seconds.)

Look at the letters in line 5 on your worksheet again. (Pause slightly.) Draw two lines under the fourth letter in the line. (Pause 2 seconds.) Now, on your answer sheet, find the number 66 (pause 2 seconds) and darken the space for the letter under which you drew two lines. (Pause 5 seconds.)

Look at the drawings in line 6 on your worksheet. (Pause slightly.) The four boxes indicate the number of buildings in four different carrier routes. In the box for the route with the fewest number of buildings, write an A. (Pause 2 seconds.) Now, on your answer sheet, darken the space for the number-letter combination that is in the box you just wrote in. (Pause 5 seconds.)

Now look at line 7 on your worksheet. (Pause slightly.) If fall comes before summer, write the letter B as in baker on the line next to the middle number. (Pause slightly.) Otherwise, write an E on the blank next to the left-hand number. (Pause 5 seconds.) Now, on your answer sheet, darken the space for the number-letter combination that you have just written. (Pause 5 seconds.)

Now look at line 8 on your worksheet. (Pause slightly.) Write a D as in dog in the circle with the lowest number. (Pause 2 seconds.) Now, on your answer sheet, darken the space for the number-letter combination that is in the circle you just wrote in.

Look at the drawings in line 9 on your worksheet. The four boxes are planes for carrying mail. (Pause slightly.) The plane with the highest number is to be loaded first. Write an E in the box with the highest number. (Pause 2 seconds.) Now, on your answer sheet, darken the space for the number-letter combination that is in the box you just wrote in. (Pause 5 seconds.)

Look at line 10 on your worksheet. (Pause slightly.) Draw a line under every number that is more than 35 but less than 55. (Pause 12 seconds.) Now, on your answer sheet, for each line that you drew a box under, darken box A. (Pause 25 seconds.)

Look at line 10 on your worksheet again. (Pause slightly.) Draw two lines under every number that is more than 55 and less than 80. (Pause 12 seconds.) Now, on your answer sheet, for each number that you drew two lines under, darken box C. (Pause 25 seconds.)

Look at line 11 on your worksheet. (Pause slightly.) Write an E in the last box. (Pause 2 seconds.) Now, on your answer sheet, find the number in that box and darken box E for that number. (Pause 5 seconds.)

Look at line 12 on your worksheet. (Pause slightly.) Draw a line under every "X" in the line. (Pause 5 seconds.) Count the number of lines that you have drawn, add 3, and write that number at the end of the line. (Pause 5 seconds.) Now, on your answer sheet, find that number and darken space E for that number. (Pause 5 seconds.)

Look at line 13 on your worksheet. (Pause slightly.) If the number in the right-hand box is larger than the number in the left-hand circle, add 4 to the number in the left-hand circle, and change the number in the circle to this number. (Pause 8 seconds.) Then, write C next to the new number. (Pause slightly.) Otherwise, write A next to the number in the smaller box. (Pause 3 seconds.) Now, on your answer sheet, darken the space for the number-letter combination that is in the box or circle you just wrote in. (Pause 5 seconds.)

Now look at line 14 on your worksheet. (Pause slightly.) Draw a line under the middle number in the line. (Pause 2 seconds.) Now, on your answer sheet, find the number under which you just drew the line and darken box D as in dog for that number. (Pause 5 seconds.)

Now look at line 15 on your worksheet. (Pause slightly.) Write a B as in baker in the third circle. (Pause 2 seconds.) Now, on your answer sheet, find the number in that circle and darken box B as in baker for that number. (Pause 5 seconds.)

Now look at line 15 again. (Pause slightly.) Write a C in the last circle. (Pause 2 seconds.) Now, on your answer sheet, find the number in that circle and darken box C for that number. (Pause 5 seconds.)

Look at the drawings in line 16 on your worksheet. The number in each box is the number of employees in a post office. (Pause slightly.) In the box for the post office with the smallest number of employees, write on the line the last two figures of the number of employees. (Pause 5 seconds.) Now, on your answer sheet, darken the space for the number-letter combination that is in the box you just wrote in. (Pause 5 seconds.)

Now look at line 17 on your worksheet. (Pause slightly.) Write an A next to the right-hand number. (Pause 2 seconds.) Now, on your answer sheet, find the space for the number next to which you just wrote and darken box A. (Pause 5 seconds.)

Now look at line 18 on your worksheet. (Pause slightly.) In the fourth box, write the answer to this question: How many feet are in a yard? (Pause 2 seconds.) Now, on your answer sheet, darken the space for the number-letter combination that is in the box you just wrote in. (Pause 5 seconds.)

Look at line 18 again. (Pause slightly.) In the second box, write the number 32. (Pause 2 seconds.) Now, on your answer sheet, find the number-letter combination that is in the box you just wrote in. (Pause 5 seconds.)

Look at line 19 on your worksheet. (Pause slightly.) In the circle with the highest number, write the second letter that I will read to you: "B" as in baker, "D" as in dog, "A" as in apple. (Pause 5 seconds.) Now, on your answer sheet, darken the space for the number-letter combination in the circle you just wrote in. (Pause 5 seconds.)

Correct Answers:
Full-Length Practice Examination

PART A: ADDRESS CHECKING

1. D	13. D	25. D	37. D	49. A	61. A	73. A	85. D
2. D	14. A	26. A	38. D	50. D	62. A	74. D	86. D
3. D	15. D	27. D	39. D	51. A	63. D	75. D	87. D
4. D	16. D	28. D	40. D	52. A	64. D	76. D	88. D
5. A	17. A	29. D	41. D	53. D	65. D	77. D	89. D
6. A	18. D	30. A	42. D	54. D	66. D	77. D	90. A
7. D	19. D	31. A	43. D	55. A	67. D	78. D	91. A
8. D	20. A	32. D	44. A	56. A	68. D	80. D	92. D
9. D	21. D	33. D	45. D	57. D	69. D	81. A	93. D
10. D	22. D	34. D	46. D	58. D	70. D	82. A	94. D
11. D	23. D	35. D	47. D	59. D	71. A	83. D	95. D
12. D	24. A	36. A	48. A	60. A	72. A	84. D	

PART B: MEMORY FOR ADDRESSES

Practice I

1. D	12. B	23. E	34. B	45. A	56. B	67. C	78. A
2. B	13. E	24. D	35. E	46. B	57. A	68. D	79. A
3. A	14. A	25. D	36. C	47. C	58. A	69. A	80. D
4. E	15. A	26. B	37. A	48. D	59. E	70. C	81. C
5. C	16. B	27. B	38. D	49. E	60. C	71. C	82. C
6. E	17. C	28. C	39. B	50. D	61. E	72. B	83. B
7. C	18. D	29. A	40. E	51. C	62. E	73. E	84. C
8. A	19. C	30. C	41. E	52. B	63. D	74. A	85. D
9. D	20. D	31. A	42. C	53. E	64. B	75. D	86. B
10. E	21. B	32. A	43. D	54. D	65. B	76. E	87. B
11. D	22. A	33. E	44. B	55. C	66. A	77. E	88. A

Practice II

1. E	12. A	23. A	34. B	45. B	56. C	67. B	78. B
2. D	13. E	24. D	35. B	46. A	57. A	68. B	79. B
3. B	14. A	25. C	36. A	47. D	58. C	69. A	80. C
4. A	15. D	26. D	37. E	48. A	59. B	70. D	81. C
5. C	16. D	27. C	38. B	49. D	60. E	71. C	82. A
6. E	17. B	28. D	39. E	50. D	61. E	72. C	83. E
7. C	18. A	29. C	40. D	51. E	62. E	73. C	84. E
8. C	19. C	30. D	41. B	52. E	63. A	74. E	85. A
9. B	20. D	31. C	42. E	53. C	64. D	75. E	86. A
10. E	21. A	32. A	43. C	54. B	65. A	76. A	87. B
11. B	22. B	33. A	44. E	55. C	66. B	77. D	88. D

Practice III

1. B	12. C	23. E	34. E	45. A	56. A	67. C	78. E
2. C	13. A	24. A	35. D	46. B	57. D	68. E	79. D
3. D	14. B	25. E	36. B	47. C	58. E	69. A	80. A
4. C	15. C	26. A	37. C	48. A	59. C	70. E	81. C
5. A	16. B	27. A	38. D	49. E	60. A	71. D	82. D
6. E	17. D	28. D	39. E	50. D	61. B	72. C	83. D
7. D	18. B	29. E	40. D	51. C	62. B	73. E	84. A
8. A	19. D	30. B	41. E	52. B	63. B	74. B	85. C
9. E	20. B	31. C	42. A	53. B	64. B	75. E	86. C
10. D	21. C	32. B	43. C	54. A	65. B	76. A	87. A
11. A	22. A	33. D	44. E	55. B	66. B	77. C	88. E

Memory for Addresses

1. A	12. C	23. C	34. C	45. A	56. E	67. C	78. D
2. C	13. E	24. D	35. C	46. E	57. C	68. E	79. C
3. E	14. E	25. C	36. E	47. C	58. A	69. D	80. E
4. E	15. C	26. A	37. A	48. B	59. E	70. A	81. D
5. A	16. B	27. E	38. E	49. B	60. E	71. A	82. B
6. A	17. C	28. D	39. B	50. D	61. B	72. D	83. C
7. B	18. B	29. B	40. A	51. A	62. D	73. B	84. D
8. D	19. D	30. B	41. D	52. C	63. B	74. A	85. B
9. E	20. D	31. E	42. B	53. A	64. D	75. E	86. C
10. A	21. A	32. A	43. C	54. A	65. B	76. A	87. C
11. C	22. A	33. C	44. E	55. C	66. D	77. C	88. E

PART C: NUMBER SERIES

Answers

1. **D**	4. **C**	7. **C**	10. **C**	13. **B**	16. **C**	19. **D**	22. **E**
2. **A**	5. **C**	8. **A**	11. **A**	14. **E**	17. **A**	20. **B**	23.. **C**
3. **E**	6. **B**	9. **D**	12. **B**	15. **E**	18. **B**	21. **A**	24. **D**

Explanations

1. **(D)** The series descends 13 12 11 10 9 8, with the number 8 appearing between each set of two numbers.
2. **(A)** Again, the series descends. This time the number 13 appears between all numbers.
3. **(E)** This time the number repeats itself before descending. The number 10 appears between each set of descending numbers.
4. **(C)** The three-number series repeats itself over and over.
5. **(C)** The series descends. The even numbers repeat.
6. **(B)** Mark the differences between numbers. The pattern that emerges is –4, +2, –4, +2, and so on.
7. **(C)** There are two alternating series. The first series begins with 7 and ascends by +1. The alternating series begins with 12 and descends one number at a time.
8. **(A)** One series, the odd numbers, repeats and ascends by +2. The alternating series, the even numbers, also ascends by +2, but does not repeat.
9. **(D)** The pattern is: –6, –6, –2, –2; –6, –6, –2, –2; etc.
10. **(C)** The pattern is: –8, repeat the number; –7, repeat the number; –6, repeat the number; –5, repeat the number; etc.
11. **(A)** The pattern is –2, ×2, –3, ×3; –2, ×2, –3, ×3; –2, ×2, –3, ×3.
12. **(B)** The easiest way to see this is to mark the pattern: –3, +5; –3, +5; etc. If, however, you see two alternating series, both ascending by +2, you will also get the correct answer.
13. **(B)** This is a +5 series with the number 5 appearing after each two numbers in the series.
14. **(E)** The pattern is: –2, –2, repeat the number; –2, –2, repeat the number, etc.
15. **(E)** The pattern is: ×2, +1, –10; ×2, +1, –10; ×2, +1, –10; etc.
16. **(C)** The series is simply 9 10 11 12 13 . . . with the number 1 appearing between each step of the series.
17. **(A)** There are two alternating series. The first series starts with 48 and descends at the rate of –2. The alternating series starts with 10 and ascends at the rate of +7.
18. **(B)** The pattern is: Repeat the number, +9, +9; repeat the number +9, +9; etc.
19. **(D)** The pattern is: –3, –6; –3, –6; etc.
20. **(B)** The pattern is 1 2 3 . . . with the numbers 7 and 8 intervening between members of the series.
21. **(A)** The series consists of repetitions of the sequence 1 2 2 1, or, if you see it otherwise, repetitions of 1 1; 2 2; 1 1; 2 2; 1 1 beginning in the repetitions of 1's.
22. **(E)** The pattern is: +11, +12; +11, +12; etc.
23. **(C)** The pattern is: +8, +2; +8, +2; etc.
24. **(D)** The pattern is: ×2, ×2, repeat the number; ×2, ×2, repeat the number; etc.

PART D: FOLLOWING ORAL INSTRUCTIONS
Correctly Filled Answer Grid

1 Ⓐ Ⓑ Ⓒ Ⓓ Ⓔ	23 Ⓐ Ⓑ Ⓒ Ⓓ Ⓔ	45 ● Ⓑ Ⓒ Ⓓ Ⓔ	67 Ⓐ Ⓑ Ⓒ Ⓓ Ⓔ
2 Ⓐ Ⓑ Ⓒ Ⓓ Ⓔ	24 Ⓐ Ⓑ Ⓒ Ⓓ Ⓔ	46 Ⓐ Ⓑ Ⓒ Ⓓ Ⓔ	68 Ⓐ Ⓑ Ⓒ Ⓓ Ⓔ
3 Ⓐ Ⓑ Ⓒ ● Ⓔ	25 Ⓐ Ⓑ Ⓒ Ⓓ Ⓔ	47 Ⓐ Ⓑ Ⓒ Ⓓ Ⓔ	69 Ⓐ Ⓑ Ⓒ ● Ⓔ
4 Ⓐ Ⓑ Ⓒ Ⓓ ●	26 Ⓐ Ⓑ Ⓒ Ⓓ Ⓔ	48 Ⓐ Ⓑ Ⓒ Ⓓ Ⓔ	70 Ⓐ Ⓑ Ⓒ Ⓓ Ⓔ
5 Ⓐ Ⓑ Ⓒ Ⓓ Ⓔ	27 Ⓐ Ⓑ Ⓒ Ⓓ Ⓔ	49 Ⓐ Ⓑ Ⓒ Ⓓ Ⓔ	71 Ⓐ Ⓑ Ⓒ Ⓓ Ⓔ
6 Ⓐ Ⓑ Ⓒ Ⓓ Ⓔ	28 Ⓐ Ⓑ Ⓒ Ⓓ Ⓔ	50 Ⓐ Ⓑ Ⓒ Ⓓ Ⓔ	72 Ⓐ Ⓑ Ⓒ Ⓓ Ⓔ
7 Ⓐ Ⓑ Ⓒ Ⓓ Ⓔ	29 Ⓐ Ⓑ ● Ⓓ Ⓔ	51 Ⓐ Ⓑ Ⓒ Ⓓ ●	73 Ⓐ Ⓑ Ⓒ ● Ⓔ
8 Ⓐ Ⓑ Ⓒ Ⓓ ●	30 Ⓐ Ⓑ Ⓒ Ⓓ Ⓔ	52 ● Ⓑ Ⓒ Ⓓ Ⓔ	74 Ⓐ Ⓑ Ⓒ Ⓓ ●
9 Ⓐ Ⓑ Ⓒ Ⓓ ●	31 Ⓐ Ⓑ Ⓒ Ⓓ Ⓔ	53 Ⓐ Ⓑ Ⓒ Ⓓ Ⓔ	75 Ⓐ Ⓑ ● Ⓓ Ⓔ
10 ● Ⓑ Ⓒ Ⓓ Ⓔ	32 Ⓐ Ⓑ Ⓒ Ⓓ ●	54 Ⓐ Ⓑ Ⓒ Ⓓ Ⓔ	76 Ⓐ ● Ⓒ Ⓓ Ⓔ
11 Ⓐ Ⓑ Ⓒ Ⓓ Ⓔ	33 Ⓐ Ⓑ Ⓒ Ⓓ Ⓔ	55 Ⓐ Ⓑ Ⓒ Ⓓ Ⓔ	77 Ⓐ Ⓑ Ⓒ Ⓓ Ⓔ
12 Ⓐ Ⓑ Ⓒ Ⓓ ●	34 Ⓐ Ⓑ Ⓒ Ⓓ Ⓔ	56 Ⓐ ● Ⓒ Ⓓ Ⓔ	78 Ⓐ Ⓑ Ⓒ Ⓓ Ⓔ
13 Ⓐ Ⓑ Ⓒ ● Ⓔ	35 Ⓐ ● Ⓒ Ⓓ Ⓔ	57 Ⓐ Ⓑ ● Ⓓ Ⓔ	79 Ⓐ Ⓑ Ⓒ Ⓓ Ⓔ
14 Ⓐ Ⓑ Ⓒ Ⓓ Ⓔ	36 Ⓐ Ⓑ Ⓒ ● Ⓔ	58 Ⓐ Ⓑ Ⓒ Ⓓ Ⓔ	80 Ⓐ Ⓑ Ⓒ Ⓓ Ⓔ
15 Ⓐ ● Ⓒ Ⓓ Ⓔ	37 Ⓐ Ⓑ Ⓒ Ⓓ ●	59 Ⓐ Ⓑ Ⓒ Ⓓ Ⓔ	81 Ⓐ Ⓑ Ⓒ Ⓓ Ⓔ
16 Ⓐ Ⓑ Ⓒ Ⓓ Ⓔ	38 Ⓐ Ⓑ Ⓒ Ⓓ Ⓔ	60 Ⓐ Ⓑ Ⓒ Ⓓ Ⓔ	82 Ⓐ Ⓑ Ⓒ Ⓓ Ⓔ
17 Ⓐ Ⓑ Ⓒ Ⓓ Ⓔ	39 ● Ⓑ Ⓒ Ⓓ Ⓔ	61 Ⓐ Ⓑ Ⓒ Ⓓ Ⓔ	83 Ⓐ ● Ⓒ Ⓓ Ⓔ
18 Ⓐ Ⓑ Ⓒ Ⓓ Ⓔ	40 ● Ⓑ Ⓒ Ⓓ Ⓔ	62 Ⓐ Ⓑ Ⓒ ● Ⓔ	84 Ⓐ Ⓑ Ⓒ Ⓓ Ⓔ
19 Ⓐ Ⓑ Ⓒ Ⓓ Ⓔ	41 Ⓐ Ⓑ Ⓒ Ⓓ Ⓔ	63 Ⓐ Ⓑ Ⓒ Ⓓ Ⓔ	85 Ⓐ Ⓑ Ⓒ Ⓓ Ⓔ
20 Ⓐ Ⓑ ● Ⓓ Ⓔ	42 Ⓐ Ⓑ Ⓒ Ⓓ Ⓔ	64 Ⓐ Ⓑ Ⓒ Ⓓ Ⓔ	86 Ⓐ Ⓑ Ⓒ Ⓓ Ⓔ
21 Ⓐ Ⓑ Ⓒ Ⓓ Ⓔ	43 Ⓐ Ⓑ Ⓒ Ⓓ Ⓔ	65 Ⓐ Ⓑ Ⓒ Ⓓ Ⓔ	87 Ⓐ Ⓑ Ⓒ Ⓓ Ⓔ
22 ● Ⓑ Ⓒ Ⓓ Ⓔ	44 Ⓐ Ⓑ Ⓒ Ⓓ Ⓔ	66 ● Ⓑ Ⓒ Ⓓ Ⓔ	88 Ⓐ Ⓑ Ⓒ ● Ⓔ

Correctly Filled Worksheet

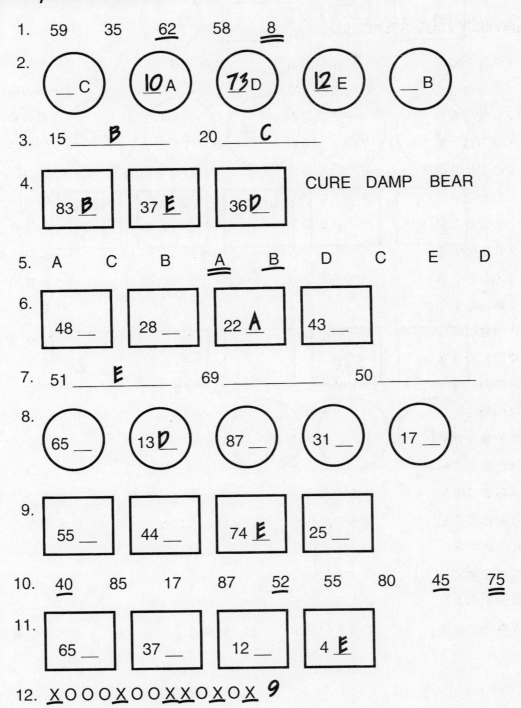

1. 59   35   <u>62</u>   58   <u><u>8</u></u>

2. (__ C) (10 A) (73 D) (12 E) (__ B)

3. 15 ___B___   20 ___C___

4. [83 B] [37 E] [36 D]   CURE DAMP BEAR

5. A   C   B   <u><u>A</u></u>   <u>B</u>   D   C   E   D

6. [48 __] [28 __] [22 A] [43 __]

7. 51 ___E___   69 _____   50 _____

8. (65 __) (13 D) (87 __) (31 __) (17 __)

9. [55 __] [44 __] [74 E] [25 __]

10. <u>40</u>   85   17   87   <u>52</u>   55   80   <u>45</u>   <u><u>75</u></u>

11. [65 __] [37 __] [12 __] [4 E]

12. <u>X</u>OOO<u>X</u>OO<u>XX</u>O<u>X</u>O<u>X</u> *9*

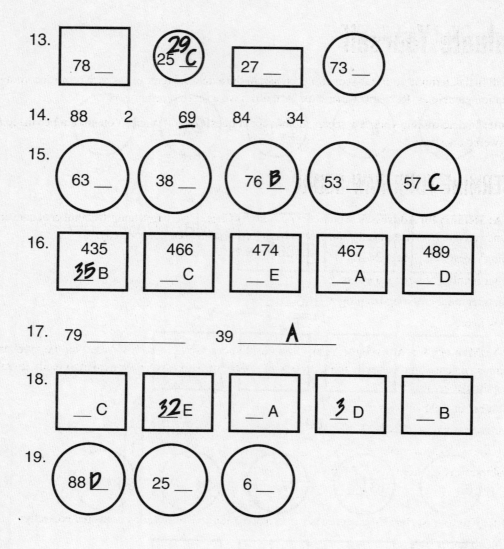

13. 78 ___   25 **29** **C**   27 ___   73 ___

14. 88   2   <u>69</u>   84   34

15. 63 ___   38 ___   76 **B**   53 ___   57 **C**

16. 435 **35** B   466 ___ C   474 ___ E   467 ___ A   489 ___ D

17. 79 _____   39 _____ **A** _____

18. ___ C   **32** E   ___ A   **3** D   ___ B

19. 88 **D**   25 ___   6 ___

Evaluate Yourself

We will first determine your raw score for each part of the exam and then assess each score according to evaluation guidelines. Remember that Parts A and B have a scoring penalty.

Note: In determining your raw scores, do not count questions left blank. You are not penalized for unanswered questions.

DETERMINE YOUR RAW SCORE

Part A: Memory for Addresses: Your score on Address Checking is based upon the number of questions you answered correctly minus the number of questions you answered incorrectly:

1. Enter number of right answers   _____
2. Enter number of wrong answers   _____
3. Subtract number wrong from right   _____

Raw Score =   _____

Part B: Memory for Addresses: Your score on Memory for Addresses is based on the number of questions you answered correctly minus one-fourth of the questions you answered incorrectly (number wrong divided by four):

1. Number of right answers   _____
2. Number of wrong answers   _____
3. Divide number wrong by 4   _____
4. Subtract answer from number right   _____

Raw Score =   _____

Part C: Number Series: Your scored is based on the number of questions answered correctly:

Enter number right   _____

Raw Score =   _____

Part D: Following Oral Instructions: Your score is based on the number of questions you answered correctly on your answer sheet:

Enter number right   _____

Raw Score =   _____

Total Score: To find your total raw score, add together the raw scores for each section of the exam:

Address Checking   _____

Memory for Addresses   _____

Number Series   _____

Following Oral Instructions   _____

Total Raw Score =   _____

Evaluate Your Score

Calculate your raw score for each test section as shown above. Then check to see where your score falls on the scale from Poor to Excellent. Lightly shade in the boxes in which your scores fall.

Part	Excellent	Good	Average	Fair	Poor
Address Checking	80–95	65–79	50–64	35–49	1–34
Memory for Addresses	75–88	60–74	45–59	30–44	1–29
Number Series	21–24	18–20	14–17	11–13	1–10
Following Oral Instructions	27–31	23–26	19–22	14–18	1–13

BIOGRAPHICAL/ACHIEVEMENT INVENTORY

Many Federal and state civil service examinations now conclude with a self-descriptive inventory that is designed to resemble a test section. This inventory is set up to look like a multiple-choice test and is timed like a test, but it is not a test at all. There are no right or wrong answers. The examiners are looking for a pattern of achievement, interests, and personality traits that they can compare to the achievement, interests, and personality profile of persons who are currently active and successful in the occupation for which you have applied.

You cannot study for this inventory. The only possible preparation is searching out old school records to refresh your own mind as to subjects that you studied (those in which you did well and those which gave you trouble), attendance records, grades, and extracurricular activities. If you cannot find your records, just answer to the best of your ability. Some questions allow for a "do not recall" response. Aside from high school and college related questions (if you did not attend college at all you are permitted to skip over a whole section of the inventory), you are asked questions about your likes and dislikes and about the impression that you make upon others. There are questions about how you rank yourself in relation to other people, about what your friends think of you, and about the opinions of your supervisors or teachers. Do not try to second-guess the test-makers to give the "right" answer. There are internal checks for consistency and honesty built into the questions. Your best bet is to answer quickly and candidly. Dwelling over the questions is not likely to help.

The inventories for different positions tend to emphasize different topics, but there is a certain similarity from one to the next. The questions below offer you a sampling of the types of questions that are often asked.

1. My favorite subject in high school was
   (A) math
   (B) English
   (C) physical education
   (D) social studies
   (E) science

2. My GPA upon graduation from high school (on a 4.0 scale) was
   (A) lower than 2.51
   (B) 2.51 to 2.80
   (C) 2.81 to 3.25
   (D) 3.26 to 3.60
   (E) higher than 3.60

3. In my second year of high school, I was absent
   (A) never
   (B) not more than 3 days
   (C) 4 to 10 days
   (D) more often than 10 days
   (E) do not recall

4. While in high school, I participated in
   (A) one sport
   (B) two sports and one other extracurricular activity
   (C) three nonathletic extracurricular activities
   (D) no extracurricular activities
   (E) other than the above

5. During my senior year in high school, I held a paying job
   (A) 0 hours a week
   (B) 1 to 5 hours weekly
   (C) 6 to 10 hours a week
   (D) 11 to 16 hours a week
   (E) more than 16 hours a week

6. In high school, I did volunteer work
   (A) more than 10 hours a week on a regular basis
   (B) 5 to 10 hours a week on a regular basis
   (C) sporadically
   (D) seldom
   (E) not at all

7. My standing in my graduating class was in the
   (A) bottom third
   (B) middle third
   (C) top third
   (D) top quarter
   (E) top 10 percent

8. In comparison to my peers, I cut classes
   (A) much less often than most
   (B) somewhat less often than most
   (C) just about the same as most
   (D) somewhat more often than most
   (E) much more often than most

9. The campus activities in which I participated most were
   (A) social service
   (B) political
   (C) literary
   (D) did not participate in campus activities
   (E) did not participate in any of these activities

10. While a college student, I spent most of my summers
    (A) in summer school
    (B) earning money
    (C) traveling
    (D) in service activities
    (E) resting

11. My college education was financed
    (A) entirely by my parents
    (B) by my parents and my own earnings
    (C) by scholarships, loans, and my own earnings
    (D) by my parents and loans
    (E) by a combination of sources not listed above

12. In the college classroom, I was considered
    (A) a listener
    (B) an occasional contributor
    (C) an average participant
    (D) a frequent contributor
    (E) a leader

13. I made my greatest mark in college through my
    (A) athletic prowess
    (B) success in performing arts
    (C) academic success
    (D) partying reputation
    (E) conciliatory skill with my peers

14. My cumulative GPA (on a 4.0 scale) in courses in my major was
    (A) lower than 3.00
    (B) 3.00 to 3.25
    (C) 3.26 to 3.50
    (D) 3.51 to 3.75
    (E) higher than 3.75

15. My supervisors (or teachers) would be most likely to describe me as
    (A) competent
    (B) gifted
    (C) intelligent
    (D) fast-working
    (E) detail oriented

16. My peers would probably describe me as
    (A) analytical
    (B) glib
    (C) organized
    (D) funny
    (E) helpful

17. According to my supervisors (or teachers), my greatest asset is my
    (A) ability to communicate orally
    (B) written expression
    (C) ability to motivate others
    (D) organization of time
    (E) friendly personality

18. In the past year, I read strictly for pleasure
    - (A) no books
    - (B) one book
    - (C) two books
    - (D) three to six books
    - (E) more than six books

19. When I read for pleasure, I read mostly
    - (A) history
    - (B) fiction
    - (C) poetry
    - (D) biography
    - (E) current events

20. My supervisors (or teachers) would say that my area of least competence is
    - (A) analytical ability
    - (B) written communication
    - (C) attention to detail
    - (D) public speaking
    - (E) self-control

21. In my opinion, the most important of the following attributes in an employee is
    - (A) discretion
    - (B) loyalty
    - (C) open-mindedness
    - (D) courtesy
    - (E) competence

22. My supervisors (or teachers) would say that I react to criticism with
    - (A) a defensive attitude
    - (B) quick capitulation
    - (C) anger
    - (D) interest
    - (E) shame

23. My attendance record over the past year has been
    - (A) not as good as I would like it to be
    - (B) not as good as my supervisors (or teachers) would like it to be
    - (C) a source of embarrassment
    - (D) satisfactory
    - (E) a source of pride

24. My peers would say that when I feel challenged my reaction is one of
    - (A) determination
    - (B) energy
    - (C) defiance
    - (D) caution
    - (E) compromise

There are no "right" answers to these questions, so there is no answer key.

IMPORTANT CIVIL SERVICE EMPLOYMENT CONTACTS

Major Federal Agencies Contact Information

Central Intelligence Agency (CIA)
Washington, DC 20505
703-482-1100
www.odci.gov

Consumer Product Safety Commission
4330 East-West Highway
Bethesda, MD 20814
301-504-0580
www.cpsc.gov

Environment Protection Agency
401 M St. SW
Washington, DC 20460
202-260-2090
www.epa.gov

Federal Bureau of Investigation (FBI)
935 Pennsylvania Ave. NW
Washington, DC 20535
202-324-3000
www.fbi.gov

Federal Communications Commission
1919 M St. NW
Washington, DC 20554
202-418-0500
www.fcc.gov

Federal Deposit Insurance Corporation (FDIC)
550 17th St. NW
Washington, DC 20429
202-393-8400
www.fdic.gov

Federal Emergency Management Agency
500 C St. SW
Washington, DC 20472
202-646-4600
www.fema.gov

Federal Highway Administration
400 7th St. SW
Washington, DC 20590
202-366-4000
www.fhwa.dot.gov

Federal Trade Commission
6th St. & Pennsylvania Ave. NW
Washington, DC 20580
202-326-2222
www.ftc.gov

Food & Drug Administration
5600 Fishers Lane
Rockville, MD 20857
301-443-1544
www.fda.gov

General Services Administration
18th St. & F St. NW
Washington, DC 20405
202-708-5082
www.gsa.gov

Health Resources & Services Administration
5600 Fishers Lane
Rockville, MD 20857
301-443-2086
www.hrsa.dhhs.gov

Immigration and Naturalization Service
425 I St. NW
Washington, DC 20530
202-514-2000
www.ins.doj.gov

Library of Congress
1st St. & Independence SE
Washington, DC 20540
202-707-5000
www.lcweb.loc.gov

National Aeronautics & Space Administration
300 E St. SW
Washington, DC 20546
202-358-2810
www.nasa.gov

National Science Foundation
4201 Wilson Blvd.
Arlington, VA 22230
703-306-1234

Securities and Exchange Commission
450 5th St. NW
Washington, DC 20549
202-942-8088
www.sec.gov

Social Security Administration
6401 Security Blvd.
Baltimore, MD 21235
410-915-8882
www.ssa.gov/ or www.nsf.gov

AUTOMATED TELEPHONE SYSTEM: LOCAL NUMBERS

ALABAMA, Huntsville	256-837-0894
CALIFORNIA, San Francisco	415-744-5627
COLORADO, Denver	303-969-7050
DISTRICT OF COLUMBIA, Washington	202-606-2700
GEORGIA, Atlanta	404-331-4315
HAWAII, Honolulu	808-541-2791
ILLINOIS, Chicago	312-353-6192
MICHIGAN, Detroit	313-226-6950
MINNESOTA, Twin Cities	612-725-3430
MISSOURI, Kansas City	816-426-5702
NORTH CAROLINA, Raleigh	919-790-2822
OHIO, Dayton	937-225-2720
PENNSYLVANIA, Philadelphia	215-861-3070
PUERTO RICO, San Juan	787-766-5242
TEXAS, San Antonio	210-805-2402
VIRGINIA, Norfolk	757-441-3355
WASHINGTON, Seattle	206-553-0888

Locations of Federal Job Information "Touch Screen" Computer Kiosks

ALABAMA:
Huntsville
520 Wynn Dr. NW

ALASKA:
Anchorage
Federal Bldg.
222 W. 7th Ave.
Rm. 156

ARIZONA:
Phoenix
VA Medical Center
650 E. Indian School Rd.
Bldg. 21, Rm. 141

ARKANSAS: Little Rock
Federal Bldg.
700 W. Capitol
First floor lobby

CALIFORNIA: Sacramento
801 I ("i") St.

COLORADO: Denver
Dept. of Social Services
Employment Center
2200 W. Alameda Ave.
Ste. 5B

CONNECTICUT: Hartford
Federal Bldg.
450 Main St.
Lobby

DISTRICT OF COLUMBIA: Washington, D.C.
Theodore Roosevelt Federal Bldg.
1900 E St. NW
Rm. 1416

FLORIDA: Miami
Downtown Jobs and Benefits Center
Florida Job Service Center
401 NW 2nd Ave.
Ste. N-214

Orlando
Florida Job Service Center
1001 Executive Center Dr.
First floor

GEORGIA: Atlanta
Richard B. Russell Federal Bldg.
75 Spring St. SW
Main lobby, plaza level

HAWAII: Honolulu
Federal Bldg.
300 Ala Moana Blvd.
Rm. 5316

Fort Shafter
Department of Army, Army Civilian Personnel Office
Army Garrison
Bldg. T-1500

ILLINOIS: Chicago
77 W. Jackson Blvd.
First floor lobby

INDIANA: Indianapolis
Minton-Capehart Federal Bldg.
575 N. Pennsylvania St.
Rm. 339

LOUISIANA:	New Orleans Federal Bldg. 423 Canal St. First floor lobby
MAINE:	Augusta Federal Office Bldg. 40 Western Ave.
MARYLAND:	Baltimore George H. Fallon Bldg. Lombard St. & Hopkins Plaza Lobby
MASSACHUSETTS:	Boston Thomas P. O'Neill, Jr., Federal Bldg. 10 Causeway St. First floor
MICHIGAN:	Detroit 477 Michigan Ave. Rm. 565
MINNESOTA:	Twin Cities Bishop Henry Whipple Federal Bldg. 1 Federal Dr. Rm. 501 Ft. Snelling
MISSOURI:	Kansas City Federal Bldg. 601 E. 12th St. Rm. 134
NEW HAMPSHIRE:	Portsmouth Thomas McIntyre Federal Bldg. 80 Daniel St. First floor lobby
NEW JERSEY:	Newark Peter J. Rodino Federal Bldg. 970 Broad St. Second floor, near Cafeteria
NEW MEXICO:	Albuquerque New Mexico State Job Service 501 Mountain Rd. NE Lobby
NEW YORK:	Albany Leo W. O'Brian Federal Bldg. Clinton Ave. & North Pearl Basement level Buffalo Thaddeus T. Dulski Federal Bldg. 111 W. Huron St. Ninth floor

New York City
Jacob K. Javits Federal Bldg.
26 Federal Plaza
Lobby

New York City
World Trade Center
Cafeteria

Syracuse
James M. Hanley Federal Bldg.
100 S. Clinton St.

OHIO:

Dayton
Federal Bldg.
200 W. 2nd St.
Rm. 509

OKLAHOMA:

Oklahoma City
Career Connection Center
7401 NE 23rd St.

OREGON:

Portland
Federal Bldg.
1220 SW Third Ave.
Rm. 376

Bonneville Power Admin.
905 NE 11th Ave.

Dept. of Army & Corps of Engineers
Duncan Plaza

PENNSYLVANIA:

Harrisburg
Federal Bldg.
228 Walnut St.
Rm. 168

Philadelphia
William J. Green, Jr., Federal Bldg.
600 Arch St.
Second floor

Pittsburgh
Federal Bldg.
1000 Liberty Ave.
First floor lobby

Reading
Reading Postal Service
2100 N. 13th St.

PUERTO RICO:

San Juan
U.S. Federal Bldg.
150 Carlos Chardon Ave.
Rm. 328

RHODE ISLAND: Providence
380 Westminster
Mall lobby

TENNESSEE: Memphis
Naval Air Station Memphis
Transition Assistance Center
7800 3rd Ave.
Bldg. South 239, Millington

TEXAS: Dallas
Federal Bldg.
1100 Commerce St.
First floor lobby

El Paso
Federal Bldg.
700 E. San Antonio St.
Lobby

Houston
Mickey Leland Federal Bldg.
1919 Smith St.
First floor lobby

San Antonio
Federal Bldg.
727 E. Durango
First floor lobby

UTAH: Salt Lake City
Utah State Job Service
720 South 2nd East
Reception area

VERMONT: Burlington
Federal Bldg.
11 Elmwood Ave.
First floor lobby

VIRGINIA: Norfolk
Federal Bldg.
200 Granby St.

WASHINGTON: Seattle
Federal Bldg.
915 Second Ave.
Rm. 110

WASHINGTON, D.C.:   Theodore Roosevelt Federal Bldg.
1900 E St. NW
Rm. 1416

WEBLIOGRAPHY OF FEDERAL EMPLOYMENT WEB SITES

Job Listings

- **Employment Index: Local and State Government Agencies' Job Listings** (www.employmentindex.com/govjob.html)—Links to the Web sites of government agencies throughout the U.S. Lists public and private sector jobs.
- **Federal Government Job Hot Line** (www.unl.edu/careers/jobs/fedhotl.html)—Job hot lines for various Federal agencies, from the University of Nebraska—Lincoln.
- **Federal Job Opportunities Bulletin Board** (fjob.opm.gov [Telnet] or ftp.fjob.opm.gov [Transfer Protocol])—Current worldwide Federal jobs, many with full announcements, salaries and pay rates, employment information, etc.; from the U.S. Office of Personnel Management. Your name and address can be left to have applications mailed to you. Accessible via *Dial-up* (912-757-3100).
- **Government and Law Enforcement Jobs** (jobsearch.tqn.com/msubgov.htm)—An annotated list of Web sites that list jobs with Federal, state and local governments, and law enforcement agencies, from the About.com Guide to Job Searching.
- **govtjobs.com** (www.govtjobs.com)—A list of jobs in the public sector.
- **HRS Federal Job Search** (www.hrsjobs.com)—A subscription job search and e-mail delivery service, which also has a lot of free information.
- **The Internet Job Source** (www.statejobs.com/fed.html)—The Federal Jobs section of this site links to job listings at numerous Federal agencies and also to online newspapers that list Federal job opportunities.
- **Jobs in State Government** (usgovinfo.about.com/blstjobs.htm)—An index of state Web sites that list government employment opportunities, with sites ranging from About.com Guide to U.S. Government Info/Resources.
- **U.S. Postal Service: Human Resources** (www.usps.gov.hrisp)—A list of vacancies in management, supervisory, administrative, professional, and technical positions only.
- **USAJOBS** (www.usajobs.opm.gov)—The official site for worldwide Federal employment listings from the U.S. Office of Personnel Management, with full-text job announcements, forms, and answers to frequently asked questions.

Applications and Other Forms

- **Electronic Forms** (www.opm.gov/forms/index.htm)—All forms and applications relating to Federal employment, from the Office of Personnel Management.
- **The Federal Job Search and Application Form** (www.usajobs.opm.gov/b1a.htm)—A description of the Federal job search as a three-step process, including three downloadable versions of the OF-612 job application form.

General Information

- **Career City: Government Jobs** (www.careercity.com/content/govcareer/index.asp)—A guide to Federal and local government employment, with links to job listings.
- **Federal Salaries and Wages** (www.opm.gov/oca/payrates/index.htm)—Rates from the U.S. Office of Personnel Management Web site.
- **The Federal Web Locator** (www.vcilp.org/Fed-Agency/fedwebloc.html#toc)—Links to agencies in all branches of the Federal government, including Federal Independent Establishments and Government Corporations.
- **Public Service Employees Network** (http://www.pse-net.com/)—A guide to government employment, including job listings.
- **The U.S. Office of Personnel Management Web Site** (www.opm.gov)—Tons of information on all aspects of Federal employment, with an index to make navigation easier.

Online Publications

- **Federal Jobs Digest Online** (www.jobsfed.com)—An online version of this well-known publication that provides job listings, federal employment news, and advice on how to get hired.
- **FederalTimes.com** (http://www.federaltimes.com)—News of interest to those in the Federal government.
- **FedForce** (www.clubfed.com/fedforce/fedforce.html)—Online service for Federal employees, with free registration.
- **GovExec.com** (www.govexec.com)—An online publication from *Government Executive Magazine,* bringing news to Federal executives and managers.

FEDERAL OCCUPATIONS THAT REQUIRE EXAMINATIONS

Test requirements are for competitive and outside-the-register appointments only, unless otherwise specified. This list does not reflect special examining provisions.

ACWA (Administrative Careers With America) examinations refer to positions that meet the criteria for ACWA.

Series	Title/Position(s)	Grade(s)	Type of Exam ACWA	Written	Performance
011	Bond Sales Promotion	5/7	•		
018	Safety & Occupational Health Management	5/7	•		
019	Safety Technician	2/3		•	
023	Outdoor Recreation Planning	5/7	•		
025	Park Ranger	5/7	•		
028	Environmental Protection Specialist	5/7	•		
029	Environmental Protection Assistant	2/3/4		•	
072	Fingerprint Identification	2/3/4		•	
080	Security Administration	5/7	•		
082	United States Marshal	5/7		•	
083	Police	2		•	
083	Park Police	5		•	
083a	Police (Secret Service)	4/5		•	
085	Security Guard	2		•	
086	Security Clerical & Assistance	2/3/4		•	
105	Social Insurance Administration	5/7	•		
106	Unemployment Insurance	5/7	•		
132	Intelligence	5/7	•		
134	Intelligence Aid & Clerk	2/3/4		•	
142	Manpower Development	5/7	•		
181	Psychology Aid & Technician	2/3		•	
186	Social Services Aid & Assistant	2/3		•	
187	Social Services	5/7	•		

Series	Title/Position(s)	Grade(s)	Type of Exam		
			ACWA	Written	Performance
189	Recreation Aid & Assistant	2/3		•	
201	Personnel Management	5/7	•		
203	Personnel Clerical & Assistance	2/3/4		•	
204	Military Personnel Clerical & Technician	2/3/4		•	
205	Military Personnel Management	5/7	•		
212	Personnel Staffing	5/7	•		
221	Position Classification	5/7	•		
222	Occupational Analysis	5/7	•		
223	Salary & Wage Administration	5/7	•		
230	Employee Relations	5/7	•		
233	Labor Relations	5/7	•		
235	Employee Development	5/7	•		
244	Labor Mgmt. Relations Examining	5/7	•		
246	Contractor Industrial Relations	5/7	•		
249	Wage & Hour Compliance	5/7	•		
270	Federal Retirement Benefits	5/7	•		
301	Misc. Administration & Program	5/7	•		
302	Messenger	2/3/4		•	
303	Misc. Clerk & Assistant	2/3/4		•	
304	Information Receptionist	2/3/4		•	
305	Mail & File	2/3/4		•	
309	Correspondence Clerk	2/3/4		•	
312	Clerk-Stenographer	3/4/5		•	•
312	Reporting Stenographer	5/6			*
312	Shorthand Reporter	6/7/8/9			*
318	Secretary	3/4		•	
319	Closed Microphone Reporting	6/7/8/9			*
322	Clerk-Typist	2/3/4		•	•
326	Office Automation Clerical and Assistance	2/3/4		•	•
332	Computer Operation	2/3/4		•	

			Type of Exam		
Series	Title/Position(s)	Grade(s)	ACWA	Written	Performance
334	Computer Specialist (for alternative B only)	5/7	•		
335	Computer Clerk & Assistant	2/3/4		•	
341	Administrative Officer	5/7	•		
343	Management and Program Analysis	5/7	•		
344	Management and Program Clerical & Assistance	2/3/4		•	
346	Logistics Management	5/7	•		
350	Equipment Operator	2/3/4		•	
351	Printing Clerical	2/3/4		•	
356	Data Transcriber	2/3/4		•	•
357	Coding	2/3/4		•	
359	Electric Accounting Machine Operation	2/3/4		•	
382	Telephone Operating	2/3/4		•	
390	Telecommunications Processing	2/3/4		•	
391	Telecommunications	5/7	•		
392	General Telecommunications	2/3/4		•	
394	Communications Clerical	2/3/4		•	
404	Biological Science Technician	2/3		•	
421	Plant Protection Technician	2/3		•	
455	Range Technician	2/3		•	
458	Soil Conservation Technician	2/3		•	
459	Irrigation System Operation	2/3		•	
462	Forestry Technician	2/3		•	
501	Financial Administration & Program	5/7	•		
503	Financial Clerical & Assistance	2/3/4		•	
525	Accounting Technician	2/3/4		•	
526	Tax Technician	5/7	•		
530	Cash Processing	2/3/4		•	
540	Voucher Examining	2/3/4		•	
544	Civilian Pay	2/3/4		•	
545	Military Pay	2/3/4		•	
560	Budget Analysis	5/7	•		

			Type of Exam		
Series	Title/Position(s)	Grade(s)	ACWA	Written	Performance
561	Budget Clerical & Assistance	2/3/4		•	
570	Financial Institution Examining	5/7	• (except FDIC positions)		
592	Tax Examining	2/3/4		•	
593	Insurance Accounts	2/3/4		•	
621	Nursing Assistant	2/3		•	
636	Rehabilitation Therapy Assistant	2/3		•	
640	Health Aid & Technician	2/3		•	
642	Nuclear Medicine Technician	2/3		•	
645	Medical Technician	2/3		•	
646	Pathology Technician	2/3		•	
647	Diagnostic Radiologic Technologist	2/3		•	
648	Therapeutic Radiologic Technologist	2/3		•	
649	Medical Instrument Technician	2/3		•	
651	Respiratory Therapist	2/3		•	
661	Pharmacy Technician	2/3		•	
667	Orthotist & Prosthetist	3		•	
673	Hospital Housekeeping Management	5/7	•		
675	Medical Records Technician	2/3/4		•	
679	Medical Clerk	2/3/4		•	
681	Dental Assistant	2/3		•	
683	Dental Lab Aid & Technician	2/3		•	
685	Public Health Program Specialist	5/7	•		
698	Environmental Health Technician	2/3		•	
704	Animal Health Technician	2/3		•	
802	Engineering Technician	2/3		•	
809	Construction Control	2/3		•	
817	Surveying Technician	2/3		•	
818	Engineering Drafting	2/3		•	
856	Electronics Technician	2/3		•	

Series	Title/Position(s)	Grade(s)	ACWA	Written	Performance
			Type of Exam		
895	Industrial Engineering Technician	2/3		•	
950	Paralegal Specialist	5/7	•		
958	Pension Law Specialist	5/7	•		
962	Contact Representative	3/4		•	
962	Contact Representative	5/7	•		
963	Legal Instruments Examining	2/3/4		•	
965	Land Law Examining	5/7	•		
967	Passport & Visa Examining	5/7	•		
986	Legal Clerk & Technician	2/3/4		•	
987	Tax Law Specialist	5/7	•		
990	General Claims Examining (One-grade interval)	4		•	
990	General Claims Examining (Two-grade interval)	5/7	•		
991	Workers' Comp Claims Examining	5/7	•		
993	Social Insurance Claims Examining	4		•	
993	Railroad Retirement Claims Examining	5/7	•		
994	Unemployment Comp. Claims Examining	5/7	•		
996	Veterans Claims Examining	5/7	•		
998	Claims Clerical	2/3/4		•	
1001	General Arts & Information	2/3/4		•	
1001	General Arts & Information	5/7	• (except fine arts positions)		
1016	Museum Specialist & Technician	2/3		•	
1021	Office Drafting	2/3		•	
1035	Public Affairs	5/7	•		
1046	Language Clerical	2/3/4		•	
1082	Writing & Editing	5/7	•		
1083	Technical Writing & Editing	5/7	•		
1087	Editorial Assistance	2/3/4		•	
1101	General Business & Industry	2/3/4		•	
1101	General Business & Industry	5/7	•		
1101	International Trade Analyst	5/7	•		

Series	Title/Position(s)	Grade(s)	Type of Exam		
			ACWA	Written	Performance
1102	Contracting	5/7	•		
1103	Industrial Property Management	5/7	•		
1104	Property Disposal	5/7	•		
1105	Purchasing	2/3/4		•	
1106	Procurement Clerical & Technician	2/3/4		•	
1107	Property Disposal Clerical & Technician	2/3/4		•	
1130	Public Utilities Specialist	5/7	•		
1140	Trade Specialist	5/7	•		
1140	International Trade Specialist	5/7		•	
1145	Agricultural Program Specialist	5/7	•		
1146	Agricultural Marketing	5/7	•		
1146	Grain Marketing Specialist	5/7		•	
1147	Agricultural Market Reporting	5/7	•		
1150	Industrial Specialist	5/7	•		
1152	Production Control	2/3/4		•	
1160	Financial Analysis	5/7	•		
1163	Insurance Examining	5/7	•		
1165	Loan Specialist	5/7	•		
1169	Internal Revenue Officer	5/7	•		
1170	Realty	5/7	•		
1171	Appraising & Assessing	5/7	•		
1173	Housing Management	5/7	•		
1176	Building Management	5/7	•		
1311	Physical Science Technician	2/3		•	
1316	Hydrologic Technician	2/3		•	
1341	Meteorological Technician	2/3		•	
1371	Cartographic Technician	2/3		•	
1374	Geodetic Technician	2/3		•	
1410	Librarian	7/9		•	
				(for applicants who do not meet certain educational requirements)	
1411	Library Technician	2/3/4		•	

Series	Title/Position(s)	Grade(s)	Type of Exam		
			ACWA	Written	Performance
1412	Technical Information Services	5/7	•		
1421	Archives Specialist	5/7	•		
1421	Archives Technician	2/3/4		•	
1521	Mathematics Technician	2/3		•	
1531	Statistical Assistant	2/3/4		•	
1541	Cryptanalysis	2/3		•	
1702	Education & Training Technician	2/3		•	
1715	Vocational Rehabilitation	5/7	•		
1801	Civil Aviation Security Specialist	5/7	•		
1801	Center Adjudications Officer	5/7	•		
1801	District Adjudications Officer	5/7	•		
1802	Compliance Inspection & Support	2/3/4		• (except Detention Enforcement Officer positions)	
1810	General Investigating	5/7	•		
1811	Criminal Investigating	5/7	•		
1811	Treasury Enforcement Agent	5/7		•	
1812	Game Law Enforcement	5/7	•		
1812	Special Agent (Wildlife)	7		•	
1816	Immigration Inspection	5/7	•		
1831	Securities Compliance Examining	5/7	•		
1854	Alcohol, Tobacco & Firearms Inspection	5/7	•		
1863	Food Inspection	5/7		•	
1864	Public Health Quarantine Inspection	5/7	•		
1884	Customs Patrol Officer	5/7		•	
1889	Import Specialist	5/7	•		
1890	Customs Inspection	5/7	•		
1896	Border Patrol Agent	5/7		• (and language proficiency)	
1897	Customs Aid	2/3/4		•	
1910	Quality Assurance	5/7	•		
1981	Agricultural Commodity Aid	2/3		•	

Series	Title/Position(s)	Grade(s)	Type of Exam		
			ACWA	Written	Performance
2001	General Supply	5/7	•		
2003	Supply Program Management	5/7	•		
2005	Supply Clerical & Technician	2/3/4		•	
2010	Inventory Management	5/7	•		
2030	Distribution Facilities & Storage Management	5/7	•		
2032	Packaging	5/7	•		
2050	Supply Cataloging	5/7	•		
2091	Sales Store Clerical	2/3/4		•	
2101	Transportation Specialist	5/7	•		
2101	Airway Transportation System Specialist (Department of Transportation Federal Aviation Administration)	5/7		•	
2102	Transportation Clerk & Assistant	2/3/4		•	
2110	Transportation Industry Analysis	5/7	•		
2125	Highway Safety	5/7	•		
2130	Traffic Management	5/7	•		
2131	Freight Rate	2/3/4		•	
2135	Transportation Loss & Damage Claims Examining	2/3/4		•	
2150	Transportation Operations	5/7	•		
2151	Dispatching	2/3/4		•	
2152	Air Traffic Control	5/7		•	
				(optional above 7)	

* mandatory for competitive appt. and inservice placement

GLOSSARY OF CIVIL SERVICE HIRING TERMINOLOGY

Glossary of Civil Service Hiring Terminology

When you're reading the announcement and filling out your application, you need to understand the government's hiring terminology. Take a few minutes to familiarize yourself with the words listed below. These are very common terms used repeatedly, both in the announcements and in any correspondence or conversation you may have with the Federal civil service, and most of the same language will also appear if you extend your job search to state and local civil service.

Career Status   To be considered a *status employee,* a Federal employee must have served for at least three consecutive years in a permanent position.

Certificate of Eligibles   This refers to the list of eligible candidates that results from responses to a vacancy announcement and an application process.

Competitive Service   Most positions in the Federal government that are subject to Title 5, US Code, meaning that candidates compete for entrance with other nonstatus applicants.

Continuously Open Positions   Positions that are open for an indefinite period. These positions, however, may be closed by the agency at any time.

Eligibles   Refers to qualified employees.

Excepted Service   Most positions in the legislative and judicial branches, and some in the executive branch, which are not in the *competitive service.*

Federal Wage System   The classification used for trade and labor jobs in the Federal government.

FWS   See *Federal Wage System.*

General Schedule   The classification for white-collar jobs in the Federal government.

Grade   Each pay category; *WG* is used to indicate pay categories for *Federal Wage System* (WS) jobs, while *GS* is used to indicated categories for *General Schedule* jobs.

GS   See *General Schedule* and also *Grade.*

High-3 Average Salary   Used to determine retirement benefits, this term refers to the average of your highest basic pay over any three years of consecutive service.

Job Family   Grouping of occupations in the *Federal Wage System* that are related in either similarity of functions performed, transferability of knowledge and skills, or similarity of material or equipment worked on.

Merit Promotion System   This system helps determine whether current employees will be promoted within the Federal government's competitive service.

Occupation   Includes all jobs at the various skill levels in a particular kind of work.

Occupational Groups   Related occupations in the *General Schedule (GS)* that are grouped together within the same multiple of 100, i.e., GS-100, 200, 300, etc.

OF-612   The Optional Application for Federal Employment.

Pay Comparability   Federal salaries, by law, are based on a comparison with private-sector jobs.

Probationary Period   A trial period before a new employee becomes permanent.

Rating and Ranking   Job candidates are evaluated and placed on a *Certificate of Eligibles* in score order.

Register   A list of qualified applicants for a specific occupation.

Reinstatement Eligibility   This provision allows former Federal employees to apply for jobs that are open to *status employees*.

Senior Executive Service   Top management in Federal agencies.

Series   All jobs in a subgroup of an *Occupational Group* that are related by subject matter, basic knowledge, and skill requirements. Includes jobs at various skill levels.

SF-171   An application form used for Federal employment.

Status Employee   An employee with *career status* is eligible to apply for other Federal jobs based on current service or reinstatement eligibility.

Temporary Appointment   An appointment that lasts one year or less and has a specific expiration date.

Term Appointment   An appointment that lasts for over one year and up to four years.

Veterans Preference   Veterans receive preference points that are added to their scores when competing for Federal jobs.

WG   See *Grade*.

Within-Grade Step Increases   Pay increases indicated by 10 steps within each *grade*. Steps are based on performance and time in grade.

Notes

Notes

Notes

Notes

Notes

Notes

Notes

WITHDRAWN

Notes

CIVIL
SERVICE

Civil service
handbook.

$12.95